Colonial Legacies

Colonial Legacies

Economic and Social
Development in East
and Southeast Asia

Anne E. Booth

University of Hawai'i Press
Honolulu

12 11 10 09 08 07   6 5 4 3 2 1

Library of Congress Cataloging-in-Publication Data
Booth, Anne.
Colonial legacies : economic and social development in
East and Southeast Asia / Anne E. Booth.
p. cm.
Includes bibliographical references and index.
ISBN 978-0-8248-3161-5 (hardcover : alk. paper)
1. Southeast Asia—Economic conditions—20th century.
2. Southeast Asia—Social conditions—20th century. 3. Southeast
Asia—Colonial influence. 4. East Asia—Economic conditions—
20th century. 5. East Asia—Social conditions—20th century.
6. East Asia—Colonial influence. I. Title.
HC441.B64 2007
330.95′041—dc22
2007006545

Designed by Paul Herr
Printed by The Maple-Vail Book Manufacturing Group

Contents

Acknowledgments

This study is the result of several years of work, and I am grateful to the School of Oriental and African Studies (SOAS) for providing me with a supportive research environment. A year's sabbatical leave in 2001, part of it spent at the Institute of Southeast Asian Studies in Singapore, allowed me to begin the thinking and background reading for what has turned out to be a more ambitious project than the one I had initially contemplated. I am also grateful to the Leverhulme Foundation, which awarded me a major research fellowship for two years from October 2004. This freed me from most of my teaching and administrative obligations, and allowed me to concentrate on writing. A project of this kind inevitably requires long hours in libraries, and I am happy to acknowledge the assistance I have had in London from staff in the SOAS library and the British Library of Political and Economic Science at the London School of Economics. In addition, I have spent valuable time in the libraries of Cornell University, the University of Wisconsin at Madison, the Menzies and Chifley libraries at the Australian National University in Canberra, and libraries at the National University of Singapore and the Institute of Southeast Asian Studies in Singapore. I am grateful to the staff of all these institutions for their patient help.

I would like to thank my colleagues in the History and Economic Development Group in London, on whom I have tried out some of the ideas that eventually found their way into this study. I have also benefited greatly from seminar presentations in London, Norwich, Canberra, Singapore, Leiden, Madison, and Tokyo. I have had valuable comments from, among others, Gregg Huff, Jean-Pascal Bassino, William Clarence-Smith, Janet Hunter, Christopher Howe, Stephen Morgan, and Howard Dick. Comments from two publisher's referees were also very helpful in preparing the final version of the manuscript. I cannot blame any of these people for the result, but I am very grateful for their help.

I am also grateful to the editor of the *Economic History Review* for permission to draw on my article to appear there in 2007 in Chapter 4 of this study.

A Note on Terminology

In this study, the colonies in East and Southeast Asia will usually be referred to by the names that came into popular use in the postcolonial era rather than by the names that were in use before 1945 or their official names in more recent decades. Thus what was the Netherlands Indies will be referred to as Indonesia, and the island of Taiwan will be referred to as Taiwan rather than Formosa or the Republic of China. Thailand will be used in preference to Siam (the official name until 1939). Korea will be used rather than Chosen and Burma rather than Myanmar. The term "British Malaya" refers to the Straits Settlements, the Federated Malay States (Selangor, Pahang, Negeri Sembilan, and Perak), and the Unfederated Malay States (Johore, Trengganu, Kedah, Perlis, Kelantan, and Brunei). During the 1950s, all these territories were often referred to as the Malayan Federation. The term "Malaysia" is used to refer to the modern state of that name, which includes all parts of British Malaya except the island of Singapore and Brunei as well as the former British protectorates of Sarawak and Sabah (formerly North Borneo). Throughout the study, the term "Southeast Asia" will be used to refer to the region now covered by the ten member states of the Association of Southeast Asian Nations (ASEAN). In 2006, these were Indonesia, the Philippines, Singapore, Malaysia, and Thailand (the original five member states) plus Brunei, Cambodia, Laos, Vietnam, and Burma (Myanmar). East Asia refers to China (including the Hong Kong SAR), Taiwan (Republic of China), North and South Korea, and Japan.

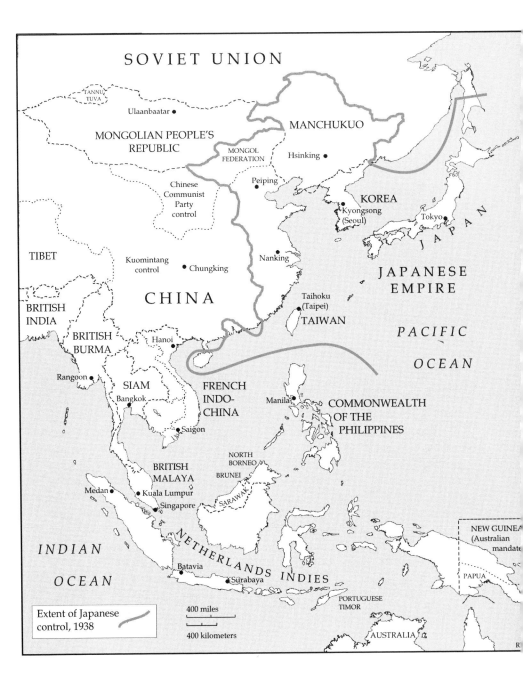

SOVIET UNION

TANNU
TUVA

MONGOLIAN PEOPLE'S
REPUBLIC

Ulaanbaatar ●

MANCHUKUO

MONGOL
FEDERATION

Hsinking ●

Chinese
Communist
Party
control

Peiping ●

KOREA

Kyongsong
(Seoul) ●

Tokyo ●

JAPAN

TIBET

Kuomintang
control

● Chungking

Nanking ●

JAPANESE
EMPIRE

BRITISH
INDIA

CHINA

Taihoku
(Taipei) ●

PACIFIC

BRITISH
BURMA

Hanoi ●

TAIWAN

OCEAN

Rangoon ●

SIAM

Bangkok ●

FRENCH
INDO-
CHINA

Manila ●

COMMONWEALTH
OF THE
PHILIPPINES

● Saigon

NORTH
BORNEO

BRITISH
MALAYA

BRUNEI

Medan ●

● Kuala Lumpur

SARAWAK

● Singapore

INDIAN

NEW GUINEA
(Australian
mandate

OCEAN

Batavia ●

NETHERLANDS INDIES

PAPUA

● Surabaya

PORTUGUESE
TIMOR

Extent of Japanese
control, 1938

400 miles

400 kilometers

AUSTRALIA

CHAPTER I

Introduction

This book attempts a comparative study of the economic and social development of colonial territories in East and Southeast Asia in the first four decades of the twentieth century and of the consequences of that development for the transition to independence after 1945. At the beginning of the twentieth century, five colonial powers were active in East and Southeast Asia. Three were European. The British controlled from Delhi the vast South Asian subcontinent that extended from the Khyber Pass in the west to the borders of Burma with China, and with the independent Kingdom of Thailand in the east. In Southeast Asia, they controlled most of the Malayan peninsula, including the strategic port of Singapore, which was developed into an important British naval base. The Dutch governed the huge Indonesian archipelago, from Sumatra to New Guinea, and the French controlled the contiguous territories of Vietnam, Cambodia, and Laos, a region known as French Indochina.

After the defeat of Spain by American forces in 1898, President McKinley decided to impose an American administration on the Philippine islands. After a bloody struggle with Philippine nationalists, William Howard Taft was dispatched in 1900 to form a civilian government. McKinley instructed Taft to promote the "happiness, peace and prosperity of the people of the Philippine Islands" (Hutchcroft 2000: 277). This reflected the strongly moralistic view that the administration took of its new colonial mission. Although Taft and several other supporters of the American occupation of the Philippines thought that the Americans could learn from both British and Dutch colonial policies in Asia, especially as they related to the development of infrastructure and commerce, by the 1920s the idea of the "exceptionalism" of American colonialism was widely held (Adas 1998: 46–50). Unlike the policies of the Europeans, who (according to many Americans) viewed their colonies as economic assets to be exploited mainly for the benefit of the metropolitan power, American policy in the Philippines was dominated by the need to prepare the population of the Philippines for self-government and ultimate independence. Crucial to this strategy was mass education. In 1935, substantial self-government was granted to the Philippines, with a promise of complete independence after a further ten years.

The fifth colonial power in Asia in 1900 was Japan. As the only Asian country to acquire colonial possessions in the twentieth century, Japan was an "anomaly" in the history of colonial Asia (Peattie 1984: 6). Japan's empire in East Asia was created between 1895 and 1913, largely as a result of military victories over two decaying imperial states, China and Czarist Russia. The island of Taiwan (or Formosa, as it was known during the Japanese period) was annexed from China under the Treaty of Shimonoseki, and an administration was established under a Japanese governor-general in March 1896. The military pacification of the island in the latter part of the 1890s was not unlike similar exercises carried out by the French in Tonkin, the Americans in the Philippines, or the Dutch in northern Sumatra at about the same time and was probably no more ruthless than these other military campaigns (ibid.: 19). By 1900, the island was largely under Japanese control. The Treaty of Portsmouth, signed in the wake of the Russo-Japanese conflict, gave Japan control over the Liaotung peninsula, which became known as the Kwantung Leased Territory. Finally in 1910, Japanese control over the Korean peninsula was consolidated in its formal annexation. Unlike in Taiwan, colonial status was fiercely resented and resisted by Korean nationalists, but their opposition was put down by massive and often brutal police and military force.

Japanese military strength in the first decade of the twentieth century was based on its growing economic and industrial might. But Japan at that time was still very much a developing economy. Its per capita national income was well below that of the European colonial powers in Asia, and little more than a quarter of that of the United States (Table 1.1). By 1910, American national income per capita had overtaken that of the United Kingdom, while the total size of the American economy exceeded that of the United Kingdom and Germany combined (Maddison 2003: tables 1a, 1b, 2a, 2b, and 5b). Compared with the economic might of the United States at this time, Japan was still a minnow.

Because Japan's per capita national income was still quite low, the economic gap between Japan and its colonies was much narrower than was the case with the other colonial powers in Asia. In 1913, per capita GDP in Taiwan and Korea was between 50 and 60 percent of that in Japan, according to Maddison (Table 1.2). Other estimates suggest that the gap was even smaller, especially for Taiwan, where per capita GDP in 1915 may well have been almost 80 percent of that in Japan, once appropriate adjustment is made for differences in the prices of goods and services in the two economies (Fukao, Ma, and Yuan 2005: table 6). This can be compared with the Philippines, which by 1913 had recovered from the devastation of war and conquest, but its per capita national income was only about 20 percent of that in the United States. A similar gap could be found between the Netherlands and Indonesia in 1913, and an even larger one existed between Britain and Burma (Table 1.2).

Table 1.1. Per Capita GDP in East and Southeast Asia as a Percentage of Per Capita GDP in the United States, 1913–2000

Year	China	India	Burma	Taiwan	South Korea	Thailand
1913	10.4	12.7	12.9	14.1	15.5	15.9
1929	8.1	10.6	n.a.	16.6	14.7	11.5
1938	9.2	10.9	12.1	21.3	23.8	13.5
1950	4.6	6.5	4.1	9.7	8.1	8.5
1960	5.9	6.6	5.0	13.2	9.8	9.5
1970	5.2	5.8	3.8	19.8	13.0	11.3
1980	5.7	5.0	4.4	31.6	22.1	13.7
1990	8.0	5.6	3.4	42.6	37.5	20.0
2000	12.2	6.8	4.8	59.2	51.0	22.5

	Malaysia	Indonesia	Philippines	Hong Kong	Singapore	Japan
1913	17.0	17.1	19.9	24.1	24.1	26.2
1929	24.4	17.0	21.8	n.a.	n.a.	29.4
1938	22.2	19.2	24.8	n.a.	n.a.	40.0
1950	16.3	8.8	11.2	23.2	23.2	20.1
1960	13.5	9.0	13.0	27.7	20.4	35.2
1970	13.8	7.9	11.7	37.9	29.5	64.6
1980	19.7	10.1	12.8	56.5	48.8	72.3
1990	22.1	10.8	9.6	75.6	61.9	81.0
2000	28.0	11.4	8.5	76.4	78.9	74.9

Source: Maddison 2003.

Note: n.a. = data not available in the source document.

Thus Japan in the early twentieth century was a colonizing power whose economic strength, while growing, was still quite restricted relative to the other colonial powers in Asia and to the regions it was controlling. This was both an advantage and a disadvantage. The main advantage was that, with the memories of its own "superbly successful modernization efforts" in the decades after the Meiji Restoration still fresh in their minds, the Japanese colonial administrators (several of whom had played key policy roles in Japan after 1870) could implement the same kind of developmental policies in the colonial territories, especially in the agricultural sector (Peattie 1984: 23). The disadvantage was that the Japanese inevitably tended to view their colonial territories as assets to be exploited in their own race to catch up with the top industrial powers. This attitude became more pronounced over the 1930s, as the Japanese state shifted to a war economy footing with inevitable consequences for its colonial territories.

The French, Dutch, and British colonies also faced different, and changing, demands from the metropolitan powers during the first four decades of

Table 1.2. Per Capita GDP in East and Southeast Asia as a Percentage of Per Capita GDP in the Metropolitan Power, 1913–2000

| Year | British Colonies | | | | |
	India	Burma	Malaysia	Hong Kong	Singapore
1913	13.7	13.9	18.3	26.0	26.0
1929	13.2	n.a.	30.6	n.a.	n.a.
1938	10.7	11.8	21.7	n.a.	n.a.
1950	8.9	5.7	22.5	32.0	32.0
1960	8.7	6.5	17.7	36.3	26.7
1970	8.1	5.2	19.3	52.9	41.2
1980	7.3	6.4	28.3	81.2	70.0
1990	8.0	4.9	31.2	106.8	87.4
2000	9.6	6.8	39.7	108.5	112.1

| | Japanese Colonies | | | Dutch | US |
	China	Taiwan	South Korea	Indonesia	Philippines
1913	39.8	53.9	59.1	22.3	19.9
1929	27.7	56.6	50.0	20.6	21.8
1938	22.9	53.2	59.6	22.4	24.8
1950	22.9	48.1	40.1	14.0	11.2
1960	16.9	37.4	27.7	12.3	13.0
1970	8.1	30.7	20.1	10.0	11.7
1980	7.9	43.7	30.6	12.7	12.8
1990	9.9	52.6	46.3	14.6	9.6
2000	16.3	79.0	68.1	14.8	8.5

Source: Maddison 2003.

Note: n.a. = not available.

the twentieth century. The United Kingdom, the Netherlands, and France all underwent considerable political and social change over these decades, with consequences for colonial policies. A particularly important trend after 1900 was the granting of the franchise to groups previously disempowered, including working-class men and eventually women. Related to this was the increased demand for government social spending on unemployment and sickness benefits, pensions, health, and housing. In all three countries, government social spending more than doubled relative to GDP between 1900 and 1930 (Lindert 2004: table 1.2). Faced with increasing demands from the home electorates, European governments were under great pressure to make their imperial possessions financially self-sufficient. This implied using a minimum of force; British colonial administrators in both Africa and Asia were expected to operate with quite small military establishments, paid for out of local budgets (Gann 1984: 510). Pride in imperial possessions undoubtedly existed among the British, the French, and the Dutch public, but increasingly after 1900, home populations wanted governments to spend more on their welfare rather than on the governance of Asians living thousands of miles away.

Assembling and Governing Empires in Southeast Asia

Japan's colonial empire was only acquired in the late nineteenth century, and Japan was deprived of all its colonial territories after defeat in 1945. Thus its colonial experience in Asia was relatively short, at most six decades. America's full colonial control of the Philippines was even shorter, from 1900 to 1935. By contrast, European colonial control over Southeast Asia was imposed in stages from the sixteenth to the nineteenth centuries, although in many parts of the region effective colonial administrative systems were only established in the late nineteenth and early twentieth centuries. In all cases, colonial governments after 1900 adopted new approaches to taxation and revenue policy, to budgetary expenditures, and to the role of government in directing economic activity (Elson 1992: 149–154).

By the late nineteenth century, probably the most dense and intrusive system of colonial governance in Southeast Asia was that built up by the Dutch in Java, although more liberal economic policies favoring private enterprise had been adopted after 1870, when the system of coercive cultivation of export crops was officially terminated. But Dutch control, both economic and political, over the other parts of the vast Indonesian archipelago was at best patchy. Lindblad has pointed out that, during the nineteenth century, many of the islands outside Java were still integrated into the wider Southeast Asian trading system and only very loosely under Dutch control (Dick, Houben, Lindblad, and Thee 2002: 82). It was only after 1900 that Dutch colony policy in Indonesia became characterized by a "systematic *mise en valeur* and an active role on the part of the state" (Wesseling 1988: 68). As the new century dawned, Dutch colonial officials were determined to transform their huge Southeast Asian colony into something more than just a loosely integrated free trade area, even if that meant disrupting traditional flows of goods, money, and people to and from regions outside Dutch control. They also became increasingly concerned about improving "native welfare," a concern that was in part prompted by a realization that a poverty-stricken colony could become a serious economic liability for the mother country (Booth 1998: 2–6).

By 1900, the phrase *mise en valeur* had also become the watchword of French officials in Indochina, who viewed ambitious infrastructure development as the main means of developing their Southeast Asian colonial possessions (Doumer 1902: 24). Although French Indochina consisted of contiguous territories in mainland Southeast Asia, rather than a chain of islands, it shared one crucial characteristic with Indonesia. Population densities varied considerably; in much of northern and central Vietnam, the pressure of people on land was as great as in Java, but southern Vietnam, Cambodia, and Laos were more lightly populated and still had considerable land available for more intensive agricultural cultivation. Like the Dutch, the French saw population movement as one way of dealing with problems of overpopulation, on the one hand, and underutilized agricultural resources on the other. For much of the period from 1900 to 1940, French officials studied Dutch colonial policies in Indonesia closely; they also examined policies relating to agriculture and public works in the Philippines, British Malaya, and India. French officials published the results of these studies in official outlets such as the *Bulletin économique de l'Indochine*.

In several respects, the two British colonies in Southeast Asia, Burma and British Malaya, had very different experiences from other parts of region, and from each other, during the first part of the twentieth century. British control over Burma was established in a series of punitive expeditions through the nineteenth century, culminating in the deportation of King Thibaw in late 1885 and the subsequent establishment of Upper Burma as a province of the British Indian Empire. For the next five decades, Burma was ruled from Delhi; it was only in April 1937 that Burma was made a crown colony in its own right, with some degree of self-government.

British Malaya by contrast was never governed as a single colony before 1942. The British established a settlement in Penang in the late eighteenth century, and in 1819, Stamford Raffles acquired the island of Singapore for the East India Company. In 1867, Singapore, Malacca, Penang, and some territory close to Penang on the mainland of peninsular Malaya were formed into a colony known as the Straits Settlements. In 1896, four Malay states in the center of the peninsula, which had come under British control between 1874 and 1889, and had accepted the presence of British advisers, were formed into the Federated Malay States (FMS), with an administrative center in Kuala Lumpur. Other parts of the peninsula, including the northern states of Trengganu, Perak, Perlis, and Kelantan and the southern state of Johore became the Unfederated Malay States (UMS) in the early part of the twentieth century. These states were more independent of British control, although government of both the FMS and the UMS was at first rather indirect, with the British administrators operating through traditional rulers. White has pointed out that Malaya was not expected to fulfill any grand imperial economic role and was indeed an "afterthought of empire," a territory that the British acquired mainly in order to protect vital sea-lanes (1999: 176). But gradually the official British attitude toward its possessions on the Malayan peninsula began to change. These changes were related to a growing awareness of the potential of the region as a producer of strategic raw materials, increasingly in demand by the rapidly industrializing economies of Europe and North America.

This growing awareness was also shared by the Dutch and the French and to an increasing extent by the Americans in the Philippines. By the late nineteenth century, it was clear that the economic future of many tropical regions lay not so much in export of foodstuffs such as rice, sugar, coffee, cocoa, tea, and spices but in new crops, such as rubber and vegetable oils, and in mineral products including tin, bauxite, and petroleum, which were crucial inputs into new and rapidly growing industries in Europe and North America. The traditional food exports remained important, but everywhere in Southeast Asia, colonial officialdom became more concerned with promoting "new exports," which would be produced by capitalist companies, usually incorporated in the metropole, using modern, large-scale production technologies. The agricultural estate, which had not, with the partial exception of Java, been widely found in Southeast Asia in the nineteenth century, became the favored vehicle for the production of new crops such as rubber and palm oil (neither indigenous to Southeast Asia), while mining companies were established to exploit reserves of minerals and petroleum.

As the production of new export commodities accelerated, colonial governments also became much more aware of the need for better infrastructure and for a disciplined labor force prepared to work long hours under arduous conditions. Ports, roads, and railways were increasingly provided by governments, using revenues raised locally through taxes and monopolies and also from foreign loans. The problem of securing a labor force was more difficult to solve, as in regions where land was abundant, local populations were understandably reluctant to abandon traditional farming activities for a harsh life as wage laborers. Increasingly labor was brought into export-producing regions in Southeast Asia from India and China, or from labor-surplus regions within the colonies; in Indonesia the Dutch encouraged Javanese workers to move to Sumatra, while the estates in Cochinchina used migrants from central and northern Vietnam.

The rapid growth of both traditional and new export industries in the decades from 1870 to 1930 transformed the economies of several regions of Southeast Asia. But although these transformations involved large flows of capital and people, their impact on the economic and social status of indigenous peoples was limited. To a considerable extent, this was the result of deliberate policies on the part of colonial officials anxious to protect local populations from what they viewed as the ill effects of exposure to "high capitalism." Urbanization in much of the region was limited, and although port cities grew, their populations were often dominated by migrants from other parts of Asia as well as from the metropoles and other parts of the world. It has been argued that Southeast Asia in 1900 was less urbanized than in the sixteenth century:

> The colonial regimes believed that they were "opening" Southeast Asian economies and societies to the world by exporting their produce and building infrastructure. In social and cultural terms the reverse was more nearly the case. As never before Southeast Asians became a peasant people

living in rural villages insulated by paternalistic officials and culturally distant traders from the changes that were transforming the world outside. (Reid 2001: 59)

This argument has important implications for the models of colonial economic development in East and Southeast Asia drawn up by economists in the postcolonial era.

How Did Colonial Economies Function?
Vent for Surplus Theory and the Open Dualistic Model of Colonial Development

Although British, Dutch, and French scholars made important contributions to the study of the precolonial history of Southeast Asia, including the study of precolonial economic systems, their work seems to have had very little impact on postcolonial studies of economic development in East and Southeast Asia. Instead most scholars who have written on the economic development of East and Southeast Asia in the second part of the twentieth century have used analytical tools drawn from Western classical and neoclassical economic theory. One influential concept, particularly associated with the work of the Burmese economist Hla Myint (1958, 1987), is that of "vent for surplus." In developing this concept, Myint drew on the work of the classical economists, especially Adam Smith.

Myint argued that many underdeveloped economies in Asia and Africa had responded to the challenges of international trade, especially after 1870, by drawing on previously underutilized resources of land and labor to produce crops such as rice, coffee, cocoa, and spices, and after 1910 new crops such as rubber for the world market. In contrast to conventional comparative advantage theory, in which producers operating in an economy where all resources are already fully employed respond to international trade by reallocating factors of production away from home goods and toward exportables, the vent for surplus approach assumes that in developing economies there are idle resources of both land and labor that can be put to work to produce more exportables without necessarily reducing output of home goods such as food and clothing. According to Myint:

> The vent for surplus theory was particularly suited to explain the rapid expansion of agricultural exports from the relatively sparsely populated countries of Southeast Asia and West Africa. After the initial opening up of these countries in the late nineteenth and early twentieth centuries, agricultural exports grew typically about 5 per cent a year for many decades. This happened without any important change in agricultural techniques, simply by bringing more land under cultivation. The additional labour was drawn from the subsistence sector. (1987: 121)

Over the years, attempts have been made to integrate the vent for surplus approach with other theories of export-led development, including the staples theory developed by Canadian economic historians. However, economic historians have not found it easy to explain why countries with apparently similar factor endowments in the late nineteenth century have evolved so differently during the twentieth century (Findlay and Lundhal 1994: 90). Why, at the end of the century, did Ghana and Burma have a much lower per capita GDP than Malaysia? Why has Argentina performed less well than Canada or Australia? According to Findlay and Lundhal, much of the explanation lies in political economy factors, including ownership patterns and the distribution of productive assets and incomes.

As is clear from the above quotation, Myint argued that the vent for surplus theory was only applicable to sparsely populated regions with considerable land resources. As we will see, several parts of East and Southeast Asia by the early twentieth century did not really fit this description. Myint's analysis has also been criticized for not taking into account the full range of products produced by the pretrade, subsistence economy, especially handicrafts. Hymer and Resnick have pointed out that the process of opening up to trade would involve not just more production for export, but also inward flows of imported manufactures that would compete down labor-intensive handicrafts produced by the subsistence sector (1971: 484–486). The extended vent for surplus model developed by Smith (1976) allows for the partial demise of the handicraft sector and also examines the implications of the failure to bring about significant technological progress in the food-crop sector.

Another analytical framework that has gained attention in the Asian context is that of the open dualistic colonial economy, developed by Hicks and McNicoll (1971) in their study of the Philippines, and Paauw and Fei (1973), who examined the economic transition from colonial to postcolonial economies in Taiwan, the Philippines, Malaysia, and Thailand. It has also been used by Ho to analyze the impact of Japanese colonialism in East Asia (1984: 380–386). In developing the model, these scholars drew on much previous work on economic development by W. Arthur Lewis, Hla Myint, Albert Hirschman, Paul Baran, Richard Caves, and Robert Baldwin, and also on a number of empirical studies of economic development in East and Southeast Asia. Variants of the model have also been used to analyze the impact of export-processing zones in Asia (Warr 1989).

At the core of the open dualistic framework are flows of commodities, labor, technology, and capital between the modern and traditional sectors of the economy, and between both these sectors and the rest of the world. In the basic version of the model, used by Paauw and Fei to describe the operation of the colony economy (1973: 4–5), the traditional sector was largely insulated from both the modern enclave and the foreign sector. The modern enclave comprises both export agriculture and the nonagricultural sector, which imports manufactures from abroad. There is also a domestic market within the enclave, where purchasing power is generated by primary exports. To complete the triangularism, the nonagricultural sector sells goods and services to the domestic market serving commercial agriculture.

> This triangular mode of the economy's operation serves to achieve colonialism's fundamental goal, the realization of profits through production and exports of primary products. Export surplus may be defined as the surplus from exports over and above imports required to maintain the existing level of production. . . . The economic goal of colonialism was to extract from the colony a tangible gain in the form of this export surplus. (Paauw and Fei 1973: 5)

Paauw and Fei argued that one of the main legacies of this "triangular mode" was that the domestic economy of the colony was compartmentalized into two largely insulated parts: a modern, export-oriented enclave and a large, backward, and stagnant agricultural sector. It was implicit in the model that investment would be concentrated in the export sector and that the pace of investment would be a function of foreign demand for the colony's exports. It was also assumed that very few "inter-industry or commercial linkages take place between the enclave and the hinterland, so the economic growth experienced by the enclave is never transmitted to the hinterland, where most of the native population reside." Furthermore the colony's exports and imports would be tightly tied to the requirements of the metropole so that bilateralism would be a strong feature of colonial trade flows (Ho 1984: 382). Thus the industrial and modern service sector, including financial services, "developed no internal momentum" of their own (Paauw and Fei 1973: 7).

Several aspects of this model seem unrealistic in the context of colonies in East and Southeast Asia in the early decades of the twentieth century. Perhaps the most serious drawback is that, unlike the vent for surplus approach, it treats the "traditional" sector as largely cut off from both the modern enclave and the foreign sector. The model thus seems to make no provision for the direct involvement of indigenous agricultural producers in the export economy. Nor is there any provision for movement of goods, labor, capital, or technologies between the traditional economy and the modern enclave. As Ho points out, the Japanese did try, with considerable success, to disseminate new technologies in the rice sector to farmers in both Taiwan and Korea. The role of government is also largely ignored, and there is no discussion of either the impact of taxation on the traditional sector or the effect of government expenditures on, for example, infrastructure development.

In their exposition of the open, dualistic model, Hicks and McNicoll abandon the assumption of a completely closed traditional sector and allow for export flows from the traditional sector and also flows of commodities such as food between the traditional sector and the modern enclave (1971: 35–37). But for a fuller exposition of both the positive and negative consequences of flows between the traditional sector and the modern enclave, we should turn to Lewis (1976: 26–30). Lewis lists a number of benefits that can accrue to the traditional sector from the development of an export enclave:

1   Payments for commodities such as food and raw materials sold to the modern enclave;
2   Payments for labor services supplied by workers from the traditional sector, some of which are likely to be remitted back to households in the sector;
3   Provision of goods and services from the modern enclave, including imported inputs and possibly credit, at cheaper prices than prevailed previously;
4   Provision of infrastructure services such as ports, railways and roads, water supplies, and health facilities, that may have been built for enterprises and residents in the modern enclave but could be also used by the population of the traditional sector, often at prices below average cost;
5   Provision of public services, including roads, irrigation, health, and education, paid for out of tax revenues that may accrue partly from the traditional sector and partly from the modern sector;
6   Provision of new crops and technologies including new agricultural staples (such as rubber) and also new public health technologies (such as smallpox vaccination) that can have important demographic implications;
7   Provision of new institutions in (for example) land and property rights or an enhanced role for local government.

To offset these possible benefits, Lewis lists a number of negative effects that the development of the modern enclave might have on the traditional sector:

1   The enclave may be predatory on the traditional sector through the enforced provision of labor, the compulsory acquisition of their lands at low or zero prices, or the compulsory provision of food and other commodities;
2   The products produced by the enclave or imported from abroad may destroy traditional handicraft industries and traditional services (e.g., railways or trucking displacing porters);
3   The above argument can be extended into the "Dutch disease" analysis of the negative impact of a booming export enclave—producing, for example, minerals—on producers of traditional traded goods through the effect of a real appreciation of the exchange rate. While in theory the negative effects can be offset by government taxation of the booming sector and use of the revenues to create jobs in nontraded goods and services, this in practice may not happen in a colonial economy where mining

and estate companies have considerable influence with the metropolitan government;

4   The development of the enclave will attract the brightest and most ambitious among the indigenous population leading to a brain drain from the traditional sector and increased polarization of the national economy;

5   It is also likely that the provision of a limited number of highly paid jobs in the modern enclave for people from the traditional sector will induce large-scale migration to and unemployment in the modern enclave;

6   The gradual dissemination of modern health technologies from the enclave to the traditional sector will lead to falling mortality and faster population growth in the traditional sector, which in turn could lead to pressure on available land and growing landlessness and rural impoverishment;

7   Although not specifically mentioned by Lewis, it is implicit in the open dualistic model that export surpluses sustained over long periods of time will reduce the growth of gross national income (as distinct from gross domestic product) and thus resources available to the domestic economy for both investment and consumption.

The above list of possible negative effects is indeed a formidable one, as Lewis acknowledged (1976: 29). It is true that these negative effects might accrue from any process of economic growth based on a dynamic export enclave and not just one taking place under a colonial government. According to Lewis, whether the net impact of the export enclave on the traditional sector is positive or negative depends crucially on whether the government "coerces or helps the traditional sectors, and on the nature of the enclaves" (ibid.). The so-called staple theory of development as well as the linkage concept stress that some export staples appear to have had a more positive effect on broad-based economic development than others, with sugar often appearing to be the "development villain" (Hirschman 1977: 92). But as Hanson has pointed out, the problem with these arguments is that the growth experience of economies producing the same staples is often very different, owing sometimes to the role of government and sometimes to the emergence of private entrepreneurs (1980: 46–50).

Questions Addressed in This Study

The debates triggered by both the vent for surplus and the open dualistic models have raised a complex set of questions that continue to be analyzed in the context of many former colonial territories, in Asia and elsewhere. Answers to these questions can in turn help us to explain the very different postcolonial outcomes that we observe in the second part of the twentieth century. That these outcomes have varied considerably in East and Southeast Asia is obvious from Tables 1.1 and 1.2. By 2000, the two former Japanese colonies of Taiwan and Korea (the Republic of Korea or South Korea) had achieved a substantial measure of "catch-up" both with the United States and with Japan. This was also true of the two city-states, one of which (Hong Kong) remained a British colony until 1997, while Singapore became an independent republic after it withdrew from the Federation of Malaysia in 1965. Of the other former colonies in Asia, India, Indonesia, Burma, and the Philippines all had lower per capita GDP, relative to the United States, in 2000 than in 1913. In other words, per capita GDP growth was slower during the twentieth century in these economies than in the United States. Far from catching up with the world's leading economy, these countries were falling further behind. Even in Malaysia, widely considered to be among the more successful economies in Southeast Asia in recent decades, per capita GDP relative to that of the United States was only slightly higher in 2000 than in 1929.

Confronted with the evidence on growth of GDP in the twentieth century, several scholars have claimed that because the two former Japanese colonies have performed better since 1950 than the former British, Dutch, French, or American colonies in Asia, or indeed than Thailand, which was never formally a colony, Japanese colonialism was exceptional, especially in its emphasis on economic development. For example, Reynolds, in a survey of economic growth in the third world since 1850, argued that "Japan has always been growth-oriented, in colonial areas as well as at home; and it is clear that Japanese rule helped to initiate intensive growth in both Korea and Taiwan" (1983: 956). Maddison argued that "Japanese colonialism was more developmental than that of other countries, because it involved a greater effort to transfer and develop technology, higher physical investment and better development of local development and human capital" (1990: 365). Similar claims for the developmental impact of Japanese colonialism in Korea have been made by Kohli (1994) and Cumings (1984a: 481).

It is possible that these writers have fallen into the trap of writing history backward and have simply concluded that because the postcolonial performance of Taiwan and South Korea has been better than elsewhere in Asia (including the independent state of Thailand), Japanese colonialism must have been more developmental. But this would be unfair to scholars with a deep knowledge of processes of economic growth and structural change in Asia and elsewhere. This study will argue that there is evidence that the Japanese approached their colonial mission in both Taiwan and Korea with different goals from those of the European colonial powers and that these goals did make a difference to the policies they adopted. But as we have seen, the Americans also believed that their colonial policies were different and were more concerned with fostering the capacity of Filipinos to govern themselves. Why then has the economic performance of the Philippines been so different from the performances of Taiwan and South Korea after 1960?

To answer this question, it is necessary to go back to the early decades of the twentieth century and to look in detail at economic trends during these decades, and then to review a number of economic and social indicators for all the colonial territories in East and Southeast Asia in the 1930s. If indeed the difference between the Japanese colonies and the rest was sufficiently striking on the eve of the Pacific War to give a clear indication of their post-1950 trajectories, then the case for Japanese developmental colonialism would seem to be confirmed. But if the differences were not obvious, then that would strengthen the case of those who argue that it was the process of decolonization itself and the policies adopted by independent regimes, some of which were intended to reverse colonial polices, that were decisive in putting the former Japanese colonies on a different development trajectory after 1945.

Chapters 2 and 3 present a review of the evidence on economic and demographic growth and structural change across East and Southeast Asia from the late nineteenth century to 1940. To what extent was agricultural growth driven by exports rather than home consumption? How important were new technologies in agricultural growth? How much industrial growth took place, and what were the effects of industrial growth on employment? And how much growth occurred in services? To the extent that growing populations were largely accommodated in agriculture, what were the implications for access to land? Was economic growth accompanied by a growing polarization of the agricultural population into landlords, tenants, and landless laborers? Or did a robust landowning peasantry manage to coexist with the large-scale estates owned by both foreign and domestic interests?

Lewis (1976) stressed that the role of government is crucial in determining the impact of enclave development on the traditional economy. Other scholars of colonial development have also stressed that colonial governments, through both taxation and expenditure policies, have played a crucial role in shaping the development environment, and that to ignore the role of government is to "omit crucial economic linkages in the development process" (Birnberg and Resnick 1975: 250). It is implicit in most criticisms of colonial economic policies, in Asia and elsewhere, that governments either had little effect at all on the economy, beyond the "nightwatchman role" of raising enough revenues to run a minimalist administration and maintain law and order, or favored the modern enclave in creating infrastructure and were coercive or even predatory in their treatment of the traditional sector. The concept of the colonial state as the precursor of the developmental state has had very little currency in Asia beyond the work of Kohli (1994) on Korea. But it is arguable that this concept has wider applicability in at least parts of Southeast Asia. The role of government in colonial East and Southeast Asia is discussed further in Chapter 4.

An important consequence of the open dualistic model, as expounded by Paauw and Fei, is that colonial economies will run large export surpluses that are used to finance remittances abroad, on either government or private account. It is also widely argued by postcolonial critics of colonial policies in East and Southeast Asia that most of these remittances went to governments or corporate enterprises, or to private citizens in the metropolitan country. A number of studies have shown that colonial trade and investment flows were usually biased in the direction of the metropolitan power (Kleiman 1976; Svedberg 1981). These arguments are reviewed in Chapter 5, which also examines the evolution of both trade and exchange rate policies in the various colonies in East and Southeast Asia in the period from 1900 to 1940 and the consequences of these policies for economic growth and structural change.

Another important strand in the postcolonial literature concerns the impact of colonial policies on the development of entrepreneurship. In the Southeast Asian context, an important concept is that of the "plural economy," which is associated with the work of Furnivall (1948, 1957). His argument was that, throughout much of the region, colonial policies encouraged in-migration from both China and India, and these migrants, together with the usually quite small European populations, mixed but did not combine with the many different indigenous groups that peopled Burma, Thailand, Malaya, Indonesia, the Philippines, and Indochina. According to Furnivall, the division of labor along ethnic lines became especially rigid in the European colonies, with each racial group performing different economic functions with little or no mobility between occupations. It has been argued that this rigidity contrasted with both the Philippines and Taiwan and Korea, where American and Japanese policies were more supportive of the development of a robust class of indigenous entrepreneurs. These arguments are evaluated in Chapter 6.

Another issue that has occasioned much debate and controversy concerns the impact of colonial economic policies on living standards of the indigenous populations. A frequent criticism is that such economic growth as occurred in the colonial era did not benefit the great majority of the population. Even while exports were booming, it is argued, food consumption per capita was stagnant or actually falling, and social indicators such as mortality rates, literacy, and educational enrollments showed little improvement. On the one hand, arguments about the "pauperization" of colonial populations have been made in the context of Korea as well as several Southeast Asian colonies. On the other hand, it has also been argued that, especially in Taiwan and the Philippines, Japanese and American policies led to improvements not just in incomes, but also in health and educational indicators. Using a range of economic and social indicators, Chapter 7 attempts to evaluate the impact of colonialism on living standards in East and Southeast Asia during the first four decades of the twentieth century.

By the late 1930s, the evidence reviewed in Chapter 7 suggests, there were significant differences between the various colonies in incomes and living standards. After the bombing of Pearl Harbor and the rapid conquest by the Japanese Imperial Army of Burma, Malaya, Indonesia, and the Philippines, together with the strengthening of Japanese control over cooperating regimes in Thailand and French Indochina, the Japanese were able to impose tight economic control over much of East and Southeast Asia. The Greater East Asian

Co-Prosperity Sphere was intended not just to destroy all vestiges of European and American control over Southeast Asia, but also to integrate both the Japanese colonies and the conquered territories of East and Southeast Asia into a huge single market, centered on Japan. Many Japanese sincerely believed this would lead to faster economic development and higher living standards throughout the region.

But in fact the years of the Japanese occupation were both an economic disaster and a political watershed for all the territories that fell under Japanese control. The reasons for this are examined in Chapter 8. It is probable that, by August 1945, when the Japanese were forced into an unconditional surrender, the lives of at least five million people in Southeast Asia had been brought to a premature end through starvation and disease. In addition, heavy Allied bombing had destroyed infrastructure and productive enterprises throughout Southeast Asia, and also in Taiwan and Korea. Virtually everywhere in the region, as well as in Japan itself, per capita domestic output was well below prewar levels, and most experts thought that the recovery period would be prolonged.

In fact there was considerable variation in the economic strategies adopted by the various governments in the region in the years after 1945, which affected both the speed of recovery and the prospects for continued economic growth and structural change. Much of the explanation for the differences lies with the very different processes of decolonization that took place after 1945. Chapter 9 examines these differences and the consequences for economic policy making in the fifteen years from 1945 to 1960. During these years several countries in Southeast Asia adopted what Myint (1967) termed inward-looking policies, which stressed national self-reliance rather than continued reliance on exports as an engine of growth. Others adopted more outward-looking policies that encouraged both the rehabilitation and expansion of traditional exports and diversification away from primary products and toward manufactures. While there is a strong consensus in the literature that countries that implemented outward-looking policies achieved faster economic growth, it is argued in Chapter 9 that other initiatives were also crucial in laying the foundations for accelerated growth after 1960. Of particular importance were policies directed toward the reform of agrarian systems and toward the elimination of the legacies of the plural economy.

To what extent do the different colonial legacies explain the different policies adopted by postindependence governments? Or were the differences in policies mainly the result of the different regimes that emerged as a result of the post-1945 decolonization process? That these regimes differed widely can hardly be disputed. By the late 1960s, many countries in Asia were ruled by regimes in which the military played a dominant role and that had little or no democratic legitimacy. This was true of South Korea and Taiwan as well as Burma, Thailand, Indonesia, and South Vietnam. But economic policies and outcomes varied considerably among these countries, in spite of the apparent similarities in the political regimes. In the Philippines and the Federation of Malaysia, from which Singapore broke away in 1965, the military had a much lower profile in government, and the political leadership was largely civilian and had greater popular support, although this hardly meant economic policies were similar in the Philippines, Malaysia, and Singapore. What explained these differences? The final chapter concludes by drawing together the main themes and arguments of the book and tries to provide some answers to the above questions.

CHAPTER 2

Economic Growth and Structural Change: 1900–1940

Population Growth

By the end of the 1930s, the population of colonial Southeast Asia together with independent Thailand amounted to around 150 million people. The population of Korea and Taiwan together came to almost 30 million. By the 1930s, all colonial governments had carried out population censuses and were also collecting a range of other data on landholdings, employment, and literacy. It is therefore possible to estimate with reasonable accuracy population growth during the early decades of the twentieth century (Table 2.1). Everywhere in East and Southeast Asia growth rates exceeded 1 percent per annum, and in Thailand, the Philippines, and British Malaya they were over 2 percent per annum, which were high growth rates for that period. Although population growth rates tended to be higher in the relatively less densely settled parts of the region, there were still, by the end of the 1930s, striking regional differences in population densities, with Java, Korea, and Taiwan having the highest populations per square kilometer of area, and Laos, Cambodia, and the Outer Islands of Indonesia the lowest.

Three variables determine the rate of growth of population in a given region or country: the birth rate, the death rate, and the rate of inward and outward migration. Changes in each of these variables had important demographic consequences in East and Southeast Asia in the early decades of the twentieth century, to varying degrees in different parts of the region. Although birth rates remained quite high virtually everywhere, mortality rates had begun to fall by the early twentieth century, mainly as a result of the dissemination of modern medical technology and the active implementation of public health measures by colonial officials. In the more land-abundant countries and regions, in-migration was often encouraged, either from more densely settled regions within the colony or from abroad. In Southeast Asia, most of the overseas migration was from either India or China. In addition, most colonial territories experienced in-migration from the metropolitan power. This migration had the biggest demographic impact in the Japanese colonies, especially Taiwan. Overseas out-migration also occurred in some areas; its

Table 2.1. Population Density and Growth in East and Southeast Asia

Colony	Population: 1939 (millions)	Population Density (per square km.)	Population Growth: c. 1913–1939 (percent annual growth)
Taiwan	5.7	160	2.1
Korea	24.0	109	1.7
Tonkin	10.4	88	1.4
Annam	8.0	54	0.7
Cochinchina	6.1	95	1.1
All Vietnam	24.5	74	1.1
Cambodia	3.1	17	1.6
Laos	1.0	4	1.3
Thailand	15.2	30	2.2
Burma	16.4	27	1.2
Philippines	16.2	53	2.4
British Malaya	5.4	39	2.5
Java	47.0	356	1.1
Outer Islands	21.4	12	1.5
All Indonesia	68.4	36	1.3

Sources: Korea: Grajdanzev 1944: 71–74; Taiwan: Barclay 1954: 13; Indonesia: Central Bureau of Statistics 1947: 6, with additional data from Boomgaard and Gooszen 1991; Vietnam: Banens 2000: 33; Cambodia and Laos: Direction des Services Économiques 1947: 271; Thailand: Manarungsan 1989: 32; Burma: Saito and Lee 1999: 7; Philippines: Bureau of Census and Statistics 1941: 13; British Malaya: Department of Statistics 1939: 36.

impact was probably greatest in Korea, where it was estimated that by the 1930s, 10 percent of the total population was "earning its bread abroad." By 1940, there were more Koreans in Japan than Japanese in Korea (Grajdanzev 1944: 76–81).

Although international migration was important in most parts of the region, its impact on the composition of populations within different colonies should not be exaggerated. Census data from the 1930s reveal that, in most parts of East and Southeast Asia, the vast majority of the population was indigenous. The main exception was British Malaya, where Chinese and Indian migrants and their descendants accounted for over half of the population in 1931 (Table 2.2). The population of Thailand who identified themselves as Chinese by race in the 1937 census amounted to more than 4 percent of the total population, although it is probable that many descendants of earlier migrants who had made Thailand their home either no longer considered themselves Chinese or did not wish to identify themselves as such in the census. Manarungsan has estimated that almost 12 percent of the population of Thailand was of Chinese descent in 1937 (1989: 32). Everywhere apart from

British Malaya, indigenous populations accounted for more than 85 percent of the total. Migrant Asians and their descendants tended to account for a higher proportion of urban populations than rural ones, although this too varied considerably by country and region. Chinese were estimated to account for 74 percent of the population of Singapore in 1931, 39 percent of the combined populations of Saigon and Cholon, but only 15 percent of the population of Batavia and the adjoining suburb of Meester Cornelis (Purcell 1965: 177; Boomgaard and Gooszen 1991: table 15.2b).

The extent of urbanization itself varied considerably across East and Southeast Asia in the early decades of the twentieth century. Although as Reid (2001) has argued, it is probable that urban populations declined as a proportion of total populations in several parts of the region after 1600, the early decades of the twentieth century did witness considerable urban growth. The most urbanized colony by the 1930s was without doubt British Malaya. Over 10 percent of the population lived in the largest city, Singapore, and more than 18 percent lived in the five largest cities. Sixteen percent lived in cities with populations in excess of 100,000 (Table 2.3). All these percentages were higher than in Taiwan, which was probably the next most urbanized colony, although

Table 2.2. Percentage Breakdown of Colonial Populations by Ethnic Background, 1930s

Colony	Europeans/Japanese/Americans	Chinese	Other Asians	Indigenous
Taiwan (1935)	5.2	1.1[a]	n.a.	93.7
Korea (1939)	2.9	0.2	n.a.	96.9
Tonkin (1937)	0.2	0.4	n.a.	99.4
Annam (1937)	0.1	0.2	n.a.	99.7
Cochinchina (1937)	0.3	3.7	n.a.	96.0
Cambodia (1937)	0.1	3.5	n.a.	96.4
Laos (1937)	0.1	0.3	n.a.	99.6
Thailand (1937)	n.a.	11.8	0.8	87.4
Burma (1931)	0.2	1.3	8.2[b]	90.3
British Malaya (1931)	0.4	39.0	15.8	44.7
Philippines (1939)	0.3	0.7	n.a.	99.0
Java (1930)	0.5	1.4	0.1	98.0
Other Indonesia (1930)	0.3	3.4	0.3	96.0

Sources: Korea: Grajdanzev 1944: 76; Taiwan: Barclay 1954: 16; Indonesia: Boomgaard and Gooszen 1991; French Indochina: Robequain 1944: tables 1 and 6; Thailand: Manarungsan 1989: 32; Burma: Saito and Lee 1999: table 1-3; Philippines: Bureau of Census and Statistics 1947: 17; British Malaya: Department of Statistics 1939: 36.

Note: n.a. = not available.

[a] Refers to citizens of mainland China and other foreigners.

[b] Includes Indo-Burmans.

by the end of the 1930s, the largest cities were Keijo (modern Seoul) in Korea, Manila in the Philippines, and Bangkok in Thailand. The least urbanized parts of Southeast Asia were French Indochina and the Outer Islands of Indonesia; less than 3 percent of the population in French Indochina lived in the five largest cities and only 2 percent outside Java (Table 2.3).

The extent of urbanization reflected the extent of economic diversification away from agriculture and toward industry and services, although by no means all nonagricultural activity was located in urban areas. By the fourth decade of the twentieth century, many colonies in East and Southeast Asia had achieved both growth in per capita GDP and considerable diversification away from small-scale agriculture. In the process, their populations diversified their sources of income by seeking new employment opportunities in addition to or in place of more traditional occupations.

Growth in National Output and Income: 1913–1938

In 1913, the United States had already become the world leader in terms of both total and per capita GDP (Maddison 2003: tables 8b, 8c). Of the major European economies, the United Kingdom still had the highest per capita GDP, followed by Belgium and the Netherlands, but in terms of total GDP, the United Kingdom had been overtaken by Germany (ibid.: table 1b). Of the

Table 2.3. Urban Populations as a Percentage of Total Populations, 1930s

Colony	Largest City	Largest Five	All Cities over 100,000	Population of Largest City (thousands)
Taiwan (1940)	5.7	13.7	10.5	313
Korea (1940)	3.8	7.6	8.3	935
Indochina (1931)	1.2[a]	2.8	2.4	256[a]
Thailand (1937)	6.1[b]	n.a.	n.a.	890[b]
Burma (1931)	2.7	4.8	3.7	400
British Malaya (1931)	10.2	18.2	16.1	446
Philippines (1939)	5.3	n.a.	n.a.	848
Java (1930)	1.3[c]	3.4	3.7	533[c]
Other Indonesia (1930)	0.6	2.0	0.6	108

Sources: Korea: Grajdanzev 1944: 80; Taiwan: Barclay 1954: 116; French Indochina: Purcell 1965: 176; Thailand: Central Statistical Office 1955: table 3; Burma: Saito and Lee 1999: table 1-4; Philippines: Bureau of Census and Statistics 1947: 18; British Malaya: Vlieland 1932: 45–47; Indonesia: Boomgaard and Gooszen 1991: tables 15.2b, 22b.

Note: n.a. = not available.

[a] Saigon and Cholon.

[b] Changwat of Phra-nakorn and Thonburi.

[c] Batavia and Meester Cornelis.

major Asian economies, only Japan had a per capita GDP that was more than one-quarter of that of the United States; in most of the colonial territories and in China, per capita GDP was well below 20 percent of that in the United States (see Table 1.1). After Japan, the highest per capita GDP in 1913, according to the Maddison estimates, was in Hong Kong and Singapore, followed by the Philippines, Indonesia, Malaysia, and Thailand. South Korea and Taiwan were below all these countries and above only Burma. Although Hong Kong was a British colony and a separate jurisdiction from China, Singapore was an integral part of the Straits Settlements, which were in turn part of British Malaya. A population-weighted average of the per capita GDP of both Singapore and the rest of British Malaya in 1913 was still below the Philippines, although above other colonial territories in the region (Table 2.4).

By 1929, Taiwan and South Korea had overtaken Thailand but were still below the other three Southeast Asian economies, according to Maddison. But his estimates have been challenged by Fukao, Ma, and Yuan (2005: table 6), who put forward a new set of purchasing-power-adjusted figures for both Taiwan and Korea, and argue that, by 1930, per capita GDP in Taiwan was 82 percent of that in Japan, compared with only 43 percent in Korea. If their figures are correct, then Taiwan's per capita GDP in 1929 would have been above the Philippines, although still below that of British Malaya, including Singapore. It has been claimed that British Malaya enjoyed very rapid output growth of per capita GDP during the second and third decades of the twentieth century, probably of around 4 percent per annum (Maddison 2003: 183). We do not yet have a comprehensive national income study for all of British Malaya for this period, but it is likely that, by 1929, average per capita GDP for all three parts,

Table 2.4. Per Capita GDP for Japan, Thailand, and Colonies in East and Southeast Asia, 1913, 1929, and 1938

	Per Capita GDP (1990 dollars)			Percentage Growth Rate	
	1913	1929	1938	1913–1929	1913–1938
Japan	1,387	2,026	2,449	2.4	2.3
Philippines	1,053	1,502	1,522	2.2	1.5
Indonesia	904	1,170	1,175	1.6	1.1
Malaysia	900[a]	1,682	1,361	4.0	1.7
Thailand	841	793	826	−0.4	−0.1
Korea	820	1,014	1,459	1.3	2.3
Taiwan	747	1,146	1,302	2.7	2.2
Burma	685	n.a.	740	n.a.	0.3

Source: Maddison 2003: 180–183.

Note: n.a. = not available.

[a] Maddison's figures refer to the contemporary state of Malaysia, which excludes Singapore. A population-weighted average of per capita GDP for Singapore and Malaysia in 1913 would have been $943.

including Singapore, was almost 90 percent of that of Japan. Other colonial territories in Southeast Asia also grew in per capita terms during these decades, although at a slower rate than British Malaya. Only Thailand, which was not a colony, stagnated.

It was only during the 1930s, a period of slow or negative growth in most parts of Southeast Asia, that the two Japanese colonies grew much faster than other parts of Southeast Asia, although in 1938 the Philippines still had a per capita GDP above either of them, according to the Maddison estimates (see Table 2.4). The revised estimates of Fukao, Ma, and Yuan (2005) suggest that Taiwan's per capita GDP was much closer to that of Japan. If their estimates are correct, then per capita GDP in Taiwan would have been above that of the Philippines by 1938, although that of Korea would still have been well below both the Philippines and British Malaya. It will be argued in subsequent chapters that there is considerable evidence to support this ranking.

The poor growth performance of most parts of Southeast Asia during the 1930s was a direct consequence of their high exposure to international markets for primary products. Not only did prices of most tropical agricultural products and most minerals fall, but many commodities became subject to international quota agreements, which restricted output. Administering these quotas became a major challenge for governments in several colonies in the 1930s. Those colonies that could sell their exports into protected markets in the metropolitan economy or in other parts of the metropolitan power's imperial possessions had a considerable advantage. The response to the problems of the 1930s varied considerably by colony, but in several cases governments responded by promoting economic diversification, including the development of manufacturing industry.

Growth of Agricultural Output

As would be expected given the generally low levels of per capita GDP in 1913, most Asian economies were predominantly agricultural, with more than 40 percent of GDP coming from the agricultural sector, except in Japan, where the share had already fallen to under 30 percent (Table 2.5). In Korea almost 60 percent of GDP accrued from agriculture and forestry, which was a higher share than in those Southeast Asian countries for which we have estimates, with the exception of Burma. Agricultural growth was certainly rapid in both Taiwan and Korea after 1913, and by 1938 value added in agriculture had doubled in Taiwan and almost doubled in Korea. The performance in Thailand, Indonesia, and Burma was not as impressive, mainly because of the very slow growth in the 1930s. But in most parts of Asia over these years, the nonagricultural sectors were growing faster than agriculture so that by 1938 the agricultural share of GDP had fallen everywhere except in Thailand. In Indonesia, by 1938 agriculture accounted for about one-third of total GDP, compared with 41 percent in Taiwan and 47 percent in Korea (Table 2.5).

The rapid agricultural growth in both Korea and Taiwan after 1913 was very largely based on smallholder agriculture. Estate agriculture was unfamiliar to the Japanese, and the colonial officials felt comfortable with the landlord-tenant regimes that existed in both colonies, which were broadly similar to that in Japan. Introducing a plantation system "would have required a radical redistribution of rural assets, a change that might be too disruptive and counter-productive" (Ho 1984: 385). There was a broad similarity between Japan and its two colonies by 1920 in the ratio of land area per male agricultural worker, output per unit of land, and output per male agricultural worker (Hayami and Ruttan 1979: tables 1-1 and 1-4). By the 1920s, growth in land per agricultural worker was negative in both Korea and Taiwan; all the growth in output per worker was due to growth in output per unit of land. It is clear that the "vent for surplus" theory had little applicability in these two colonies.

Instead, the explanation for growth in agricultural output must be sought in technological change that led to rapid growth in crop yields, especially of rice. After the serious shortages and rice riots of 1918, the Japanese government began to facilitate the transfer of Japanese high-yielding rice varieties to both Taiwan and Korea, in the hope that both colonies could provide Japan with rice. The *ponlai* variety in particular diffused rapidly, and fertilizer use increased in both colonies (Hayami 1973: table 2.1; Lin 1973: 17–19; Lee and Chen 1979: 82–86; Myers and Yamada 1984: 437–439). Government investment in irrigation also grew, which led to an increase in double cropping, especially in Taiwan. By 1925, Korea was supplying Japan with more than 5 percent of its total rice consumption and Taiwan a further 2.8 percent (Ka 1995: 135). Taiwan also became an important supplier of sugar to Japan, dis-

Table 2.5. Index of Growth of Real Value Added in Agriculture for Japan, Thailand, and Selected Colonies, 1913, 1929, and 1938

Country	Index of Value Added in Agriculture			Percentage Annual Growth	Agriculture as a Percentage of NDP/GDP[a]	
	1913	1929	1938	1913–1938	1913	1938
Japan	100	118	129	1.0	28.9	15.6
Korea	100	133	184	2.5	63.3	47.1
Taiwan	100	132	202	2.8	53.8	41.2
Thailand	100	129	168	2.1	44.7	44.3
Burma	100	125	129	0.9	68.6	54.3
Philippines	n.a.	n.a.	n.a.	n.a.	60.4	46.6
Indonesia	100	131	148	1.6	40.5	33.7

Sources: Japan, Korea, and Taiwan: Mizoguchi and Umemura 1988: 230–239; Thailand: Manarungsan 1989: 251; Indonesia: van der Eng 2002: 171–172; Burma: Aye Hlaing 1965: 289; Philippines: Hooley 1968: table 1.

Note: n.a. = not available.

[a] NDP for Japan, Korea, Taiwan, and Burma; GDP for Indonesia and Thailand.

placing imports from Java (Lin 1973: 17). There can be little doubt that the introduction of a "Meiji agrarian strategy," including considerable investment in irrigation and rural infrastructure, and the large market in metropolitan Japan served to accelerate the pace of agricultural growth in both Korea and Taiwan, and by the late 1930s, rice yields were much higher than in other parts of Asia (Table 2.6). The impact of Japanese agrarian policies on the welfare of the rural population will be discussed further in subsequent chapters.

In much of Southeast Asia after 1900, colonial governments were also actively seeking to promote agricultural growth, both for home and foreign markets. The growth of rice production was quite rapid in the decades after 1910 in land-abundant parts of Southeast Asia such as the Philippines, Malaya, and Thailand, and in southern Vietnam (Cochinchina), although nowhere was it faster than in Taiwan (see Table 2.6). Much of this growth was due to the reproduction of traditional varieties over more land; where the cultivation frontier was pushed out to less fertile land, average yields tended

Table 2.6. Growth of Rice Production, 1916–1920 to 1937–1939, Per Capita Availability, and Planted Area per Agricultural Worker in East and Southeast Asia, 1937–1939

Colony/ Country	Output Growth 1916/1920 to 1937/1939[a] (% per annum)	Yields 1937/1939 (tons/ha.)	Per Capita Availability[b] 1937/1939 (kg. per year)	Irrigation Ratio[c]	Planted Rice Area per Agricultural Worker (ha.)
Taiwan	3.4	2.1	129[d]	83.7	0.47
Korea	2.9	2.1	91	68.5	0.21
Indochina	1.6	0.7	140[e]	n.a.	n.a.
Thailand	2.6	0.8	142	9.7	0.56
Burma	0.6	0.8	122	11.8	1.20
Malaya	2.7	1.1	178	n.a.	0.24
Philippines	2.3	0.8	97	24.8	0.57
Java	1.4	1.1	85	30.6	0.30

Sources: Rose 1985 with additional data from van der Eng 1996: tables A.3 and A.6; Saito and Lee 1999; Grajdanzev 1942: 54; Grajdanzev 1944: 291; Boomgaard and van Zanden 1990: 96; Barnett 1947: table 26. Data on per capita rice availabilities for Taiwan and Korea from Johnston 1953: 270, for the Philippines from Mears et al. 1974: 355, for Java from Mears 1961: 246, for Burma from Richter 1976: 6, for Thailand from Manarungsan 1989: 210–211, for British Malaya from Grist 1941: table 32, for Indochina from *Bulletin économique de l'Indochine* 52:5 (May 1949): 146.

Note: n.a. = not available.

[a] Output growth for British Malaya: 1917/1919 to 1937/1939; Korea: 1917/1918 to 1937/1938; Indochina: 1916/1918 to 1936/1938.

[b] Milled rice.

[c] Irrigated area as a percentage of harvested area of rice in the late 1930s.

[d] Average for 1938/1939 and 1939/1940.

[e] Average for 1934–1938.

to fall. In Burma and Thailand, yields of paddy per hectare either stagnated or declined between 1916–1920 and 1936–1940 (Saito and Lee 1999: 80–81; Manarungsan 1989: 50–51). Value added in agriculture in Burma (as estimated by Aye Hlaing) did not expand as rapidly as land under occupation during the period from 1901–1902 to 1936–1937 (Table 2.7). In the Philippines, Hooley found that land under cultivation also grew faster than agricultural output, especially after 1918 (1968: 16–18). He did not, however, consider that falling land productivity in the 1920s and 1930s was solely due to the extension of the cultivation frontier to less fertile regions.

Stagnant or falling land productivity, because of falling yields of food crops, was not characteristic of all parts of Southeast Asia in the first four decades of the twentieth century. In peninsular Malaya, yields per acre of wet paddy increased by 57 percent between 1925–1926 and 1938–1939, while area under cultivation increased by around 23 percent (Barnett 1947: table 26). In other words, significant yields growth was achieved at the same time culti-vated area expanded. The yields growth reflected investment in irrigation and also a program to disseminate new seed varieties (Lim 1977: 190). The Dutch in Java also tried to encourage greater use of fertilizer and to develop new vari-eties; these facilitated double cropping and thus increased production (Barker, Herdt, and Rose 1985: 58; van der Eng 1996: 81–91). Van der Eng estimates that land productivity grew by 0.5 percent per annum in Java between 1900 and 1920, and 1.2 percent per annum between 1920 and 1937 (1996: 39). Dur-ing these four decades, the real value of agricultural output almost doubled, while land area increased by only 38 percent (see Table 2.7).

From the latter part of the nineteenth century, in peninsular Malaya, in

Table 2.7. Index of Growth of Value Added in Agriculture and Cultivated Land, 1901 to 1938: Burma, the Philippines, and Java (1938 = 100)

	Burma		Philippines[a]		Java	
Year	Value Added	Land	Value Added	Land	Value Added	Land
1901–1902	76.0	65.6	40.9	29.4	53.6	72.3
1906–1907	67.5	76.9	n.a.	n.a.	61.5	74.7
1911–1912	76.1	81.8	n.a.	n.a.	72.6	84.6
1916–1917	109.9	86.2	89.8	66.8	77.1	90.1
1921–1922	77.2	90.3	n.a.	n.a.	73.7	94.4
1926–1927	94.2	94.9	95.6	n.a.	89.4	97.1
1931–1932	124.5	96.9	n.a.	n.a.	97.2	99.6
1936–1937	117.1	99.2	n.a.	n.a.	91.3	98.8
1938–1939	100.0	100.0	100.0	100.0	100.0	100.0

Sources: Burma: Saito and Lee 1999: 37, 214; Philippines: Hooley 1968: tables 1 and 5; Java: van der Eng 1996: tables A.1.2. and A.4.

Note: n.a. = not available.

[a] Figures for the Philippines refer to calendar years 1902, 1918, 1928, and 1938.

Sumatra, and in southern Vietnam, the British, Dutch, and French colonial authorities facilitated the acquisition of land by large estate companies to grow crops such as tobacco and rubber, while in Java the area under sugar (much of it rented from small farmers by the estate companies) increased rapidly after 1870. In the Philippines, there were few large-scale agricultural proprietors in the latter part of the nineteenth century (Legarda 1999: 185–186). The largest landlord was the Catholic church, which was induced to sell most of its lands by the incoming American administration. During the American period, large estates producing sugar, fruits, and other crops were built up, many of them owned by Filipinos. In parts of Southeast Asia where large estates emerged, whether owned by foreigners, migrants from other parts of Asia, or locals, tensions frequently erupted over landownership and cultivation rights. These tensions and their consequences are examined in more detail in the next chapter. But to the extent that they were important by the interwar era, they suggest that the simple vent for surplus theory is not entirely satisfactory in explaining agricultural growth in Southeast Asia. Land was increasingly becoming a scarce and contested asset.

By and large, estate companies in the late nineteenth and early twentieth centuries in most parts of Southeast Asia sought to increase output by replicating known cultivation technologies over more land and did not try to increase yields through development of higher-yielding varieties or by other means until the interwar years. The most striking exception to this lack of interest in improving cultivation technologies was the case of sugar in Java, where several research stations were established and funded by estate companies in the late nineteenth century (van der Eng 1996: 78). They achieved considerable success in developing and disseminating improved cane varieties to estate companies, and by 1910–1914 sugar yields in Java were higher than in any other producing region except Hawai'i. Yields remained much higher in Java than in either the Philippines or Taiwan until the end of the 1930s (Evenson and Kislev 1975: table 3.4). Unfortunately, falling prices meant that real monetary returns per hectare did not increase at the same rate as yields (Booth 1988: 222–223).

Tree crop production for export in Southeast Asia did not just occur on large estates owned by foreigners. One of the most remarkable developments in Indonesia and British Malaya from the late nineteenth century until 1942 was the rapid expansion of smallholder production. For some crops such as coffee, smallholder cultivators proved themselves better able to cope with problems of crop disease and fluctuating prices. In the 1870s, only 12 percent of coffee in Indonesia was produced by smallholders; by the 1920s, they accounted for almost half of total output (Booth 1988: table 6.5). After 1920, smallholder production of rubber grew rapidly in Sumatra, Kalimantan, and Malaya so that by the late 1930s almost half of all rubber production came from small producers in Indonesia and about 30 percent from small producers in Malaya (Table 2.8).

Table 2.8. Percentage of Rubber from Large Estates, in British Malaya and Indonesia, 1929–1938

	Total Production (thousand tons)		Percentage from Estates	
	Malaya	Indonesia	Malaya	Indonesia
1929	457	263	54	59
1930	452	244	52	63
1931	435	255	55	65
1932	417	212	58	71
1933	460	288	52	60
1934	479	379	55	51
1935	377	300	64	52
1936	364	313	64	52
1937	501	454	63	54
1938	360	322	68	54
1939	360	383	68	52

Sources: British Malaya: Sundaram 1988: table 3.4; Indonesia: Creutzberg 1975: table 10.

The robust response of smallholder producers to the opportunities provided by the rapid growth of world demand for a range of crops was often unanticipated by colonial officials and posed problems for them in the interwar years when they tried to implement output restriction schemes. The smallholder phenomenon gave the lie to colonial views on the supposed lack of entrepreneurial initiative on the part of indigenous cultivators. It also meant that the crude version of the open dualistic model that viewed the export enclave as exclusively the preserve of foreign capitalist enterprises did not conform to the realities of the Southeast Asian situation in the early part of the twentieth century. As well as providing employment and income in the production of export commodities, the rapid growth of the smallholder sector also gave new employment opportunities in processing, trade, and transport. The next section examines the diversification that occurred in greater detail.

Growth of Nonagricultural Activities

Turning from agricultural to industrial growth, there were differences between the two Japanese colonies both in the growth of manufacturing between 1911 and 1938, and in the size of the sector by the late 1930s. From a very small base in 1911, industrial growth in Korea was more rapid than in mainland Japan; between 1911 and 1938, there was an almost tenfold increase in real value added from the mining and manufacturing sectors (Mizoguchi and Umemura 1988: 239). Growth was particularly rapid during the 1930s, and by 1938, manufacturing and mining accounted for around 16 percent of Korean net domestic product. The industrial growth in the 1930s has been attrib-

Table 2.9. Percentage of Total NDP/GDP Accruing from Nonagricultural Sectors, 1900–1938

Year	Taiwan	Korea	Indonesia	Burma[a]	Thailand	Philippines[b]
1900	34.4[c]	n.a.	55.5	36.4	56.3	45.0
1913	46.2	36.7	59.5	36.6	55.3	n.a.
1916	55.4	37.4	59.6	35.3	n.a.	39.6
1921	56.0	37.5	63.1	49.6	n.a.	n.a.
1926	55.0	42.4	62.1	49.0	n.a.	46.3
1931	55.6	46.0	62.7	42.4	56.2[d]	n.a.
1936	60.3	54.6	64.6	45.6	n.a.	n.a.
1938	58.8	52.9	66.3	48.7	55.7	53.4

Sources: Mizoguchi and Umemura 1988: 234, 238; Saito and Lee 1999: 214; van der Eng 2002: 171–172; Manarungsan 1989: 251; Hooley 1968: table 1.

Note: n.a. = not available.

[a] Figures for Burma refer to fiscal years 1901–1902, 1911–1912, 1916–1917, 1921–1922, 1926–1927, 1931–1932, 1936–1937, and 1938–1939 respectively.

[b] Figures for the Philippines refer to 1902, 1918, 1928, and 1938.

[c] 1903.

[d] 1929.

uted to the establishment of large capital-intensive plants by Japanese *zaibatsu* including Mitsui, Mitsubishi, and Sumitomo in sectors such as chemicals, metals, and textiles (Grajdanzev 1944: 152–171; see also Ho 1984: 364–369 and Woo 1991: 35). Until the mid-1930s, light industry accounted for around 60 percent of total industrial production, but that share fell as heavy industry, especially chemicals and metals, expanded rapidly. By 1943, heavy industry accounted for almost half of total industrial production (Chung 2006: 221). Adding in construction and services, which also grew rapidly after 1920, non-agricultural output accounted for more than half of total net domestic product in Korea by 1938 (Table 2.9).

In Taiwan, industrial growth was slower than in Korea, especially in the 1930s, but because the manufacturing and mining sector was larger to begin with, it accounted for a greater share of net domestic product by 1938 than in Korea, around 24 percent (Mizoguchi and Umemura 1988: 234–235). In 1938, almost 60 percent of net domestic output in Taiwan accrued from nonagricultural sectors, including manufacturing, construction, transport, and other services. However, employment in the nonagricultural sectors was a small proportion of total employment in both Taiwan and Korea. Especially in Korea, it appears that industrial development was very capital intensive so that the percentage of the labor force employed in industry was lower than in Taiwan (Table 2.10). Suh argued that total employment in manufacturing actually fell in absolute terms in the 1930s (1978: 47–51); this decline was entirely due to a very sharp decline in the employment of women. This in turn may have been linked to a decline in cottage and small-scale industry during the 1930s, although Chung has argued that there is little evidence that traditional handicrafts did decline in Korea during the Japanese period (2006: 236–237).

It is often asserted that, right up until 1940, the industrialization that took place in Southeast Asia was largely restricted to agricultural and mineral processing. British, French, and Dutch colonial regimes were supposedly intent on preserving colonial markets for their own manufactures and had little interest in encouraging either their own nationals or anyone else to establish industrial plants in their colonies. In fact, the evidence does not support these rather crude generalizations, especially in the interwar era. The increase in national income that undeniably took place between 1900 and 1930 in British Malaya, Indonesia, and the Philippines, and to a lesser extent in Burma and Indochina, did lead to increased demand for a range of manufactures, some of which by reasons of high transport costs or perishability could profitably be produced in the home market, even without tariff protection. We have already seen that the world slump of the 1930s had a serious impact on agricultural exports (in terms of both quantity and price) in most parts of Southeast Asia and forced many colonial officials to consider economic diversification as a means of insulating their populations against the vagaries of world markets. "Among the solutions offered none was seized upon with more enthusiasm than industrialization" (Shepherd 1941: 4). The flood of manufactured exports from Japan into several Southeast Asian colonies during the interwar years also served to increase colonial support for industrialization; after all, if Japan could industrialize using its abundant supplies of cheap labor, why not Java or Vietnam?

Already by 1930, the industrial labor force accounted for more than 10 percent of total employment in British Malaya, Burma, Indonesia, and the

Table 2.10. Occupational Distribution of the Employed Population, Japan, Thailand, and Colonies, c. 1930

Country / Year	Agriculture	Industry	Other	Total
Japan (1930)	49.6	20.1	30.3	100.0
Taiwan (1930)	73.0	8.6	18.3	100.0
Korea (1930)	79.6	6.3	14.1	100.0
Thailand (1929)	84.2	2.2	13.6	100.0
Burma (1931)	69.6	11.0	19.4	100.0
British Malaya (1931)	60.8	12.3	26.9	100.0
Philippines (1939)	69.0	12.2	18.8	100.0
Indonesia (1930)	70.0	10.4	19.6	100.0

Sources: Japan: Grajdanzev 1944: 77; Korea: Suh 1978: table 2; Taiwan: Grajdanzev 1942: 33; British Malaya: Vlieland 1932: 99; Burma: Saito and Lee 1999: table 1.6; Indonesia: Mertens 1978: 51; Philippines: Kurihara 1945: 16; Thailand: Ingram 1971: 57, 144.

Philippines, which were higher percentages than in Taiwan and Korea (see Table 2.10). Much of this employment was in small-scale and cottage industry, but the estimates of van der Eng indicate that value added in the industrial sector in Indonesia (manufacturing, utilities, and construction) comprised around 15 percent of GDP in 1930 (2002: 171). Indeed, since 1900, output from the nonagricultural sectors in Indonesia accounted for a higher proportion of GDP than in either Taiwan or Korea (see Table 2.9). Under a relatively liberal trade regime, the manufacturing sectors that emerged in Indonesia were those that enjoyed a degree of natural protection. As Dick has shown in his study of the manufacturing sector in Surabaya, in 1921 the dominant sector was not food processing or textiles and clothing but engineering workshops (2002: 268–269). The reason for this was the strong presence of the sugar refining sector in East Java, which together with ship repair facilities and railway yards provided demand for a variety of spare parts. Rather than wait several months for spare parts to be brought from Europe, it was in the interests of all these important sectors to obtain spare parts from local engineering workshops.

Foodstuffs were imported in large quantities from Europe and Australia, while textiles were increasingly sourced from Japan. It was only in the latter part of the 1930s, as a result of more activist government policies, that these and other industries expanded within the colony. During the 1930s, the Dutch regime made considerable efforts to attract foreign investment into the large-scale manufacturing sector, with considerable success. Companies such as Goodyear, National Carbon, Unilever, and Bata all built Indonesian plants during the decade, and in addition, cement plants, breweries, paper mills, canneries, and several large weaving and spinning mills were established or enlarged (Booth 1998: 44). By 1941, the industrial sector accounted for around 20 percent of GDP (van der Eng 2002: 172).

Although French policies in Indochina were not supportive of industrialization that might compete with French imports, as in Indonesia official attitudes began to change in the interwar years, especially with regard to yarn and textiles. In densely settled Tonkin, concern about rural unemployment led to some support for both the spinning and weaving industries, which also assisted small producers. Large-scale spinning and weaving factories were established in North Vietnam, which supplied local craftspeople with yarn and also produced cloth. The factory cloth was of a different quality from that produced by small weavers and did not directly compete with their output. Certainly many managed to survive the competition from larger enterprises; a government survey of 1940 found that Tonkin had 55,000 weavers and a total of 120,000 textile workers (Norlund 1991: 86–89; see also Shepherd 1941: 30–31).

In the Philippines, much of the industry that emerged in the American period was based on agricultural and mineral processing. The Philippine market, although small by American standards, was nevertheless an important export destination for some categories of American products. Official American estimates showed that in 1936 the Philippines was the largest export market for American cigarettes, steel sheets, wheat, and dairy products, and the second largest market for cotton textiles, rubber goods, and chemical fertilizers (Joint Preparatory Committee 1938: 32). Thus powerful interests in the United States wanted to preserve the Philippine market for American goods. For their part, some Philippine commentators were arguing that only complete autonomy in tariff matters would allow the Philippines to industrialize (Espino 1933: 11–12).

But even under a tariff system that gave most American manufactures duty-free access to the local market, the manufacturing industry still accounted for around 21 percent of gross value added in 1938 (Hooley 1968: tables 1 and 3). Output from all nonagricultural sectors comprised around 53 percent of total GDP, which was about the same as in Taiwan (see Table 2.9). Goodstein's estimates suggest that an even higher proportion of net value added originated from the nonagricultural sectors of the economy, almost 70 percent (1962: table IV-2). By late 1938, the manufacture of clothing and embroideries together with "native textiles" employed almost 170,000 workers according to the 1939 population census, the great majority women. Manufacturing industry as a whole employed over 11 percent of all workers (Kurihara 1945: 16–17).

The evidence on growth of output and employment in manufacturing industry and in other nonagricultural sectors such as construction and transport in many parts of colonial Asia since 1900 hardly seems to support the deindustrialization argument associated with writers such as Furnivall (1957: 161–164) and Resnick (1970). It may well have been true that imported textiles and other products did lead to the demise of traditional handicrafts in some parts of Southeast Asia in the latter part of the nineteenth century. Legarda discussed the decline of native textile production in southern Panay (around Iloilo) and in Ilocos, and argued that the social costs of this decline may have been considerable (1999: 154–156). In contrast, Shepherd, in his survey of industrial growth in Southeast Asia, stressed that Ilocano weavers responded to the threat of imported cloth by "concentrating their attention on specialized articles for which there is both a domestic and foreign demand" (1941: 89). He pointed out that in the Philippines, as in other parts of Asia, there was considerable consumer prejudice in favor of finely made handicrafts that allowed traditional industries to survive and even flourish.

Other indigenous manufactures had a harder time in the face of foreign competition. In Burma, Furnivall pointed out, spinning and weaving, salt manufacture, and shipbuilding all declined in the last part of the nineteenth century. Shepherd argued that the large shipyards in Manila, which survived until the end of the nineteenth century, disappeared during the American era. Ingram produced evidence for the decline of native industry in Thailand (1971: chap. 6). The figures on the decline in female employment in Korea in the 1930s have already been mentioned; it is likely that these women were engaged in small-scale manufacture of textiles and other products that could no longer compete with cheap imports from Japan. In all these cases, it may have been difficult for displaced workers to find alternative employment either in production of export staples or in nontraded sectors such as trade and transport. In addition, as Resnick (1970) argued, increased specialization in export production left many people vulnerable to swings in the terms of trade. This had an especially harsh impact on the interwar years.

Lessons

What lessons can we draw from this review of trends in output and in economic structure in colonial Asia in the early decades of the twentieth century? Taken together, the evidence would hardly seem to constitute an overwhelming case for "Japanese colonial exceptionalism" on grounds of economic growth leading to rapid structural change away from agriculture and toward industry and the modern services sector. Per capita GDP growth was quite rapid in both Taiwan and Korea in the twenty-five years from 1913 to 1938, but it only outpaced that in Southeast Asia after 1929, when the effects of the world crisis of the early 1930s were more severe. Certainly the growth in rice yields was impressive, especially in Taiwan, but rice production also grew rapidly in some of the land-abundant parts of Southeast Asia, at least partly as a result of increased yields. There was no parallel in either Taiwan or Korea to the remarkable expansion of smallholder agricultural exports of tree crops that characterized several parts of Southeast Asia after 1870.

Nor does it appear that industrial growth was more rapid in Taiwan and Korea than in some parts of Southeast Asia. In fact, Taiwan resembled economies such as the Philippines, Indonesia, and British Malaya in that industrialization was mainly based on agricultural processing, at least until the 1930s. In Korea, industrial growth was rapid but from a very low base, and the acceleration during the 1930s was largely the result of investment in heavy industry by Japanese conglomerates. It is probable that women workers in particular were displaced from traditional industries by Japanese imports. There were parallels with Indonesia, where there was also quite rapid growth in manufacturing industry based on investment from foreign multinationals in the latter part of the 1930s, although government policy in the 1930s was more protective of labor-intensive sectors such as textiles. It seems probable that by 1940 industry accounted for roughly the same share of gross domestic production in both Korea and Indonesia, although it employed a higher share of the labor force in Indonesia. One historian of Korea has claimed that "colonial industrial growth was a powerful historical earthquake" (Park 1999: 158). If that was the case, earthquakes of a similar or stronger force were also felt in parts of Southeast Asia.

It must be stressed that the growth in output and GDP that occurred in much of the region between 1900 and 1930 did not automatically lead to improved incomes and living standards for the bulk of the population or even for those directly employed in the dynamic export sectors. To begin with, tenure arrangements often penalized agricultural producers, even when they had access to land. Those with little or no land of their own were vulnerable to exploitation from politically powerful landlords. As Lewis pointed out, large estates or mining companies could be predatory on the traditional sectors, usually by encroaching on land or by coercing labor (1976: 28). Large foreign-owned companies also remitted profits abroad, and even where they were taxed by colonial governments, the resulting revenues were not always used in ways that benefited the local populations. Indeed colonial governments were not infrequently accused of taxing smallholder producers more heavily than the large companies.

In following chapters, these arguments are reviewed in more detail. I begin with a discussion of issues relating to land tenure, land alienation, and the emergence of a rural landless class.

CHAPTER 3

Agricultural Expansion, Population Growth, and Access to Land

Vent for Surplus in Theory and Practice

It was pointed out in Chapter 1 that the vent for surplus theory has been widely used by economists to explain the rapid growth in production for export in several parts of Southeast Asia from 1870 onward. A crucial assumption of this theory and the models derived from it was that "land suitable for the cultivation of food is not a scarce factor" (Findlay and Lundhal 1994: 89). In his discussion of the applicability of the vent for surplus theory to West Africa, Hopkins emphasized three further implications of the theory: "the massive growth in the volume of exports was achieved without a comparable increase in population, without a significant reduction in the amount of land and time involved in the production of traditional goods and services, and without the adoption of any major improvements in agricultural techniques" (1973: 232).

It is implied not just that there is abundant land available for producing export crops, but also that underutilized labor could easily be drawn out of subsistence food production to meet increased world demand for agricultural exports, whether food crops, which had always been cultivated, or exotic tree crops such as rubber and coffee, which indigenous cultivators would never have grown had there not been an expanding world market. It is further implied that the land tenure system functioned in such a way that any household willing and able to cultivate larger holdings could easily obtain more land on favorable terms. How realistic are these assumptions in the context of East and Southeast Asia by the early twentieth century?

It was pointed out in the previous chapter that the growth in agricultural production for export in both Taiwan and Korea was due in part at least to adoption of improved cultivation techniques in rice agriculture. Much of the growth that occurred in both Japanese colonies, especially after 1920, was due to growth in output per unit of land cultivated and the amount of land per agricultural worker contracted (see Table 2.6). Furthermore, there is evidence, reviewed below, that the increase in sugar exports from Taiwan was achieved at the expense of food-crop cultivation, while the growth in rice exports from Korea led to a steep decline in availability for domestic consumption. Vent for surplus would therefore not seem helpful in explaining the export growth that occurred in either of these colonies.

The Southeast Asian evidence is more complex. There is little doubt that export volume growth was faster than population growth in many parts of the region from the late nineteenth century to 1930, even though population growth was itself quite rapid compared to other parts of Asia. It was noted in the previous chapter that in both Burma and the Philippines land area grew more rapidly than agricultural output after 1900 (see Table 2.7). This indicates a land-extensive process of agricultural growth, consistent with the vent for surplus theory. But did land area grow faster than population or that part of the population largely dependent on agriculture for its income? And even if area cultivated did expand rapidly, was it the case that land was freely available to all those who wished to cultivate it?

Of particular importance in the Southeast Asian context was the effect of the expansion of estate agriculture on land available to smallholder producers. Does it really make sense to assume that there was so much land relative to the population in Southeast Asia that both smallholder and estate production could expand without any competition for land? The impact of vent for surplus production of export crops on land tenure was not directly addressed by Myint in his original exposition of the theory; he was mainly concerned with the argument that vent for surplus was a more suitable theoretical tool for analyzing response to growing world trade than neoclassical comparative advantage theory. But it is obvious that over time, the growth in demand for tropical crops made land a more valuable commodity, even if it was still in relatively abundant supply.

As exports expanded in the last part of the nineteenth century, land markets developed where none had existed before, and colonial administrations reacted to the increased demand for land by introducing new concepts of land titling, usually imported from other parts of the world and quite alien to indigenous populations. In both Thailand and the Philippines as well as in parts of British Malaya, the Torrens system of land titling from Australia was introduced. This system had been developed in Australia to give European farms a secure title to land so that they could then invest in improvements and capital works. The system required a detailed land cadastre that did not exist in most parts of Southeast Asia, even in the more densely settled areas, let alone in the frontier zones. Especially in the Philippines, funds were very limited for both surveying and the drawing up and issuing of title deeds, and many smallholders never received any legal title, thus making them vulnerable to land grabs on the part of the rich and powerful who could hire lawyers and where necessary pay bribes to get titles and expropriate traditional cultivators (Miranda 1991: 58–59; Pelzer 1945: 109–110). In Thailand, land titles were given to cultivators in the central plains, but in many other parts of the country, cultivators received no official recognition of their claims to land (Feeny 1982: 96–97).

As large estate companies expanded their operations, especially in Indonesia, Malaya, and the Philippines, they used their influence with both colonial administrations and home governments to get access to large blocks of land on long leases or freehold tenure. Many small cultivators developed hitherto underutilized land close to their food-crop farms so that they could grow more rice or tree crops such as coffee and rubber. This was sometimes a reasonably peaceful process, with the smallholder acquiring extra assets and an extra source of cash income. But often there was the risk of expropriation by powerful land grabbers, both local and foreign, who had the tacit if not open support of colonial and indigenous ruling elites. In the case of British Malaya, Sundaram argued that the imposition of colonial land laws and the large-scale alienation of land to estates meant that many shifting cultivators were deprived of their traditional livelihoods (1988: 86–87). In the Philippines, those most vulnerable to predatory behavior were cultivators who had migrated to the so-called frontier regions, where they developed homesteads and smallholdings. In his discussion of the growth of sugar production in Negros Occidental in the Philippines, Larkin argues that the peopling and exploitation of the western Negros wilderness had

> much in common with the global frontier phenomenon taking place at this time. The expansion of agriculture onto hitherto underutilized territory of the Americas, Eurasia, Africa, and Oceania happened in response to social, economic, and political pressures, as well as to an imperative to feed the machines of the Industrial Revolution. The cycle of initial pioneering, succeeded by intense cash-crop agriculture, the encumbering of land, the harnessing of labor, and the gradual imposition of a full range of civilization's amenities and restraints, was repeated on Negros, as on other frontiers. As elsewhere, forest lands were reduced and the local aboriginal population displaced as a rising entrepreneurial elite rapidly accumulated wealth. (1993: 60)

No doubt mindful of its own recent pioneering history, the American administration in the Philippines was, according to Larkin, keen to follow "America's own ideal of turning the frontier into the realm of the yeoman farmer" (1993: 68). The Homestead Act of 1902 granted a maximum of sixteen hectares of public land to each settler family. This was a generous amount for many poor families, and numbers of applications grew steadily over the ensuing years. But a large number of applications for homesteads failed, partly because many potential settlers were often not aware of the legal status of the land they wished to settle. If the land was not considered to be in the "public domain," the application was refused. In addition, if the homesteader was not able to cultivate at least one-fifth of the land allocated within five years, he lost the claim, which was then given to another applicant (Pelzer 1945: 110–114). In parts of Luzon, some homesteaders found that the land they had cleared and farmed was registered by some of the powerful landlords in the area and in effect taken from them by a legal titling procedure of which the homesteaders were ignorant (McLennan 1969: 673–674).

Other colonial administrations also stated that their goal was to establish an agrarian system based on small owner-cultivators. If necessary, the government would facilitate the opening up of "empty lands" with agricultural potential on which to settle migrants from the densely settled areas. French policy in southern Vietnam from the 1860s onward was "intended to settle the majority of the population on the land, and thereby create a secure social order based on small proprietors" (Brocheux 1995: 30). After 1900, the Dutch began an ambitious land settlement program that involved moving landless families from Java to Sumatra and Sulawesi (Pelzer 1945: chap. 7). In the delta regions of southern Vietnam, central Thailand, and southern Burma, large tracts of agricultural land were opened up for cultivation in the latter part of the nineteenth and early twentieth centuries (Siamwalla 1972). The impact of these ambitious schemes differed over time and space, but often it led to consequences unintended by the governments that had initiated the process of land expansion.

It was noted in the previous chapter that, in the 1930s, agriculture was the main source of employment for a large part of the labor force in East and Southeast Asia (see Table 2.10). In the five decades or so from 1890 to 1940, rural populations dependent on agriculture for most, if not all, of their incomes grew in absolute terms everywhere in the region. In the relatively densely settled regions, the growth of the agricultural labor force outstripped the growth of arable land so that, by the end of the 1930s, planted area per agricultural worker was well below one hectare in Korea, Taiwan, Java, and Thailand (Table 3.1). In all these regions (except Thailand, where reliable labor force data were not available before 1937), the growth in the agricultural labor force in the decades from 1918 to 1938 exceeded growth in arable area (Table 3.2). In British Malaya, Burma, Tonkin, and Annam, population growth was faster than growth in area under rice cultivation between 1913 and 1938, while in Thailand, Cochinchina, and the Philippines, it was roughly the same (Table 3.3). By the latter part of the 1930s, planted/cultivated area per head of population was below 0.2 hectares in both Korea and Taiwan and in some parts of Southeast Asia (Table 3.1).

These data suggest that the notion of "unlimited supplies of agricultural land" was becoming more and more problematic not just in Taiwan and Korea, but also in several parts of Southeast Asia by the 1930s. On the one hand, indigenous population growth rates were accelerating, at least in part because of improved access to modern medical technologies. On the other hand, it was becoming more difficult for growing populations to be absorbed in tradi-

Table 3.1. Planted Area of Main Crops per Agricultural Worker and Per Capita, 1930s (hectares)

Colony / Country	Planted Area per Agricultural Worker	Planted Area Per Capita
Taiwan (1940)	0.84	0.21
Korea (1938)	0.65	0.19
Tonkin (1939)	n.a.	0.17
Annam (1939)	n.a.	0.30
Cochinchina (1939)	n.a.	0.39
Thailand (1937)	0.62	0.26
Burma (1931)	1.62	0.48
FMS (1931, indigenous)	2.20	0.71
FMS (1931, total)	2.12	0.62
British Malaya (1939)	n.a.	0.40
Philippines (1939)	1.38	0.30
Java (1940)	0.74	0.20

Sources: Taiwan: Lee and Chen 1979: table T-4; Barclay 1954: table 2. Korea: Grajdanzev 1944: 291; Suh 1978: 49. Java: Central Bureau of Statistics 1947: 36–39; van der Eng 1996: table A-3. FMS: Lim 1977: 259; Vlieland 1932: table 132. British Malaya: Grist 1941: tables 3 and 4. Burma: Saito and Lee 1999: tables 1.1, 1.6, 11.1. Philippines: Bureau of Census and Statistics 1947. Thailand: Central Service of Statistics c. 1946 with additional data on rubber cultivation from Manarungsan 1989: table 3.4. Tonkin, Annam, and Cochinchina: Banens 2000 and Giacometti 2000a: annexes.

Note: n.a. = not available.

Table 3.2. Growth in Agricultural Labor Force and Arable Land, 1918–1920 to 1938–1940: Taiwan, South Korea, and Java (1918–1920 = 100)

	Growth in Agricultural Labor Force	Growth in Arable Land
Korea (southern)	110.2	102.2
Taiwan	124.7	116.1
Java	124.4	111.9

Sources: Ban 1979: table K-4a; Lee and Chen 1979: table T-4; van der Eng 1996: tables A.3 and A.4.

tional food-crop agriculture. The rate of growth of land of arable potential was slowing down, and there was increasing competition for such land on the part of migrants from the same country or colonial jurisdiction, from other parts of Asia, or from large capitalist enterprises—whether indigenous, from the metropole, or elsewhere—who were in turn often backed by colonial governments. Scrambles for land on the part of an assortment of competing claimants became more and more frequent in the early decades of the twentieth century.

Table 3.3. Growth in Population and Cultivated Area, c. 1913–1938

	Population Growth (annual average)	Cultivated Area Growth[a] (annual average)
Tonkin	1.4	0.5
Annam	0.7	0.4
Cochinchina	1.1	1.1
Thailand	2.2	2.3
Burma	0.9[b]	1.1
Philippines	2.4	2.5

Sources: Thailand: Manarungsan 1989: tables 1.1 and 2.7; Burma: Saito and Lee 1999: 15, 37; Philippines: Bureau of Census and Statistics 1941: 13; Owen 1972: 59; Tonkin, Annam, and Cochinchina: Banens 2000 and Giacometti 2000a: annexes.

[a] In Thailand, Tonkin, Annam, and Cochinchina, cultivated area refers only to rice land. In the Philippines, it refers to all cultivated area, and in Burma net sown area.

[b] Indigenous population only.

Changing Agrarian Structures under Different Colonial Jurisdictions

What was the effect of the increased competition for available land on agrarian structure and tenancy? In both Korea and Taiwan, what had emerged by the 1930s was a broadly "Japanese" agrarian structure, in which a significant proportion of holdings were in the smaller holding sizes and where many holdings were not owner-cultivated but were farmed under various types of tenancy arrangements (Tables 3.4 and 3.5). The agricultural surveys carried out in both Taiwan and Korea in the 1930s indicated that over 50 percent of all operated holdings were below one hectare. In both Korea and Taiwan, two-thirds of all holdings were either wholly or partly tenanted. In both colonies, a significant proportion of land in the larger holdings was owned or controlled by Japanese interests. Lee argued that by 1930 Japanese individuals and companies in Korea controlled over 11 percent of the total taxable land area (1936: 148). Chung states that by 1944 the Japanese share had increased to 16 percent (2006: 246). Ka estimated that by 1939 Japanese-owned land in Taiwan accounted for more than 15 percent of the total (1995: 147).

In spite of the American aim of encouraging the growth of "yeoman farmers" settling and cultivating their own land in the Philippines, what actually emerged by the 1930s was a pattern of tenure in which around half the holdings were under two hectares in size, while 13 percent were over five hectares (see Table 3.4). More than 40 percent of all cultivated land was in holdings over five hectares (Pelzer 1945: 85). As in Korea and Taiwan, tenancy was widespread. Only 49.2 percent of all farmers in 1939 were owners of the land they worked; a further 15.6 percent owned part of the land, and the rest were tenants, mainly sharecroppers. Pelzer considered the extent of tenancy in the Philippines "astonishingly high" and attributed it to Spanish

Table 3.4. Distribution of Operated Holdings by Size: Japan, Taiwan, Korea, and the Philippines, 1930s

Holding Size[a]	Korea 1938	Japan 1937	Taiwan 1930	Philippines 1938
Under 0.5	38.4	33.8	30.3	
0.5–0.99	24.9	34.2	22.9	22.6[b]
1.0–1.99	19.7	22.7	23.7	29.9
2.0–2.99	10.9	5.7	18.6[c]	18.7
3.0–4.99	4.7	2.3		15.8
Over 5.00	1.4	1.4	4.5	13.0
Total	100.0	100.0	100.0	100.0

Source: Grajdanzev 1944: 113; Grajdanzev 1942: 79; Bureau of Census and Statistics 1947.

[a] The Korean and Japanese data are in *cho* (0.99 hectares); the Taiwanese data are in *ko* (0.96 hectares). The Philippine data are in hectares.

[b] Percentage of holdings under one hectare.

[c] Percentage of holdings between two and five *ko*.

Table 3.5. Average Holding Size and Extent of Tenancy, 1930s (hectares)

Colony/ Country	Average Holding Size	Percentage of Holdings Tenanted	Percentage of Land under Tenancy
Taiwan (1932)	1.9	31.7	53.5
Korea (1938)	1.5	52.6 (15.5)[a]	n.a.
Thailand (1937)	n.a.	n.a.	15.7
Burma (1938)	n.a.	n.a.	59.0
Philippines (1939)	2.4 (4.1)[b]	35.1 (15.6)[c]	32.5 (15.0)[d]

Sources: Korea: Grajdanzev 1944: 291–294; Taiwan: Grajdanzev 1942: 76–79; Thailand: Ingram 1971: 268; Philippines: Bureau of Census and Statistics 1947: table 44; Burma: Pfanner 1969: table 15.

Note: n.a. = not available.

[a] Figures in parentheses refer to holdings "chiefly tenanted."

[b] Figure in parentheses refers to total land rather than cultivated land.

[c] Percent of holdings cultivated by part owners.

[d] Percent of cultivated land farmed by part owners.

policies that favored local chiefs *(cacique),* many of whom acquired substantial holdings and reduced the traditional cultivators to the status of tenant (1945: 86–89). McLennan stressed the importance of the *pacto de retroventa* arrangements, whereby moneylenders (often of mixed Chinese-Filipino ancestry) acquired parcels of land when loans secured on the land were in default (1969: 659–662; 1980: 97). He also argued that royal grants and purchase of land, or acquisition by occupation were important means by which haciendas were established during Spanish rule. By the late nineteenth century, haciendas of between 100 and 500 hectares proliferated, with ownership by one family quite common (McLennan 1980: 97).

American policy, while ostensibly favoring the owner-cultivator, in fact did little to reduce the extent of tenancy, which could have increased in the first four decades of the twentieth century, although the available evidence does not permit a clear conclusion on this. Owen argued that the large amounts of land acquired from the church (the friar lands) could have been used to settle landless families but were in fact sold to wealthy speculators (1972: 50), while Larkin pointed out that, in the sugar-growing areas, small landowners were not infrequently dispossessed by "the new breed of planters" seeking to build up large haciendas and were forced into a precarious living as agricultural laborers on large plantations, with few alternative sources of income (1993: 61). But although the high rates of tenancy in the Philippines have attracted considerable critical attention from subsequent scholars, the proportion of land under tenancy was in fact lower than in Taiwan or indeed in Burma by the late 1930s (see Table 3.5). Even in the central plains of Thailand, the agricultural census of 1937 found that around one-quarter of all land was in tenanted holdings, while in Lower Burma it was estimated that almost 60 percent of arable land was operated under tenancy by the late 1930s (Pfanner 1969: 221). The reasons for these high rates of tenancy are examined further below.

The rather small amount of cultivated land per capita in Thailand by the end of the 1930s (less than in Burma and about the same as in the Philippines) together with the quite high rates of tenancy, especially in the central plains, would suggest that, even in a country that was not a colony and where foreign-owned estates were largely absent, competition for agricultural land was becoming more intense by the 1930s, and land was not always freely available to all those wishing to cultivate it. The rural survey conducted by Zimmerman in 1930–1931 indicated that around 36 percent of all households in central Thailand owned no land at all (Table 3.6). It is probable that most landless households were able to access some land through tenancy arrangements, but in many cases they would have had to supplement income from tenant farming with wage labor and handicraft activities. A further rural household survey

Table 3.6. Owned and Cultivated Land in Thailand by Region, 1930–1931

Region	Average Holding Size		Percentage Owning No Land	Number of Parcels per Holding
	Owned or Squatted (ha.)	Cultivated (ha.)		
Central	4.5	3.9	36.0	1.64
Northern	1.5	1.6	27.4	1.32
Southern	1.2	1.0	14.5	2.08
Northeast	0.9	1.1	18.0	1.30

Source: Zimmerman 1999: 25–36.

conducted by Andrews in 1934–1935 found that income from craft activity, labor, and trade accounted for around 35 percent of current income in central Thailand and a higher proportion elsewhere (Wilson 1983: 99).

In Java, where by 1930 the average holding size was below one hectare, by the early decades of the twentieth century, a substantial part of the indigenous population had little or no access to agricultural land, either as owners or as tenants, and were largely, if not entirely, reliant on handicrafts, trade, and wage labor for their incomes. Data collected in 1905 as part of the Declining Welfare Surveys found that on average only 5.3 percent of all those engaged in agriculture could be classified as tenants, although the percentage was twice as high in parts of West Java and in Yogyakarta (Pelzer 1945: 257). The breakdown of the population of Java given by Meijer Ranneft and Huender in the 1920s indicated that poor farmers comprised 27 percent of the population and sharecroppers with no land a further 3.4 percent. Landless laborers were estimated to comprise 32 percent of the population. Thus over 60 percent of the population was "land poor" (Wertheim 1964: 232). A practice that became increasingly common in the 1920s and 1930s was the leasing of land in return for an advance payment; usually the landowner continued to work the land, and the lessee received a share of the crop. Such arrangements were informal and seldom registered, but surveys indicated they were widespread; in one district of East Java in 1939 it was found that almost three-quarters of landowners had leased part of their land in order to obtain cash (Pelzer 1945: 172).

In northern Vietnam (Tonkin) by the 1930s, the amount of cultivated hectares per person was even smaller than in Java (see Table 3.1). As in Java, landholdings were often divided into small parcels, with the great majority of cultivators operating very small and often fragmented holdings. Gourou argued that it was not possible to establish how many households owned no land at all (1945a: 278), although Popkin has estimated that, by 1930, 69 percent of all families in Tonkin were either landless or cultivated less than 0.36 hectares (1979: 156). As in Java, most cultivators were cultivating small plots with their own labor, and there was relatively little land available to be rented or sharecropped out. Much the same was true in Annam, where 94 percent of all holdings were under 0.5 hectares in 1930, and almost 90 percent of holdings were cultivated directly by owners (Henry 1932: 211–213).

The situation in Cochinchina, in southern Vietnam, was very different. Between 1880 and 1910, land under cultivation almost trebled, from 522,000 to 1.52 million hectares. Thereafter, the rate of expansion slowed (Gran 1975: table 2-2; see also table 3.7). This was the only part of Vietnam where growth in area under rice cultivation kept up with population growth in the early decades of the twentieth century (see Table 3.3). In order to bring more land under cultivation, the French invested heavily in land reclamation, dredging, and canal building, and to recoup these expenditures, government policy was to sell concessions. Especially after 1913, land was sold "to the highest bidder" (Brocheux 1995: 30). The result was that agricultural land was very inequita-

Table 3.7. Growth of Population, Rice Area, and Rice Exports: Three Deltas, 1880–1930s

	Population (millions)	Cultivated Area (thousand hectares)	Rice Exports (thousand tons)
Thailand			
1881–1885	6.2 (1880)	1,046 (1885)	220
1906–1910	8.3 (1910)	1,755 (1910)	929
1936–1940	15.0 (1938)	3,481 (1936–1940)	1,475
Cochinchina			
1880	1.7	522	295
1910	3.1	1,528	1,109
1936	4.6	2,110	1,711
Burma [a]			
1880	3.7 (1881)	1,255	807
1910–1914	6.2 (1911)	4,116	2,383
1935–1939	8.9 (1941)	4,965	2,909

Source: Manarungsan 1989: 32, 51, 61; Gran 1975: 63; Saito and Lee 1999: 7, 83.

[a] Population data refer to Lower Burma only.

bly distributed; in several provinces between 39 and 66 percent of all agricultural land was in holdings over fifty hectares (Henry 1932: 189). The process of land surveying and land titling was often farmed out to private companies who "carried out their duties unsystematically and sluggishly" (Brocheux 1995: 36). Disputes over land rights erupted when squatters were evicted by new owners, who farmed the land out to tenants, often on short leases (Gran 1975: 252).

In the rest of this chapter, the impact of population and agricultural expansion on access to land is examined, first by looking at the competition for land to grow different crops and then by examining the conflict that emerged between estates and smallholders, and between foreign and local claimants to land. These conflicts varied over time and across regions but in all cases gave rise to problems that governments were forced to wrestle with in the early decades of the century and that were often not resolved by 1940. They remained for the governments that emerged in the post-1945 era to deal with in very different ways.

Growth in Rice Production and Land Tenure

Rice was not only the main food staple for the vast majority of the population in East and Southeast Asia, but also, by the early twentieth century, an important export crop for both Korea and Taiwan as well as Burma, Thailand,

and southern Vietnam. In the two Japanese colonies, the rice export economy was developed primarily to feed metropolitan Japan, while in the three delta regions of Lower Burma, central Thailand, and southern Vietnam, the export surplus was sold on regional and world markets, although in the case of Burma, the British Indian market was given priority in times of scarcity. But even in the major rice-exporting regions, there were significant differences in policies used to expand production and the exportable surplus.

In Korea, it appears that the growth in rice exports occurred at the expense of domestic consumption; between 1912 and 1930, the index of rice consumed per capita within Korea declined from 100 to 62 (Lee 1936: 275). By 1930, Korea was supplying over 700,000 tons of rice to the Japanese market, or about 7.4 percent of total Japanese consumption. In 1933, as a result of increases in production and low prices in Japan, the Koreans were urged to eat more rice themselves and export less (Chung 2006: 233). The impact of this policy on rice consumption in Korea will be examined in Chapter 7. But by 1938, as a result of the expansion of the Japanese empire into China, rice shortages were again feared by the Japanese government, and Korea was expected to provide an export surplus. Korean people were told to stop eating rice. The amount supplied to Japan increased sharply in 1938; in that year Korea was supplying 12.7 percent of total Japanese requirements (Ka 1995: 135). How did the colonial government in Korea manage to extract the exportable surplus from Korean farmers? Were they coerced into supplying the Japanese market at the expense of their own consumption?

Some historians have argued that there is little evidence that direct coercion was used and that the main reason for the continuing large supplies to the Japanese market, even during the 1930s when that market was oversupplied and prices were falling, was that the export marketing networks were far better developed than internal ones (Gill 1998: 133). Infrastructure development also facilitated the export of food grains; thus it was very much in the interests of surplus producers to sell their output to Japan (Cha 1998: 733). It is likely that a significant proportion of the exportable surplus came from large farms owned by Japanese and cultivated by Korean tenants; the Japanese landlords would have had close ties with rice traders in Japan. The issues of tenancy and foreign ownership are examined in more detail below; in the Korean case, Japanese landownership was concentrated in the fertile rice-growing plains in the southern part of the peninsula. In this area, around 70 percent of farms were tenanted (Lee 1936: 148–161).

In Taiwan, the growth in rice exports to Japan was also rapid until the mid-1930s; in 1934, Taiwan was supplying almost 7 percent of Japanese total rice requirements and a much higher proportion of rice entering the urban markets. The high-yielding *ponlai* variety introduced by the Japanese was grown almost entirely for export, with the local population eating inferior varieties often grown on poorer land. But by the early 1930s, the Japanese government was concerned with oversupply to the home market and the political consequences of declining rice prices and farm incomes in Japan. In the latter part of the 1930s, the colonial government intervened to discourage rice production in Taiwan and encourage production of other crops such as sugar. Area under paddy cultivation declined in the latter part of the 1930s, while that under sugarcane increased. The sugar companies, mostly owned by Japanese business groups, acquired dry land in the central and southern part of the island. In these areas, land concentration increased, while in the northern rice-growing areas, tenancy declined and land fragmentation increased (Ka 1995: 150–152). It would appear that sugar and rice production did not compete for land in Taiwan to the same extent as in other parts of Southeast Asia, so the switch from rice to sugar production for export could have led to increased rice availability for home consumption. Certainly by the late 1930s rice availability per capita in Taiwan was well above that in Korea, in Java, and in the Philippines (see Table 2.6). The implications of rice availability for home consumption vis-à-vis living standards are discussed further in Chapter 7.

It has already been argued that the growth of export production in Korea and Taiwan after 1918 hardly seems to accord with the vent for surplus theory, in that land area per worker was falling, and much of the increased output of rice was derived from growth in yields, in turn the result of using new seeds and production techniques (see Tables 2.6 and 3.2). In contrast, the growth of rice production in the delta regions of Southeast Asia in the last part of the nineteenth century and the early twentieth century has often been used as an example of vent for surplus, in the sense that large tracts of jungle in the delta regions were rapidly brought under rice cultivation using existing technologies. Much of the increased output was exported. Rice exports increased faster than population, and unlike in Korea, there was little evidence that this increased output was at the expense of domestic consumption.

In Burma, rice exports grew rapidly in the last part of the nineteenth century; by 1880 exports amounted to over 800,000 metric tons (see Table 3.7). By 1910–1914, land under cultivation had increased from 1.2 to 4.1 million hectares, and rice exports had increased almost threefold. Adas has described how internal migration was important in opening up the delta regions of southern Burma, especially from the dry zone in the center of the country (1974: chap. 2). British policy was certainly important in removing the restrictions on the export of rice and in facilitating internal population movements, but the story of the Burma delta in the last part of the nineteenth century is essentially one of indigenous populations responding to the opportunities created by expanding regional and world markets. The British administration, while not preventing the rapid growth of land settlement in the delta, did not provide much assistance in bringing land under cultivation. The migrants themselves had to find the funds to turn jungle into rice land, and this led to increased reliance on Indian moneylenders.

Adas also stressed that new settlers relied heavily on the rather primitive rice technologies with which they had been familiar in the dry zones in the center of Burma (1974: 62–65). The crude harrow adopted in many parts of the delta had been used in central Burma for a thousand years, and cultivators applied little or no fertilizer of any kind, beyond some use of cattle manure. The cultivator in Lower Burma "seldom took time to select better seeds" but relied on traditional varieties which produced low yields (ibid.: 64). The situation regarding the adoption of improved cultivation technologies was little different in Thailand and Vietnam, with the result that yields were lower than in Malaya and Java, and much lower than in Taiwan and Korea by the 1930s (see Table 2.6).

In both Thailand and Cochinchina, the expansion of land under rice cultivation and rice exports were also rapid after 1880 (see Table 3.7). In Thailand, Siamwalla pointed out that the liberalization of the rice trade that occurred in the latter part of the nineteenth century was not immediately followed by the elimination of the corvée system or of slavery (1972: 17–18). He suggested that "the first group of people who responded to the signal of rising prices were the people who had control over labor and who were thus in a position to exploit the labor under their control for commercial gains for the first time" (ibid.). In addition, many farmers may have taken new land into rice cultivation on their own initiative and used the extra money they gained to buy out their obligations to their patrons. This would explain the relative lack of long-distance migration in the Thai case as compared to Burma. It might also explain the slower growth in area under rice cultivation in Thailand between 1880 and 1910 compared with Burma and Cochinchina (see Table 3.7).

There has been considerable debate among economic historians of Thailand about the failure on the part of government to invest in the development of irrigation systems after 1900. The expansion of irrigation in the Rangsit area of the central plains was largely carried out by a private company and the improved land sold off to members of the Bangkok elite, who cultivated it with tenants (Siamwalla 1972: 28–29). A Dutch expert with considerable experience in Indonesia, J. Homan van der Heide, was asked by the Thai government to investigate the feasibility of expanding irrigated agriculture in central Thailand, and he submitted several reports and memoranda between 1903 and 1908. But most of his recommendations were not taken up. Brown argued that the main reason was budgetary; the Thai government gave priority to expenditures on railways and strengthening the capacity of the military in order to defend the country's political sovereignty against encroachment from the British and the French (1988: 174–175).

The experience of Cochinchina was different again; it has already been noted that the French invested heavily in land reclamation in the Mekong delta around the turn of the century and often disposed of the resulting land in large tracts to both expatriates and local residents who had either the money to buy the land in auctions or the political influence to acquire it as grants. The population of the delta area expanded rapidly after 1880, although how much of the growth was from natural increase, how much from local migration within southern Vietnam, and how much from longer distance migration from northern and central Vietnam and from Cambodia is difficult to judge from the existing data. Owen argued that much of the migration was from less fertile and more crowded parts of Cochinchina (1971: 127), while Brocheux has shown that the numbers of Cambodians in western Cochinchina more than doubled between 1886 and 1908 (1995: table 1). By 1908, Cambodians accounted for almost 16 percent of the population. Many were probably squatters on land to which they had no legal title and were increasingly vulnerable to dispossession after 1900.

Most studies of the development of the agricultural economy of Cochinchina in the first three decades of the twentieth century have relied heavily on the work of Henry (1932), who carried out the only detailed survey of land distribution in Indochina around 1930. His findings have been widely cited by all subsequent writers, although it is difficult to judge how accurate they are; Gourou suggested that they were "perhaps not incontestable" but used them anyway (1945a: 339). Henry claimed that in Cochinchina there were only 255,000 agricultural holdings, of which almost 72 percent were below five hectares (Henry 1932: 212). If we adopt the population estimates of Banens (2000: 33), then it would appear that the total population of Cochinchina in 1929 was almost 5.5 million. If it is further assumed that the average household comprised six people and that 75 percent were largely or wholly dependent on agriculture, we can derive a rough estimate of around 680,000 agricultural households. If indeed only 255,000 (fewer than 40 percent) owned land, then it is clear that a substantial majority of all agricultural households were either tenants or agricultural laborers.

This indeed has been assumed by several subsequent writers (Gourou 1945a: 339–344, 516; Murray 1980: 420–421; Ngo 1991: 28). It seems a reasonable assumption; even if Henry's estimates of the numbers of landowning households were to be increased by 50 percent, there would still have been a significant minority (around 40 percent) of households that were either tenants or agricultural laborers. Sansom argued that the "attitudes of the landlords on matters of production and estate management were determined by their efforts to maximize the rent output from their fields while minimizing the administrative costs" (1970: 31). Although rentals were a fixed percentage (usually 40 to 60 percent) of the crop, there is little evidence that landlords made any attempt to increase yields through better cultivation methods. Gourou found that rice cultivation techniques in southern Vietnam were not very different from those used in Tonkin and Annam (1945a: 355–356). He argued that a substantial part of the income of landowners came from lending money to their tenants, and many had little interest in improving cultivation technologies.

If indeed tenancy was widespread in all the major rice-exporting regions of East and Southeast Asia by the early part of the twentieth century, what were the explanations? In both Korea and Taiwan, tenancy was probably widespread before the consolidation of Japanese rule, although in both cases the penetration of Japanese capitalism into the rural economic structure brought about considerable changes in land tenure and in the distribution of land. In the case of Korea, Lee argued that the main result of Japanese colonialism was a polarization of landholdings into a small number of large, often Japanese-owned holdings and a large number of very small, Korean-owned or -tenanted holdings (1936: 161). Cha suggested that, during the 1930s, many farmers suffered declining incomes and could not pay off debts incurred for irrigation and other land improvements (1998: 734). They were compelled to sell land and become tenants. While it may have been true that the widespread distress sales of land in the 1930s came about as "a result of economic forces and not from a colonial conspiracy to deprive Koreans of their land," the evidence suggests that landholdings became more concentrated, and many Japanese individuals and corporations acquired land from Korean cultivators (Gragert 1994: 148–149).

Ka argued that in Taiwan, where a system of perpetual tenancy had evolved that gave strong usufruct rights to the tenants, the Japanese did not try to implant another system but rather modified the existing one to achieve their own aims of increasing rice and sugar exports (1995: 39). In the delta areas of Southeast Asia, where large amounts of new land were brought under cultivation, tenancy evolved either as a direct consequence of government land policy (in Cochinchina and to a lesser extent in Thailand) or because the new settlers depended heavily on loans from private moneylenders, and when defaults occurred, the landowners were forced to surrender their land and became either tenants or laborers on land that they had formerly owned.

Even as rice exports were increasing rapidly from the two Japanese colonies and the three deltas, other colonies in Southeast Asia were, by the early twentieth century, becoming rice importers, dependent on supplies from Cochinchina, Burma, and Thailand to make up the difference between domestic demand and supply. In the Philippines, the switch from net rice exporter to rice importer appears to have begun after 1870 (Legarda 1999: 164–173). On the one hand, exports from Cochinchina were competing with those from the Philippines, especially in the China market, while, on the other hand, many Filipino cultivators found other crops, such as sugar and hemp, more profitable. Reliance on imports increased in the early years of the twentieth century, and in the six years from 1917 to 1922, imports amounted to more than 8 percent of home production (Mears et al. 1974: 355).

Indonesia also became a major rice importer after the 1870s, and from 1917 to 1922, imports to Java amounted to more than 9 percent of domestic production (Boomgaard and van Zanden 1990: 46). Imports to the islands outside Java also increased rapidly after 1900 and by 1925 exceeded imports to Java; we do not have production data for Sumatra before 1940, but it is probable that the ratio of imports to local production was much higher than in Java. But from 1920 to 1940, the largest rice importer, both in absolute terms and relative to local production, was British Malaya. Imports seldom dropped below 400,000 metric tons from 1923 to 1940 and in 1938–1940 were above 600,000 tons. For much of the 1920s, imports were more than twice as high as domestic production (Grist 1941: table 32).

The high and growing reliance on imports of the key food staple worried both British and Dutch officials. In Malaya, from the late nineteenth century onward, government policy supported the development of irrigation, although as Lim has pointed out, expansion of irrigated land was impeded by the insistence that irrigation works could only be carried out where the capital outlay could be recouped with interest (1977: 42). The Dutch in Java were less concerned with financial rates of return, and in fact water charges were not levied in the schemes that were initiated or enlarged after 1900. The ethical policy, introduced in 1901 in order to increase the prosperity of the Indonesian, and especially the Javanese, population placed considerable emphasis on irrigation as a means of increasing agricultural productivity. This emphasis appears to have led to a rapid expansion of harvested area; one estimate suggests that it more than doubled between 1880 and 1937 (van der Eng 1996: 67). But still the reliance on imported rice continued, as population growth more than offset growth in area under rice production, and no breakthrough was achieved in yields.

The Growth of Sugar as an Export Crop

By 1910, the three deltas had become virtually monocrop rice economies. But in other parts of the Asian region, new export crops emerged that in some cases competed with rice for land. The most prominent example of a competitor crop was sugar, and sugar cultivation developed rapidly in the latter part of the nineteenth century in Java and the Philippines, and after 1900 in Taiwan. By the latter part of the 1920s, Java was exporting over 2 million tons, and Taiwan and the Philippines about 1.1 million tons between them (Table 3.8). Elsewhere in Southeast Asia, sugar cultivation for export never took off, in spite of favorable agroclimatic conditions in several parts of the region. Ingram has pointed out that for some years after the Bowring Treaty, it was expected that sugar would become one of Thailand's main export crops (1971: 123–127), and in the 1860s a British firm obtained a grant of over one thousand hectares of land from the Thai government at a very low rental. The plan was to grow cane and also develop sugar-processing facilities, but low world prices and an unfavorable domestic tax regime together prevented the growth of sugar exports; by the 1880s, they had practically ceased.

Low prices and stiff international competition also prevented the development of sugar cultivation in Vietnam, in spite of some government efforts to import new varieties from the Caribbean (Thompson 1937: 140–141). The low world prices in the last decades of the nineteenth century were due to the

Table 3.8. Growth of Sugar Exports from Taiwan, the Philippines, and Java: 1870–1874 to 1935–1939 (thousand metric tons)

	Taiwan	Philippines	Java
Exports			
1870–1874	n.a.	92.1	185.5
1900–1904	30.3	78.6	848.2
1910–1914	158.8	184.3	1,431.2
1920–1924	340.0	292.4	1,661.0
1925–1929	537.1	555.4	2,137.4
1930–1934	738.9	949.0	1,503.5
1935–1939	1,003.1	806.0	1,093.5
Yields			
1928–1932	29.3	20.4	56.4

Sources: Ka 1995: 68; Larkin 1993: 150, 202, appendix A; Java: Creutzberg 1975: 73–76. Yields data from Evenson and Kislev 1975: table 3.4.

Note: Yields are in short tons per acre; n.a. = not available.

rapid growth of a subsidized beet industry in Europe and also the growth of exports from some parts of the tropics, including Java and Cuba. In addition, the American industry in both Hawai'i and several southern states expanded after the end of the civil war and reduced the American reliance on imports, further depressing world market prices. These factors seem to have been crucial in encouraging the mainly Chinese-owned sugar estates in Malaya to switch to other crops, such as rubber, which by the end of the nineteenth century were facing more buoyant world markets and also required less labor (Jackson 1968: 172–175). In addition, official British policy was to encourage the growth of rice cultivation on irrigated land, rather than sugar or other crops that officials considered "speculative."

The industries in both Java and the Philippines were also affected by the difficult world market conditions in the last part of the nineteenth century, but by then they had become sufficiently strongly established to weather the unfavorable international conditions. The Javanese industry had developed during the period of the cultivation system *(cultuurstelsel),* when smallholders were induced, or coerced, by various means to grow export crops for delivery to government agencies and sale in the Netherlands. By 1840, production amounted to 58,000 tons, and this figure almost trebled over the next three decades (Creutzberg 1975: 52). After the demise of the cultivation system and the introduction of the so-called liberal policy, the industry developed rapidly, although problems in the 1880s led to a thorough restructuring of the industry, with some firms going out of business. Output had reached 744,000 tons by 1900. Large sugar factories using imported equipment were built, usually with foreign capital, although the factories themselves owned little land and obtained most of their cane from land rented in from indigenous landowners. By the early years of the twentieth century, Java had become one of the world's leading producers, and also one of the most efficient, with higher yields than any other producing region except Hawai'i (Evenson and Kislev 1975: table 3.4).

The industry in the Philippines also developed rapidly in the second part of the nineteenth century, with foreigners playing an important part in supplying credit and technology (Larkin 1993: 46–53). British and American trading firms controlled the export trade, although the role of Philippine-Chinese merchants became more important in the final decades of the century, partly because of Spanish attempts to lessen the stranglehold of other foreign firms. Spain was not an important customer for Philippine sugar; most of the exports went to Britain and to other Asian markets, including China and Japan, which took mainly lower quality output. The share of sugar in total Philippine exports between 1846 and 1895 fluctuated considerably but seldom fell below one-third and was, with abaca, the most important export commodity.

The third Asian colony to emerge as an important sugar exporter after 1900 was Taiwan. Here there can be little doubt that the Japanese government played a crucial role in the early development of the industry. Sugar had been grown in Taiwan for several centuries, but the Japanese considered the Taiwanese industry to be primitive. Although there were over one thousand mills on the island, "not a single mill had adopted the modern, mechanical method of manufacturing, and all of them used animal power" (Foreign Affairs Association 1944: 926). The Japanese colonial authorities were determined to increase production to supply the Japanese domestic market and thus lessen dependence on imports from other parts of Asia. Ho has argued that the Japanese strategy was to cooperate with private Japanese capital and create a corporate business structure that would then lead to the virtual elimination of Taiwanese capitalists from the industry, while at the same time encouraging Taiwanese farmers to grow more cane in order to supply large-scale mills with enough raw material to allow them to operate at full capacity for most of the year (1971: 320–321). Government investment in infrastructure, including roads, railways, and irrigation, was an important part of the policy package, but more direct assistance was also needed.

A regulation issued in 1902 clarified the extent of the government subsidies to both cultivators and factories. Any cultivator who grew more than five acres of sugar could apply for fertilizer subsidies and "sugarcane shoot subsidies." In addition the government was prepared to subsidize up to 50 percent of the construction costs of irrigation and drainage projects that benefited sugar cultivation. Sugar manufacturers using approved government machinery could claim up to 20 percent of its cost, and there were additional subsidies for companies with grinding capacity above a certain limit. Lastly, government lands could be cleared and used for cane cultivation without rent, and such lands could also be used without cost for irrigation construction. Other inducements provided by the colonial regime included tax concessions, reduced rail freight rates, and some legal privileges (Ho 1971: 321).

The Taiwanese sugar industry was granted further assistance through high tariffs imposed on imported sugar from outside the Japanese empire in the domestic Japanese market (Chang and Myers 1963: 445; Schneider 1998: 164). The colonial government encouraged Japanese firms operating in Taiwan to form a powerful cartel that regulated output price and exports. With such a favorable package of inducements, the industry expanded rapidly; between 1905 and 1920, both land under sugar cultivation and output increased four-fold (Grajdanzev 1942: 59). Between 1925 and 1940, the land controlled by sugar companies, through ownership and tenancies, grew by a further 44 percent; by 1940 the land controlled by sugar companies amounted to 13.7 percent of total arable land. By the 1930s, the sugar companies owned most of the land under sugar cultivation and either farmed it themselves or leased it to tenants. Less than 25 percent of land under sugar was owned by smallholders (Ka 1995: 99). But in spite of all the government assistance to the industry, it remained less productive than the world leaders in Java and Hawai'i; in the 1930s yields per hectare were only about half what was achieved in these two producing regions (Grajdanzev 1942: 46). Taiwanese producers also remained almost completely dependent on the protected Japanese market, and when that was withdrawn after 1945, production levels dropped markedly.

Ka contrasted the development of the sugar industry in Taiwan with that in Java, where after 1870 the industry developed rapidly by renting in land from indigenous owners (1995: 98–101). The Javanese industry ran into severe problems in the mid-1880s, caused by disease and falling world prices, and many sugar companies were unable to meet their loan obligations and were taken over by banks. Smaller firms went under, and the larger ones became limited liability companies owned mainly by shareholders in the Netherlands (Boomgaard 1988: 160). It was at this time that the companies began to invest in the development of new varieties that greatly increased yields. Most writers have claimed that a strong element of compulsion was involved in the renting of land to the companies, who wanted large blocks of irrigated land of one thousand hectares or more delivered to them for use over at least fifteen months on a recurring cycle (Geertz 1963: 86–89; Gordon 1979: 256). While many Dutch civil servants of an "ethical" cast of mind may have been unhappy with the consequences of this policy, the sugar companies usually got their land.

The effects of this policy on agricultural development in Java have been much debated. Most scholars agree that the rental paid to the landowner by the company did not fully compensate for the value of the farm production lost over fifteen months, and sometimes the land was returned in poor condition and needed work before it could be planted again with rice. But it has also been argued that, taking into account all the payments made by the sugar companies for labor and other services, the "direct social returns from sugar production were substantially higher than the shadow value of farm production" (van der Eng 1996: 223). But if this argument is true, then why did the companies not encourage farmers to grow cane themselves and supply it to factories, using either rice land or other land? It was the element of coercion that some Dutch officials and many subsequent scholars have criticized. Geertz argued that the effect of the sugar industry in Java was to make the Javanese cane worker a coolie while he also remained a peasant farmer (1963: 89), although it is probable that many of the coolies employed by the sugar companies either as factory hands or field workers did not themselves own irrigated land.

The sugar industry on Java clearly created employment; it has been estimated that at its height in the late 1920s, the factories employed up to 175,000 workers, and the cultivation of cane needed 800,000 to 1 million seasonal workers (Boomgaard 1988: 164). Another 250,000 were needed for cutting and carting the cane. When output began to contract after 1930, many of these jobs were lost. While the landowners no longer had to surrender their land, many poorer Javanese lost an important source of cash income. Between 1930 and 1935, sugar output contracted from 3 million tons to little over 500,000 tons (Creutzberg 1975: 53). This loss was almost entirely due to loss of markets, especially in the British empire after the policy of imperial preference was adopted. Unlike the Taiwanese and Philippine industries, there was no protected market into which Javanese producers could sell. The Netherlands itself was a small market, and the home government had to consider the interests of its own beet producers.

By the latter part of the 1930s, exports from both Taiwan and the Philippines had almost caught up with those from Indonesia (see Table 3.8). The Philippine story is particularly interesting, as the sugar industry seemed to be facing a bleak future in the early American period. Production and exports had plunged during the hostilities with America, as both refining facilities and ports were shut down. Competition from Java in Asian markets intensified, and increased imports from Taiwan cut the Philippines out of the Japanese market. Several of the British and American trading companies that had provided credit to growers and arranged exports were virtually bankrupt by 1900 (Larkin 1993: 53–54). In addition, American land policy appeared to favor smallholdings over large land grants, and powerful American cane and beet sugar producers supported politicians in Congress who opposed the establishment of large agricultural estates in the new colony (Pelzer 1945: 105).

And yet, by 1916, the industry had recovered and sugar exports from the Philippines had more than regained the peak levels attained in the early 1890s (Larkin 1993: appendix A). One reason for the resurgence was that potential investors in the sugar factories (centrals) were able to exploit loopholes in the 1902 Public Land Act, which placed ceilings of sixteen hectares on land grants to individuals and of 1,024 hectares on grants to corporations. An American syndicate was able to purchase 18,000 hectares in Mindoro in 1909, and although this venture failed, other American-led ventures acquired land in Luzon. In addition, other sugar centrals negotiated long-term milling contracts with local growers that gave them guaranteed supplies of cane (ibid.: 58–59). With the establishment of the Philippine National Bank in 1916, local investors were able to access credit to expand milling operations; they were further helped by government spending on transport infrastructure and higher world prices during the First World War. In addition, sugar from the Philippines was given favorable access to the American market, while the Panama canal reduced freight rates from Southeast Asia to the huge markets of the American eastern seaboard. By the 1920s, sugar planters from Luzon and Negros had formed a powerful lobby "capable of shaping national government policy on tariffs, investment policy, and relations with the United States" (McCoy 1992: 124).

Thus three colonial regimes used rather different strategies to build up important sugar export industries in the early decades of the twentieth century, while neighboring colonies with similar resource endowments failed to do so. The Javanese industry did not have a large protected home market to sell into; it grew through substantial investments in raising productivity, which allowed it to compete on world markets even in periods of falling prices. It is unlikely that the Taiwanese industry, which remained technically less developed than the Javanese one until 1940, would have developed if it had not had the protected Japanese market to sell into and if the colonial government had not provided a range of subsidies. The Philippine industry was also technically backward and benefited from a protected market in the United States.

The industry in the Philippines was unique in that most of the assets, both in land and in processing plants and equipment, were owned not by foreign interests but by indigenous Filipinos who had by the 1920s become both very wealthy and politically powerful. Exports grew rapidly between 1921 and 1934, with the American market becoming more and more important; after 1930 almost all exports went to the United States (Larkin 1993: table 10). But the industry remained, like the Taiwanese one, technically backward, and growers had little incentive to increase yields or adopt more modern refining facilities, a fact that worried American officials, if not the growers themselves (Davis 1932: 24). The industry remained protected by favorable access to the American market after 1935 and indeed after full independence was granted in 1946. The sugar barons remained politically powerful well after independence, with consequences for the country's economic and political development that few could have predicted in the early years of the twentieth century.

Estates and Smallholders

The sugar companies that developed in Taiwan, the Philippines, and Java in the latter part of the nineteenth and early twentieth centuries, whether owned by locals or by foreigners, were capitalist enterprises in that the processing factories were large-scale and required heavy investment in plant and equipment as well as substantial amounts of wage labor. The companies sold their output either to protected metropolitan markets or to third countries, and they were required by owners to return a profit. But at the same time they were often reliant on indigenous smallholders for supplies of land; in some parts of the region they depended on independent growers or tenants to supply them with cane. In that sense they were different from the fully integrated estate enterprises that had evolved in Indonesia after the policy changes of the 1870s and in other parts of the region such as British Malaya later in the century, which were almost always foreign-owned. These enterprises acquired substantial amounts of land either in perpetuity or on long-term leases and grew crops largely if not entirely for export. Where processing was necessary before export, this was done on the estate; for both cultivation and processing, the estate depended on wage labor.

The term "estate" is not infrequently used in the literature to refer to any large landholding (say over twenty hectares in size) that is too big to be operated by a normal farm household so must either be tenanted or operated by wage labor or some combination of both. As we have seen, tenancy was widespread in most of the rice-exporting regions of Asia by the 1930s, albeit for different reasons in different countries. It was also widespread in the Philippines. But were large holdings operated by tenants always owned by foreign interests? In the case of Korea and Taiwan, tenancy appears to have been at least partly associated with increased landownership by Japanese individuals and corporations, although there were some indigenous landlords as well. Lee estimated that, by 1930, Japanese owners accounted for 11 percent of taxable land area (1936: 147–148), and a substantial part of this was in large holdings of over 100 hectares that must have been cultivated by either paid labor or tenants. Ka showed that by 1939 Japanese interests owned substantial landholdings in Taiwan, mainly in the southern, sugar-growing areas, which in some cases were cultivated by tenants rather than directly by the companies (1995: 146–147).

In Burma, the growth in tenancy was at least partly the result of land being claimed by Indian moneylenders when loans were in default, although even as late as 1937, only about half the land occupied by nonagriculturalists was the property of the chettyars (Andrus 1948: 70). Adas argued that at least until the first decade of the twentieth century, most landlords were successful farmers who through luck or good management had been able to acquire more land than they were able to cultivate themselves (1974: 71), although the term "estate" does not seem to have been used to refer to their holdings, even when they amounted to hundreds of hectares. But increasingly landlords and others acquired land when owners could not pay back loans, whether to indigenous or Indian lenders.

Brocheux has shown that in Cochinchina, where tenancy was widespread by 1930, European ownership accounted for only about 147,000 hectares, while "Asian settlement" accounted for almost 1.4 million hectares (1995: table 4). Henry reported that there were 6,300 holdings over fifty hectares in Cochinchina (1932: 212), but it seems that the majority were owned by Vietnamese, in some cases with French nationality, rather than Europeans (Sansom 1970: 51). In Thailand, there was little alienation of land to foreign individuals or companies, and most of the land in large holdings was owned by members of the aristocracy, often funded by Chinese merchants. In the Philippines, tenancy appears to have been a means of sharing out the available land to all households willing and able to operate it, but there were also large holdings operated by managers and hired labor. The 1939 census showed that about 3.5 percent of all cultivated land was in such holdings, and the average size of these holdings was 88.3 hectares (Bureau of Census and Statistics 1947: 137–140). But how many of these managed holdings were foreign-owned or fully integrated estate enterprises is difficult to discern from the available data.

It is easier to distinguish foreign-owned, fully integrated estate enterprises from other types of large holdings in the Indonesian and British Malayan figures. This is because colonial statistics made a sharper distinction between estates and smallholdings not just on grounds of size, but also on grounds of legal status. The statistics reflected official concern about alienation of indigenous land to "foreign interests," including not just European companies, but also migrants from other parts of Asia, especially the Chinese. Such alienation was increasingly subject to legal controls after 1870 in Indonesia and after 1913 in British Malaya (Lim 1977: chap. 4). By the early twentieth century, fairly accurate statistics were available on land controlled by estate companies in both Java and the Outer Islands and the conditions of tenure (Creutzberg 1975: table 6). In 1900, around 920,000 hectares of land in Java and 850,000 hectares of land outside Java were available to commercial estates through various concessions and leasing arrangements, including the letting of village land in Java to sugar companies.

By the early 1920s, land controlled by estates outside Java was roughly equal to that in Java, but after that there was a contraction in Java and an increase elsewhere (Table 3.9). By the late 1930s, the amount available to estates in Java had dropped to slightly over 1 million hectares, or about 13 percent of the land cultivated by indigenous Indonesians. But even in Java, only about 55 percent of the land controlled by estates was actually cultivated, while the proportion was lower elsewhere (Table 3.9). In Java, apart from the irrigated land rented to the sugar estates, most of the land controlled by estates was dry and often hilly, and used for the cultivation of tea, coffee, and rubber.

But by the 1930s many landless and near-landless indigenous cultivators were eager to cultivate even dry uplands with food crops such as corn and cassava. Disputes over access to land between the estates and local populations were to become more intense after 1942.

Outside Java, the land controlled by estates was used for a variety of crops, although by the 1920s rubber had become the most important. Rubber cultivation in Indonesia took off more slowly than in British Malaya; by 1910, planted area of rubber on estates was only about 60 percent of that in peninsular Malaya. But by 1940 planted area in Indonesia had almost caught up with Malaya. Particularly striking was the huge area estimated to be under smallholder cultivation outside Java by 1940 (Table 3.10). After 1920, there was also rapid growth in area under smallholder rubber in southern Thailand, although the total area remained less than in British Malaya or Indonesia up until 1940.

The emergence of large, fully integrated estates producing crops such as tobacco or rubber for export was viewed by many colonial officials as inevitable. They were convinced that economies of scale existed in agricultural production as much as in industry and that the best way to "modernize" agriculture was to facilitate the emergence of the large-scale capitalist producer, who hired in labor and sold the output at a profit on world markets. But these views were contradicted by the rapid growth of smallholder production of tree crops, which was one of the most remarkable aspects of agricultural development in both British Malaya and Indonesia after 1900. In neither colony was government policy strongly supportive of smallholder production, and in British Malaya official attitudes to smallholder rubber production remained overtly hostile until 1940.

British officials were convinced that smallholdings were badly cultivated, and yields would decline progressively compared to the large estates managed on "scientific" principles (Drabble 1991: 138). They remained impervious to any evidence to the contrary, and increasingly the relationship between estates and smallholders became more competitive, not just over land but also over

Table 3.9. Area Controlled by Estates in Java and the Outer Islands, 1921–1940

| | Area Controlled (million hectares) | | Planted Area as a Percentage of Controlled Area | | Planted Area of Estates as a Percentage of Peasant Area |
	Java	Outer Islands	Java	Outer Islands	Java
1921–1925	1.33	1.31	42	24	18
1926–1930	1.23	1.56	54	29	16
1931–1935	1.10	1.55	55	35	14
1936–1940	1.06	1.41	55	41	13

Sources: Department of Economic Affairs 1941: 70–73; van der Eng 1996: table A.4.

access to other support services such as improved seeds and credit. In Indonesia, official attitudes were probably more positive, especially on the part of officials anxious to encourage smallholders to diversify their output and incomes, although the growth in smallholder cultivation of rubber took place mainly outside the estate areas. Pelzer pointed out that only about 42,000 of the estimated 715,000 hectares under smallholder rubber cultivation in 1940 were in East Sumatra, where most of the large estates were located (1978: 53). Most smallholders were in central and southern Sumatra and in western Kalimantan, where there were few barriers to smallholders taking more land under rubber cultivation.

It is undoubtedly true that the smallholder rubber boom in Indonesia and Malaya would not have taken place if estates together with agency houses and banks had not pioneered the financing, cultivation, and marketing of what was an exotic export crop about which indigenous Southeast Asian farmers knew nothing until the early years of the twentieth century. It is striking that rubber cultivation never took off at all in the southern Philippine island of Mindanao, where there was abundant land and a climate well suited to the crop. Pelzer suggested that the main reason was that American rubber capital was deterred by the 1,024-hectare limit on plantations and turned instead to Malaya and Sumatra (1945: 105), although immediately after the formation of the Federated Malay States, instructions to residents limited the amount of land that could be alienated to one individual to 640 acres (260 hectares) in Perak and a lower amount elsewhere (Drabble 1973: 23). These restrictions were lifted or circumvented when corporate capital became more involved in rubber cultivation, both in the FMS and in Johore.

In southern Vietnam, the amount of land under rubber cultivation was small relative to both Malaya and Indonesia and confined entirely to production on large plantations, located mainly in the "gray" and "red" lands to the north of Saigon. There is little evidence that much smallholder production was undertaken; certainly it was never encouraged by the French colonial regime. The only region where smallholder cultivation was established before 1940

Table 3.10. Planted Area of Rubber (Hevea), 1910–1940: British Malaya, Java, Outer Islands of Indonesia, and Thailand, 1910–1940 (thousand hectares)

Year	British Malaya		Java		Outer Islands		Thailand
	E	S	E	S	E	S	S
1910	172	53	64	n.a.	40	n.a.	0.4
1921	522	369	165	n.a.	204	n.a.	11.2
1930	754	476	229	n.a.	344	n.a.	60
1940	848	541	241	16	385	715	273

Sources: Drabble 2000: 53; Creutzberg 1975: table 10; Manarungsan 1989: 109.

Note: E = estate area, S = area under smallholdings; n.a. = not available.

outside Malaya and Indonesia was southern Thailand, where farmers managed to get access to seedlings from across the border. By 1940, planted area was around 273,000 hectares, although only about 120,000 hectares were tappable (Manarungsan 1989: 109). This area was much smaller than in either Malaya or Indonesia, but tappable hectarage was to expand rapidly after 1950.

The main problem facing the large estates in Malaya, Vietnam, and Indonesia after 1900 was recruiting and retaining sufficient labor. Local populations who themselves had access to land were reluctant to work under what were seen as demeaning conditions for low wages, and companies had little alternative but to seek migrant workers. In Malaya, the recruitment was mainly from the huge labor pools in China and India, while in Indonesia and Vietnam, the colonial governments encouraged recruitment from the more densely settled areas within the colony where land was becoming scarce. The growth of large estates was thus an important factor in the development of a wage labor force in several parts of Southeast Asia in the early decades of the twentieth century, although by no means the only one.

The Emergence of a Wage Labor Force

By the 1920s, a skewed pattern of landholdings had emerged in many parts of East and Southeast Asia, where ownership was highly concentrated. In many regions, tenancy was used to distribute land to households who were willing and able to operate it, but tenants operating small plots of land were often in a very precarious position and probably little better off than those who depended mainly on wage labor for their incomes. In fact, it was frequently difficult to make a clear distinction between households owning very small plots, households who leased small amounts of land, and the wholly landless, as all three categories were dependent on wage labor and various types of self-employment to make ends meet. As we have seen, by the 1920s, it was estimated that around 60 percent of the population of Java was "land poor," in the sense that they operated either no land at all, only very small plots, or house gardens. In Tonkin (northern Vietnam), almost 62 percent of households owned less than one *mau* (0.36 hectares), and a further 30 percent owned less than five *mau* (1.8 hectares). Gourou argues that a household cultivating three *mau* (1.1 hectares) and owning a buffalo was in "easy circumstances" by Tonkin standards, but the majority were below this threshold (1945a: 279).

For such households everywhere in Asia, the options were to try to acquire more land through purchase or rental/sharecropping arrangements, to earn some extra cash in various types of self-employment (food processing, weaving, petty trade, and so on), or to seek wage employment either in agriculture on in other activities (mining, construction, manufacturing, transport, trade, and so on). A further option was to migrate to a place where land was in greater abundance and establish a new holding. Long-distance migration did occur without government assistance, as in the case of the Irrawaddy delta. There were also attempts at government-sponsored land settlement schemes. In Indonesia, the Dutch colonial authorities viewed the movement of poor families from Java to Sumatra and Sulawesi as an integral part of the ethical policy. But movement of colonists to new settlements was costly and subject to a number of bureaucratic rules. In the early years of the twentieth century, the numbers moved were small, although they accelerated in the 1920s, especially to Lampung in southern Sumatra. As Pelzer pointed out, the government settlement program had to compete with the recruiting agencies of the Sumatran plantations, which were by the early years of the twentieth century almost entirely dependent on Java for their labor supply (1945: 196–197).

The numbers of "coolies" working on the estates of East Sumatra increased over the first three decades of the century to a peak of almost 303,000 in 1929 (Lindblad 1999a: 72). Around 90 percent were Javanese, and most of the remainder were Chinese. Large numbers of Javanese also moved to other estate areas in Sumatra and southeastern Kalimantan; in 1929, the total number of coolies working on estates outside Java amounted to almost 535,000, of whom the great majority were Javanese (Lindblad 1999b: 101). By 1930, people born in Java formed 31 percent of the total population of the region along the east coast of Sumatra where most large estates were located and about 10 percent of the entire population of Sumatra (Pelzer 1945: 260). During the 1930s, all the estates in Indonesia reduced their labor force, and by the end of the decade, the numbers of contract coolies had diminished to a few thousand. Recruitment in Java largely ceased, and most workers were "free," that is, locally recruited. Over the same decade, the numbers of colonists moved by the government increased, but even in 1940, the stock of Javanese transmigrants settled outside Java was lower than the numbers of estate workers (206,000 compared with 331,000). Taken together, official land settlement and the recruitment of estate workers from Java to the Outer Islands represented the largest movement of labor *within* a colonial territory in East or Southeast Asia in the early part of the twentieth century.

In addition, large numbers of workers were employed as wage laborers on sugar estates on Java. Life as a coolie worker on a large estate was hard for the Javanese, especially for those working many hundreds of miles away in Sumatra or Kalimantan. Workers were not infrequently recruited with false promises of wages and conditions, and mistreated after their arrival. In spite of the establishment of the Labor Inspectorate early in the twentieth century, conditions remained harsh for contract workers until the 1930s. Unpleasant and demeaning working conditions often resulted in attacks by coolies on their European supervisors (Houben 1999: 119). Rates of desertion peaked in the late 1920s, although they were never higher than around 3 percent of the total number of coolies (Lindblad 1999a: 76). But the lack of employment opportunities in most parts of Java ensured a steady supply of labor, both to the sugar estates in Java and to the plantations of Sumatra and Kalimantan.

This also appears to have been the case on the rubber estates in southern Vietnam, which by 1930 employed over 55,000 workers, of whom around 31,000 were on contracts and the balance were free workers (Brocheux 1975: 63). During the early 1930s, the rubber estates employed more workers than the mining sector, which was the other large-scale employer of wage workers in Indochina.

As in Sumatra, there was criticism of the conditions under which the laborers had to work; the harsh conditions and high incidence of malaria made it difficult for the estates to recruit in the Saigon area, where alternative work was increasingly available in the 1920s in the port and in industry. Murray states that in the buoyant years of the late 1920s, noncontract workers were paid around 60 cents a day, sufficient to buy around four kilograms of rice (1980: 284). But they had to pay for food and lodgings. Unskilled workers in Saigon were paid at a slightly higher rate (between 65 and 79 cents) and would have been able to lodge with family or friends. The plantations were increasingly forced to look north to Tonkin and Annam for workers (ibid.: 272). Labor recruiting was done through private agents, and as in Java, it appears that workers were often lured through false promises of high wages that did not eventuate. Workers were contracted for three years, and those who broke their contracts were subject to various penalties. Even so, there was a very high turnover of workers. In order to maintain an effective labor force of around 22,000 workers, estates found they had to recruit up to 75,000 (Brocheux 1975: 63). This turnover was partly due to high mortality, although better medical care led to a decline in death rates during the 1930s. But many workers simply broke their contracts and either went home or joined the ranks of the wage labor force in other parts of the south.

It is not possible to estimate the size of the wage labor force in Southeast Asia or in Korea and Taiwan in the colonial period; labor force data are not available broken down by category of worker. There can be little doubt that several million workers in the region were largely if not entirely dependent on wage labor by 1930. The world depression in the early 1930s meant that many large enterprises, both estates and others, cut back on employment. In Indonesia, the total number of coolies working on estates outside Java more than halved between 1929 and 1934; there was also a sharp decline in numbers employed on rubber estates in British Malaya (Thoburn 1977: 285–286). In the case of Burma, many Indian workers returned home in the early 1930s as a result of the decline in wage labor opportunities. But by the latter part of the 1930s, as world economic conditions improved, recruitment of wage labor in the estates sector began to recover. By then other forms of wage employment had also become important. In Indonesia, by 1939 wage payments in industry exceeded those in estates, while earnings of Indonesians employed in government service had also risen in real terms over the 1930s (Polak 1943: tables 7.3, 8.2, and 10.3).

A striking aspect of labor markets in several parts of Southeast Asia was the apparently high degree of nominal wage rigidity; as employment declined in the early 1930s, money wages either stayed constant or declined quite slowly in Java, Sumatra, Thailand, and Vietnam. As prices of key staples such as rice were falling rapidly during these years, the real purchasing power of money wages often increased. Conversely, in the latter part of the 1930s, as exports and employment began to recover, money wages did not keep pace with increasing prices. Virtually everywhere in Asia, the amount of rice that daily wages could purchase declined in the latter part of the 1930s (Table 3.11). As would be expected, rice wages were lowest in the land-scarce areas of Java and Tonkin, although in neither case were they as low as in Korea. By the end of the 1930s, the highest wages were found in Manila and Bangkok, although in both cases government regulation of urban labor markets was increasing. In Manila, minimum wage legislation pushed urban wages well above rural ones and probably restricted employment growth as well. In Bangkok, the post-1932 government began to restrict Chinese in-migration and impose quotas on Chinese employment in urban areas (Phongpaichit and Baker 1995: 179). By the late 1930s, many rural Thais were joining the urban wage labor force, which must have depressed real wages in sectors such as rice milling, formerly a Chinese preserve.

A more complete discussion of the functioning of labor markets, wage trends, and their implications for living standards of both indigenous and migrant workers will be undertaken in Chapter 7. Here we can conclude by making three points about the interaction between land and labor markets in the context of export-oriented economies with rapid population growth. First, by the 1920s, land was becoming an increasingly scarce and contested asset in many parts of East and Southeast Asia. At the same time, labor was becoming more abundant, partly because of natural increase and partly because of in-migration. It is thus probable that land rentals were increasing relative to wages, even in those parts of the region that in the mid-nineteenth century were land abundant. Data on this point are limited, but in Thailand Feeny's estimates indicate that, between 1915 and 1940, land prices increased by more than 40 percent, while wage rates for unskilled labor grew by only about 6 percent (Feeny 1982: tables 3-8 and 3-10).

A second point concerns the role of migrant workers. In Southeast Asia, labor migration, by the early twentieth century, was increasingly important, although it varied over time and place. In Indonesia, French Indochina, and the Philippines, the policy of the Dutch, the French, and the Americans was to restrict in-migration, especially from China, while at the same time facilitating movement of workers and families from regions where land was scarce to regions where it appeared to be more abundant. These policies were also adopted after 1932 in Thailand. The Japanese in Korea and also the Dutch in Java began to encourage international migration. But everywhere in the region, the goal of a nation of prosperous homesteaders cultivating their own holdings remained elusive. More and more people worked for wages, even if

Table 3.11. Daily Wages in Kilograms of Rice: Agricultural and Urban Workers, 1934–1938

Colony / Country	1934	1935	1936	1937	1938
Korea					
Male agricultural	3.3	2.9	n.a.	n.a.	n.a.
Taiwan					
Farm wage	7.8	7.9	7.1	5.6	5.7
Straits Settlements					
Rubber: male	11.4	6.1	6.3	6.9	7.1
Rubber: female	7.3	4.9	5.0	5.5	5.6
Peninsular Malaya					
Rubber estates	7.7	5.7	6.2	6.6	5.9
Sumatra					
Tobacco: male	10.8	10.0	10.4	8.8	8.7
Ditto with supplements	12.2	11.2	11.4	9.7	5.1
Tobacco: female	6.8	6.0	5.9	4.9	5.1
Ditto with supplements	8.1	7.2	7.0	5.9	6.2
Java					
Sugar coolies: male	7.2	5.4	4.3	3.5	4.2
Ditto: female	5.9	4.5	3.9	3.1	3.6
Sugar: regular workers	12.0	8.4	6.6	5.2	5.6
Sugar: artisans	25.3	18.6	13.7	10.6	11.4
Saigon					
Unskilled male	16.9	12.9	10.7	7.8	5.9
Unskilled female	13.2	9.5	7.6	5.3	4.0
Artisan male	36.5	27.4	22.1	14.9	12.0
Hanoi					
Unskilled male	4.8	4.5	n.a.	n.a.	2.1
Unskilled female	3.2	3.0	n.a.	n.a.	1.3
Artisan male	10.3	9.7	n.a.	n.a.	4.1
Bangkok					
Coolies	14.7	11.5	11.0	11.3	12.0
Carpenters	26.6	20.9	20.0	20.5	21.7
Philippines					
Manila: laborer	n.a.	n.a.	n.a.	15.5	12.2
Sugar: laborer	n.a.	n.a.	n.a.	n.a.	5.1 (1939)

Sources: Taiwan: Rose 1985: 39. Korea: Rose 1985: 90. Singapore: Department of Statistics 1939: 127–130. Malaya: Thoburn 1977: 286. Sumatra and Java: Department of Economic Affairs 1941: 248; rice prices from Creutzberg 1978: table 3. Saigon and Hanoi: Giacometti 2000b: 189, 204–205, with additional price data from Takada 2000: 136. Bangkok: Central Service of Statistics 1940: 515, 522. Manila: Bureau of Census and Statistics 1947: 239; Runes 1939: 12.

Note: n.a. = not available.

they had to move over long distances to do so. In Thailand and Burma, and in British Malaya, governments did not control in-migration but instead tried to regulate the land market, albeit with varying success. Migrant Chinese and Indians were largely confined to urban labor markets and to large estates in British Malaya. In Burma, the alienation of land to Indians occurred through the credit market, which was left largely unregulated until the late 1930s.

The third point concerns the role of government in regulating markets for land, labor, and credit. There can be little doubt that during the first four decades of the twentieth century, colonial governments in most parts of the region grasped the fact that in order to control, or at least influence, production, they would have to be able to control factor markets. But the policies used differed over time and place, according to the priorities of the various governments and the instruments that were available. As we saw in the case of the sugar industry, the Dutch used coercion to control land rentals, while Japanese policy was to subsidize Japanese companies in order to establish processing facilities, while at the same time making sure that they were able to access sufficient land to produce the cane needed to supply the factories. In the Philippines, where the cultivation and processing of cane was largely in indigenous hands, the industry itself became a powerful lobby able to influence government policy in its interests.

A More Nuanced View of Vent for Surplus?

Critics of the vent for surplus model as originally set out by Myint have stressed in particular the overly simplistic way in which he dealt with the precolonial economy (Smith 1976: 433). The assumption that the population was only involved in subsistence agricultural production was clearly unrealistic, both in Southeast Asia and in other regions such as West Africa. In addition, in the Southeast Asian context, the assumption that before the imposition of European colonialism much of the region was effectively closed to foreign trade is also questionable. Not only was there a significant indigenous handicraft sector within the region, but there had also been quite extensive involvement in long-distance trade within Asia, which had given rise to large port cities where many people were employed in transport and commerce. Although this diversified commercial economy had declined in the seventeenth and eighteenth centuries even before the intrusion of European colonial institutions, that intrusion brought about a substantial restructuring of domestic economic activity.

It was pointed out in Chapter 2 that, in many parts of Southeast Asia in the late nineteenth and early twentieth centuries, there is evidence of a decline in handicraft production as cheaper imports not just from the metropolitan powers but also from Japan flooded in. The decline was by no means total, and the census evidence suggests that many handicraft producers survived and even flourished into the 1930s, partly because imported inputs of yarn and cotton cloth actually helped activities such as weaving and batik manufacture. In addition, the growth of exports created employment in processing industries, and these workers together with the many millions of smallholder producers of crops such as rice and rubber were able to use their extra income to purchase a range of both home-produced and imported goods. But at the same time, the export boom inevitably made land a more valuable asset, and struggles over access to land became more intense in the first four decades of the twentieth century. The casual assumption that underpins some discussions of vent for surplus, that agricultural land was easily available to all those willing and able to cultivate it, was far from the truth in many parts of Asia after 1900. Even in the so-called frontier regions, scrambles for land intensified, and the victors were often those with the best connections to the colonial establishment.

Other factors also affected the extent to which export growth benefited indigenous populations. One of the most important was the role of government. Implicit in much of the critical writing on the role of colonialism was the argument that governments were at best neutral in their impact on indigenous populations and at worst extremely negative. The next chapter tries to assess some of the main effects of government policy, paying particular attention to the evolution of taxation and expenditures.

CHAPTER 4

What Were Colonial Governments Doing?
The Myth of the Night Watchman State

Alternative Views of the Role of the Colonial State

One influential view of the role of government in colonial territories was put forward by Morris in the context of nineteenth century India: "Government policy during the nineteenth century, despite its authoritarian characteristics, was in its economic aspects essentially *laissez faire*. The British *raj* saw itself in the passive role of night watchman, providing security, rational administration, and a modicum of social overhead on the basis of which economic progress was expected to occur. The Indian government obviously had no self-conscious programme of active economic development" (1963: 615).

In a footnote, Morris pointed out that while the British certainly felt that the welfare of Indian society was an important objective, the prevailing ideology in Britain at the time made a more assertive policy of economic development impossible. It is important to note that Morris was only discussing nineteenth-century British policy, although there is little evidence to suggest that government revenues and expenditures in British India increased significantly after 1900 or that economic policy became more "developmental" in other respects. Nor was Morris implying that colonial governments in other parts of Asia were pursuing similar policies to those in British India. Nevertheless the phrase "night watchman state" has gained a place in the literature on European and especially British colonialism in Southeast Asia; for example, Emerson argued in the case of the Straits Settlements that "until very recent times, the government has not interpreted its function more broadly than in terms of police power" (1937: 306). Huff argued that government in Singapore "conceived of its role as primarily to enforce law and order and to secure property rights" (1994: 168), while Bayly and Harper thought that before the Pacific War, "large parts of the state across the whole region had been content to operate as the classic night watchman" (2004: 463–464), although they did concede that there had been progress in the development of infrastructure.

It was pointed out in Chapter 1 that the "night watchman" view of the colonial state has been challenged by writers who view the government's role in colonies as mainly concerned with encouraging the rapid exploitation of resources for export. Some writers have argued that, in most tropical colonies, "there were few constraints on state power. . . . The colonial powers set up authoritarian and absolutist states with the purpose of solidifying their control and facilitating the extraction of resources" (Acemoglu, Johnson, and Robinson 2001: 1375). A third view on the economic role of the colonial state has been put forward by writers who support Japanese exceptionalism and who argue that the Japanese colonies were characterized by activist governments; in the case of Korea, Kohli claimed:

> The colonial state in Korea was a busy state. While pursuing the imperial interests of Japan, it evolved a full policy agenda, including the goal of Korea's economic transformation. The broad strategy of transformation was two-pronged: The state utilized its bureaucratic capacities to directly undertake numerous economic tasks, and, more important, the state involved propertied groups—both in the countryside and in the cities, and both Japanese and Koreans—in production-oriented alliances aimed at achieving sustained economic change. (2004: 40)

Was such a policy agenda unique to the Japanese colonies? The role of government in colonial jurisdictions is a complex issue and must be addressed from several angles. This chapter attempts a comparison of government taxation and expenditure policies in colonial East and Southeast Asia; the involvement of the state in promoting production and controlling factor markets is discussed further in Chapter 6.

Tax and Expenditure Policies: An Overview

By the first decade of the twentieth century, all the colonial powers in East and Southeast Asia were trying to establish effective administrative structures that prioritized the centralization and reform of fiscal systems (Elson 1992: 149–154). Independent Thailand also carried out major reforms of government revenue policy (Ingram 1971: chaps. 8 and 9). On the revenue side, the metropolitan powers wanted tax systems under the direct control of the colonial administrations, which were sufficiently buoyant to provide enough revenues to fund current expenditures while at the same time providing a surplus for investment. Old practices of revenue farming were eliminated during the last decades of the nineteenth and the early twentieth century in favor of more "modern" revenue systems relying on trade taxes, domestic excises, and sales taxes, and in some cases on corporate and individual income taxes (Butcher 1993).

In the Japanese colonies, considerable resources were devoted to drawing up land cadastres so that land taxes could be levied (Ho 1984: 355; Grajdanzev 1944: 54). Detailed cadastral surveys were also carried out in Burma and Java, and in some of the more settled regions outside Java, on the basis of which land taxes were levied as a fraction of the income that cultivators were assumed to be deriving from the land. Furnivall, who had extensive knowledge of the Burmese system and studied the Dutch colonial land tax in Java in the 1930s, argued that the Javanese tax was simpler and in some respects more equitable than that in Burma (Furnivall 1934a). Less progress was made in the frontier regions of Indonesia outside Java and in French Indochina, where cadastral surveys were far less accurate and the assessment of land taxes a hit-or-miss affair (Thompson 1937: 193–194, 232–233).

Revenue policy reform in Southeast Asia in the early twentieth century was in part directed to the abolition or at least the downsizing of politically embarrassing revenues such as those derived from the sale of opium. In the Philippines, the American administration was committed to replacing the "repressive" Spanish revenue system with one that would enhance economic and social uplift (Luton 1971: 133). Not surprisingly given these aims, the opium levy was seen as especially reprehensible, although it only accounted for about 7 percent of total revenues in the final phase of Spanish rule. The Americans fought hard for the prohibition of opium trading, except for medical purposes, throughout Asia in the early part of the twentieth century, although other colonial powers, including the British, were reluctant to support more than its "gradual" withdrawal (Foster 2003: 112). Indeed Bayly and Harper have argued that British rule in both Burma and Malaya was "supported by narco-colonialism on a colossal scale" (2004: 33).

By the early 1920s, this was probably an exaggeration. Certainly the governments of the Straits Settlements and the Unfederated Malay States (UMS) were still dependent on the sale of opium products for a considerable share of total government revenues, although during the 1920s and 1930s the proportion did fall, as other revenue sources became more important. In 1926, the governments of Kedah and Johore (which together accounted for 87 percent of total revenues raised in the Unfederated Malay States) derived about one-third of their revenues from licenses, including those from the sale of opium. Revenues from other sources such as customs duties were larger and growing more rapidly (Colonial Reports 1929: appendix B). By 1938, the Straits Settlements and the FMS were deriving less than 10 percent of total revenues from opium, although tax revenues accounted for less than half of the total (Table 4.1). In Indochina, the sale of opium became a state monopoly under the Doumer reforms implemented at the end of the nineteenth century; thereafter net receipts tended to stagnate (Descours-Gatin 1992: 226). But Vietnam remained reliant on a range of nontax revenues, including the opium, salt, and alcohol monopolies, for around 40 percent of revenues until the 1930s. In Thailand, Taiwan, and Korea, the proportion from nontax sources was even higher (Table 4.1).

Table 4.1. Percentage Breakdown of Total Government Revenues, c. 1938

	Customs Revenues and Direct Taxes (incl. land taxes)	Other Indirect Taxes (incl. excises)	Other Revenues[a]	Total
FMS (1938)	38.2	2.8	59.0 (8.2)	100
Straits Settlements (1938)	0	25.2	74.8 (9.2)	100
Thailand (1938/1939)	45.3	6.7	48.0 (8.7)	100
Vietnam (1938)	41.0	17.0	42.0 (17.6)	100
Philippines (1938)	28.1	35.9	36.0	100
Burma (1938/1939)	66.8	16.0	17.2	100
Indonesia (1938)	45.0	17.9	37.1	100
Taiwan[b] (1937)	25.8	20.2	54.0 (32.5)	100
Korea[b] (1938)	25.5	27.5	47.0 (16.2)	100

Sources: FMS and Straits Settlements: Department of Statistics 1939: chap. 33; Thailand: Central Service of Statistics 1940: 274–279; Vietnam: Bassino 2000b: table 2; Philippines: Bureau of Census and Statistics 1941: 164–166; Burma: Andrus 1948: table 37; Indonesia: Central Bureau of Statistics 1947: 127–133; data on total revenues taken from Creutzberg 1976: table 4; Taiwan: Grajdanzev 1942: 133–135; Korea: Grajdanzev 1944: 212–214.

[a] Includes profits from government monopolies and government enterprises. Figures in parentheses show revenues from opium monopolies and, in the case of Vietnam, Taiwan, and Korea, all government monopolies.

[b] To ensure better comparability with other data, revenues exclude government loans and carryovers from previous fiscal years.

On the expenditure side, all the colonial governments had by 1900 begun to assume responsibility for a much broader range of activities than simply the maintenance of law and order and the collection of revenues. Increasingly it was recognized that ambitious programs of infrastructural development would have to be funded by government rather than the private sector, with government funds derived in part at least from loan finance. In Indonesia, where government expenditures had grown in real terms continuously after 1870, public works (including railways) accounted for 40 percent of total government expenditure in 1920 (Booth 1990: table 10.5). In Burma, civil public works accounted for almost 24 percent of government expenditures by 1901–1904, although the percentage fell somewhat thereafter (Aye Hlaing 1965: table 22). In Indochina, especially the three provinces composing what is now Vietnam, public works already accounted for 20 percent of total government expenditures in 1901; by 1909, the share had risen to more than 40 percent (Booth 2007: table 2). The concept of *mise en valeur,* stressed by successive French administrators after 1900, meant in effect increased expenditures on public works in order to facilitate the exploitation of the colony's natural resources (Doumer 1902: 24; Simoni 1929).

To what extent was government spending biased in favor of infrastructure in the export enclaves? French investment in land development in the south of the country was intended to boost rice production for export, although it was pointed out in the previous chapter that most of the beneficiaries were Vietnamese, not French settlers. In other parts of Southeast Asia, several colonial regimes (notably the Americans in the Philippines, but also the Dutch in Indonesia and the British in the Federated Malay States) were devoting a growing proportion of budgetary expenditures to increasing food-crop production through improved rural infrastructure, especially irrigation, as well as to health and education. Official rhetoric began to stress commitments to "uplift the natives" and gradually equip them for life in a modern economy. American policy in the Philippines was strongly influenced by such aims, and after 1901, Dutch colonial policy shared many of the goals of the Americans. The ethical policy made the enhancement of the welfare of the indigenous population of the huge Indonesian archipelago the key objective of colonial policy. Irrigation development, the expansion of health and education services, an ambitious land settlement program, and the development of rural credit facilities all received significant budgetary funding after 1900 (Boomgaard 1993; Cribb 1993).

In Taiwan and Korea, there was also a strong emphasis on increased provision of rural infrastructure, although in both colonies the main concern of the Japanese was to increase rice, and in Taiwan also sugar, production for supply to the market in Japan. In the early years of the Japanese occupation of Taiwan, government expenditures were concentrated on the agricultural sector and on transport infrastructure. By 1920 these two heads of expenditure accounted for almost 60 percent of the total (Table 4.2). Government capital formation (GCF) peaked at around 6 percent of GDP in 1912, although it fell thereafter (Figure 4.1). In Korea, government expenditures were far more skewed toward public order and administration, although spending on transport accounted for a growing share, especially after 1920 (Table 4.2). Government capital formation was a lower percentage of GDP than in Taiwan until the latter part of the 1930s.

The considerable differences in outcomes of revenue and expenditure policies in different parts of colonial Asia can be appreciated by examining revenues and expenditures per capita, converted into US dollars. Government revenues per capita in 1910 varied between around one dollar per capita in Vietnam to fifteen dollars in the Federated Malay States (FMS) (Table 4.3). Although several of the colonies with low revenues per capita in 1910 improved their revenue performance over the next two decades, none caught up with either the FMS or the Straits Settlements. By 1929, government revenues in Indonesia, the Philippines, Korea, and Burma were around five to six dollars per capita, more than in Thailand and Vietnam but still well below Taiwan and the three components of British Malaya. With the onset of the world depression, revenues fell in terms of dollars per capita in most colonies and had not recovered to 1929 levels by 1938.

Table 4.2. Government Expenditures Broken Down by Category: Taiwan and Korea, 1900–1938 (percentage of total expenditures)

Year	Agriculture	Education	Transport	Public Order	Administration/ Salaries
Taiwan					
1900	7.7	4.3	35.1	13.4	19.1
1910	30.7	10.4	20.9	18.3	11.0
1920	29.9	4.1	29.3	5.6	24.1
1925	37.4	5.9	24.5	8.7	20.3
1930	28.2	8.2	28.4	10.9	20.0
1935	24.7	6.9	26.7	12.9	23.4
1938	21.6	6.2	26.4	22.3	17.1
Korea					
1910	9.6[a]	23.8	5.7	30.3	30.6
1920	5.0	10.1	23.3	35.4	20.8
1925	4.3	6.0	31.4	25.2	21.6
1930	4.8	5.9	29.5	26.2	18.2
1935	6.5	5.6	30.1	29.4	13.3
1938	4.0	4.2	40.0	28.8	9.6

Source: Mizoguchi and Umemura 1988: 288–293.

Note: Excludes local government expenditures. Percentages do not always add to 100, as certain categories of expenditure are omitted.

[a] Includes expenditures on industry and commerce as well as agriculture.

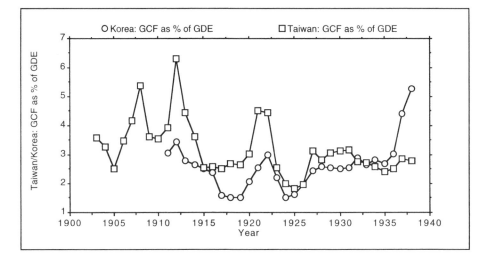

Figure 4.1. Government capital formation as a proportion of gross domestic expenditure, market price, Taiwan and Korea. (Source: Mizoguchi and Umemura 1988: part 3, tables 5, 7, 54, and 57)

Table 4.3. Government Revenues Per Capita in Southeast Asia, Taiwan, and Korea, 1910–1938 (US dollars)

Country	1910	1920	1929	1934	1938
Vietnam[a]	1	3	3	3	2
Netherlands Indies	2	5	5	4	4
Philippines	3	6	6	4	5
Thailand	3	3	4	3	3
Burma	3	5	6	6	4
UMS[b]	5	6	11	10	10
Straits Settlements	8	21	29	17	15
FMS	15	24	28	19	18
Taiwan	8	16	16	8	12
Korea	1	4	6	4	7

Sources: Vietnam: Bassino 2000b and Banens 2000; Indonesia: Creutzberg 1976: table 4; van der Eng 2002: 171–172; Philippines: Birnberg and Resnick 1975: table A.38; Thailand: Ingram 1971: appendixes B and C; Burma: Shein, Thant, and Sein 1969: appendix 2; National Planning Commission 1960a–b; Andrus 1948: tables 37 and 38; British Malaya (FMS, UMS, and Straits Colonies): Emerson 1937: chaps. 4, 5, and 6, with additional data from Lim 1967: appendix 9.2; Fraser 1939: appendix A for the Federated Malay States; exchange rates: van Laanen 1980: table 8; Direction des Services Économiques 1947: 288; Ingram 1971: 337; Emerson 1937: 522. Taiwan and Korea: Mizoguchi and Umemura 1988: 256, 288–293; exchange rates from Japan Statistical Association 1987.

[a] Data refer to 1913, not 1910. Local and (after 1931) provincial revenues and expenditures are included.

[b] Data refer to 1911 and 1921, not 1910 and 1920. The 1911 data refer to Johore and Kelantan only.

The striking differences in revenues per capita that were obvious by the 1920s must have reflected significant differences in revenues as a ratio of GDP. We do not yet have complete national income data for all parts of the Southeast Asian region in the first part of the twentieth century; the available evidence indicates that by 1929 the highest per capita GDP was in British Malaya. It was not much higher than in the Philippines, but about 40 percent higher than in Indonesia (see Table 2.4). Thus revenues as a proportion of GDP must have been much higher in the Straits Settlements and the FMS than in the Dutch, American, or French colonies, or in independent Thailand. Whether they were higher than in the Japanese colonies is unclear. In Taiwan, government revenues peaked at around 26 percent of GDP in 1912 and fell thereafter, although they seldom dropped below 17 percent of GDP. The ratio was much lower in Korea until the 1930s, when there was rapid convergence. The same is true for the ratio of government expenditures to GDP (Figures 4.2 and 4.3).

Changes in revenues per capita in colonial Asia were broadly matched by changes in expenditures per capita (Table 4.4), although colonial budgets were not always balanced in every fiscal year. During the 1920s, several colo-

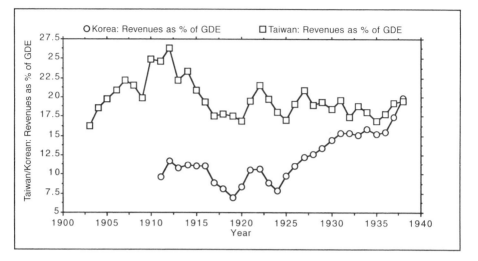

Figure 4.2. Government revenues as a proportion of gross domestic expenditure, Taiwan and Korea. (Source: Mizoguchi and Umemura 1988: part 3, tables 5, 7, 53, and 56)

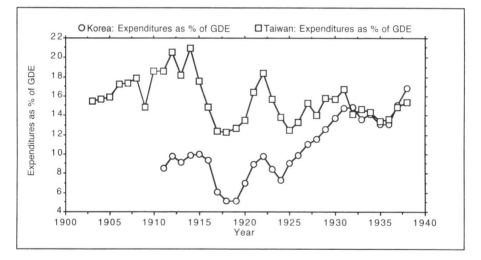

Figure 4.3. Government expenditures as a proportion of gross domestic expenditure, Taiwan and Korea. (Source: Mizoguchi and Umemura 1988: part 3, tables 5, 7, 54, and 57)

nies ran budget surpluses; as revenues fell in the early 1930s, some budgets swung into deficit. This was the case in Indonesia, the Federated Malay States, the Philippines, and Vietnam in the early 1930s, although not in Burma and Thailand or in Taiwan and Korea (Table 4.5). These deficits hardly reflected a conversion to Keynesian economics on the part of colonial officials, but rather an inability to cut expenditures as rapidly as revenues fell with falling export

Table 4.4. Government Expenditures Per Capita in Southeast Asia, British India, Taiwan, and South Korea, 1910–1938 (US dollars)

Country	1910	1920	1929	1934	1938
Vietnam[a]	1	3	3	3	2
Indonesia	2	7	5	5	4
Philippines	3	6	6	4	5
Thailand	3	4	4	3	4
Burma	2	4	4	3	3
UMS[b]	5	8	11	7	10
Straits Settlements	6	20	19	15	17
FMS[b]	13	33	29	15	28
India	1	2	3	2	2
Taiwan	6	13	13	6	9
Korea	1	3	6	4	6

Sources: Vietnam: Bassino 2000b and Banens 2000; Indonesia: Creutzberg 1976: table 4; van der Eng 2002: 171–172; Philippines: Birnberg and Resnick 1975: table A.38; Bureau of Census and Statistics 1941: 13; Thailand: Ingram 1971: appendixes B and C; Burma: Shein, Thant, and Sein 1969: appendix 2; National Planning Commission 1960a–b; Andrus 1948: tables 37 and 38; British Malaya (FMS, UMS, and Straits Colonies): Emerson 1937: chaps. 4, 5, and 6, with additional data from Fraser 1939: appendix A for the Federated Malay States; Department of Statistics 1939: 245–246; exchange rates: van Laanen 1980: table 8; Direction des Services Économiques 1947: 288; Ingram 1971: 337; Emerson 1937: 522. Taiwan and Korea: Mizoguchi and Umemura 1988: 256, 288–293; exchange rates from Japan Statistical Association 1987. India: Reddy 1972.

[a] Data refer to 1913, not 1910. Local and (after 1931) provincial revenues and expenditures are included.

[b] Data refer to 1911 and 1921, not 1910 and 1920. The 1911 figure refers to Johore and Kelantan only.

prices. In several colonies, such as the FMS and Indonesia, it proved difficult to cut back on expenditures on salaries and pensions. Independent Thailand found it easier to make cuts in spending. Virtually everywhere in the region, government expenditures on capital investments fell more rapidly than current spending after 1930. The main exception was Korea, where there was a steep rise in government capital formation relative to GDP in the latter part of the 1930s, due in part to the increased expenditures on transport infrastructure (see Figure 4.1 and Table 4.2).

Determinants of Revenue and Expenditure Growth

There is strong evidence that both revenue and expenditure growth in Southeast Asia in the first four decades of the twentieth century were tightly linked to export growth. Long-run elasticities of both government revenues and expenditures with respect to exports were close to unity in most parts of the

Table 4.5. Budgetary Revenues as a Percentage of Expenditures, 1900–1939 (five-year averages centered on the year shown)

Year	Vietnam	Burma	FMS	Thailand	Indonesia
1902	n.a.	153	122	100	95
1907	n.a.	146	121	94	100
1912	112[a]	139	110	94	94
1917	104	142	134	100	84
1922	96	143	95	88	87
1927	89	146	108	97	104
1932	81	162	93	104	75
1937	104	108[b]	107[c]	97	88

	Philippines	Straits Settlements	Taiwan	Korea
1902	96[d]	97	107	n.a.
1907	104	103	126	n.a.
1912	101	129	125	117
1917	105	142	136	134
1922	97	118	124	112
1927	102	110	134	109
1932	97	97	123	107
1937	107[c]	117[c]	129[e]	117[e]

Sources: As for Tables 4.3 and 4.4.

Note: n.a. = not available.

[a] Average for 1913/1914.

[b] Average for 1937/1938 and 1938/1939.

[c] Average for 1935–1938.

[d] Average for 1902–1904.

[e] Average for 1936–1938.

region, which indicates that they increased in the same proportion as export revenues (Booth 2007: table 6). The reasons are not difficult to find; by the early years of the twentieth century, the revenue base had become, at least in part, dependent on trade taxes that fluctuated with the fortunes of the export sector. Income taxes were levied in most colonies, although not in British Malaya, and they were a minor source of revenue in the Philippines and Thailand. By contrast, they were important in Indonesia; by 1912–1916 they accounted for about 22 percent of total tax revenues and more than 30 percent in 1936–1940 (Booth 1990: table 10.4). But in an open and trade-dependent economy, income taxes would also have depended on export earnings to a considerable extent, as would land taxes. Even consumption taxes whose incidence fell on the lower income groups (such as opium and alcohol excises) would have fluctuated with export earnings, especially in British Malaya.

As already noted, expenditures did not always move in step with revenues, and in Vietnam, the Philippines, and Indonesia the elasticity of expenditures with respect to exports was slightly higher than revenues. This elasticity partly reflected the tendency to run deficits in years when revenues fell sharply; it could also have reflected the fact that, in boom periods when exports were growing rapidly, it was easier for governments to access loan finance to fund increases in expenditures. It has been estimated that during the period 1900–1925 loans covered about 21 percent of the cost of all public works carried out by the central and local governments in French Indochina (Simoni 1929: 141). In Indonesia, the ethical policy led to a rapid increase in budgetary expenditures and a widening deficit by the end of the second decade of the twentieth century; by 1923 the public debt amounted to 21 percent of GDP and debt service charges around 6 percent of exports. Through the 1920s, the government implemented a more austere spending policy, but by the early 1930s, the debt to GDP ratio had increased, not just because of heavier borrowing but also because of a contraction in nominal GDP (Booth 1998: 146).

Even in fiscally conservative Thailand, government debt and debt service charges grew in the early part of the twentieth century (Manarungsan 1989: 176). In Taiwan, the early years of the Japanese occupation were difficult in that the domestic revenue base was far too weak to sustain the development expenditures that the new colonial power felt were essential to develop the island's agricultural potential. Subsidies from the Japanese government and government debt issue covered more than half of all budgetary expenditures until 1897 and around one-third until 1903 (Chang and Myers 1963: 447). Direct subsidies ended in 1904, but as Ho has pointed out, other forms of budgetary assistance continued until 1914 (1971: 290). Thereafter, Taiwan was considered fiscally self-sufficient, although the financial crisis of 1927 led to another bond issue being floated to recapitalize troubled banks (Moulton 1931: 176). By the late 1930s, the budget surplus in Taiwan was around 4 percent of GDP (Mizoguchi and Umemura 1988: 289). In Korea, the goal of fiscal autonomy proved far more elusive. The budget continued to receive direct grants from the Japanese budget until the end of the 1930s; in addition, loan finance continued to be important until the end of the Japanese occupation (Moulton 1931: 176–177; Grajdanzev 1944: 212–213).

Looking at the four decades from 1900 to 1940 as a whole, it seems clear that different factors were driving colonial revenue and expenditure policy from those that were determining such policies in the metropolitan powers. In most European states and in the United States and Japan, the first three decades of the twentieth century saw an increase in government revenues and expenditures in per capita terms. This change was due to the increase in military expenditures associated with the war against Russia in Japan and the 1914–1918 war in the European metropolitan powers and in the United States. There were also growing demands on governments for provision of infrastructure, education, and social security. Relative to GDP, social transfers (government spending on welfare, unemployment, pensions, health, and housing subsidies) increased between 1890 and 1930 in France, the Netherlands, the United Kingdom, the United States, and Japan, although they were much lower in Japan than in the other countries (Lindert 2004: table 1.2).

These pressures toward increasing government spending were not felt to the same extent in the colonial territories; in every colony in Southeast Asia, government revenues and expenditures fell relative to those in the metropolitan power after 1910 (Booth 2007: table 7). In the FMS, where government expenditures per capita were almost two-thirds of those in the United Kingdom in 1910, the ratio had fallen to only 17 percent by 1934. In Vietnam, where both revenues and expenditures per capita were low in comparison with other colonies, they fell relative to those in metropolitan France after 1920. In Taiwan, government revenues per capita in 1900 were higher than in Japan, and government expenditures only slightly lower, although they fell relative to Japan thereafter. Only in Korea did revenues and expenditures increase relative to the metropolitan power from 1910 to 1934, although they fell between 1934 and 1938 (Table 4.6).

Changing Expenditure Priorities

By the third decade of the twentieth century, public works dominated government expenditures in many parts of Southeast Asia, although in Indonesia expenditures on capital works were cut sharply after 1920 in order to eliminate the budget deficit (Booth 1998: 145). In the Federated Malay States, where by 1920 government expenditures per capita were much higher than elsewhere in the region, expenditures on capital works accounted for almost 40 percent of total government expenditures in the early 1920s. Railways accounted for around half of capital expenditures, while public buildings and roads took up much of the rest (Maxwell 1922: 7). In Vietnam, expenditures on public

Table 4.6. Per Capita Government Revenues and Expenditures in Taiwan and Korea as a Percentage of Japan, 1900–1938

Year	Taiwan		Korea	
	Revenues	Expenditures	Revenues	Expenditures
1900	110.3	89.3	n.a.	n.a.
1910	95.4	87.1	8.2	8.2
1920	66.9	59.5	17.6	16.3
1929	69.4	55.6	25.4	23.3
1934	52.0	42.5	26.6	24.5
1938	32.8	28.3	20.8	19.5

Sources: Japan: Ohkawa and Shinohara 1979: 370–377, 392–393; Taiwan and Korea: Mizoguchi and Umemura 1988: 256, 288–293.

Note: n.a. = not available.

works accounted for at least 25 percent of budgetary expenditures through the decade (Booth 2007: table 2).

The comparative study produced by Schwulst showed that in 1931, when the effects of the world depression were only just beginning to affect government budgets in most parts of Southeast Asia, public works still accounted for around 30 percent of government expenditures in French Indochina and 20 percent in the Federated Malay States (Schwulst 1932: 57; Booth 2007: table 8). The Philippines stood out as the colony where a high proportion of budgetary expenditures were devoted to education and health. In both Indonesia and Siam, defense expenditures accounted for more than 20 percent of total expenditures. Elsewhere the proportion was much lower. Nowhere in Southeast Asia did defense expenditures account for as high a proportion of budgetary expenditures as in British India, where they fluctuated between 40 and 65 percent of all outlays (Lal 1988: table 8.11A).

As the impact of the world slump increasingly affected government revenues in most parts of Southeast Asia in the early 1930s, spending priorities changed in most colonies. By 1935, expenditures on public works had fallen to around 13 percent of total expenditures in the Straits Settlements and less than 10 percent in the Federated Malay States. In the FMS, debt charges and pension payments accounted for almost 30 percent of the total (Department of Statistics 1936: 229–232). Military expenditures also increased in most parts of the region in the latter part of the 1930s. This was especially the case in Indonesia and Thailand, where by the latter part of the 1930s, the governments were devoting more than 25 percent of budgetary expenditures to defense-related expenditures (Central Bureau of Statistics 1947: table 193; Central Service of Statistics 1940: 388–389). In the Philippines, by contrast, national defense only accounted for around 10 percent of budgetary outlays in 1939–1940 (Bureau of Census and Statistics 1941: 165). In Vietnam, central government expenditures on the military were even smaller, at around 5 percent of the total in 1939 and 1940 (Bassino 2000b: 287). These differences reflected different perceptions of external (especially Japanese) threats by the various colonial powers, although in the event military preparedness proved inadequate everywhere in the region.

In Korea and Taiwan, expenditures on public order and defense accounted for 29 and 22 percent of total budgetary outlays respectively in 1938. In Taiwan, there had been an increase in the share over the 1930s, while in Korea there had been little change in the share since 1910 (see Table 4.2). After 1925, there had been a continual decline in the share of budgetary outlays on agriculture in Taiwan, although agriculture always commanded a higher share than in Korea. It was noted in Chapter 2 that the two Japanese colonies both experienced faster growth during the 1930s than the Southeast Asian colonies; in the case of Korea in particular, revenues and expenditures grew faster than GDP, so that by 1940, the ratios of expenditure and revenues to GDP had caught up with Taiwan (see Figures 4.2 and 4.3). Between 1910 and 1938, government revenues per capita, in terms of nominal US dollars, increased seven-fold in Korea, which was faster than in any other part of Asia (see Table 4.3). The rapid growth in total revenues relative to national income meant that the Japanese authorities in Korea could increase expenditure in priority areas such as transport infrastructure without incurring increasing deficits. The impact of this increased expenditure on the welfare of the Korean population will be assessed in the next section.

The emphasis on spending on transport infrastructure in both Korea and Taiwan meant that, by the end of the 1930s, length of both road and rail per unit of area was higher in the two Japanese colonies than in most other Southeast Asian colonies. The main exception was Java, where dense road and rail networks had been developed by the early 1930s. As in Taiwan, part of this infrastructure was intended to serve the sugar industry, although it served other sectors of the economy as well and facilitated the mobility of people. Electricity generation capacity was also higher in Taiwan and Korea than in Southeast Asia, with the exception of British Malaya (Table 4.7).

The Incidence of Taxation and Expenditures

Most scholars in the postcolonial era who have examined government rev-enue and expenditure policies in colonial Asia in the decades from 1900 to

Table 4.7. Infrastructure Endowments, Late 1930s

Country/Year	Roads (km. per thousand square kilometers)	Railways (km. per thousand square kilometers)	Electricity[a] (installed capacity)
Philippines (1939)	70.5	4.5	4.76
Indonesia (1940)	27.7	3.9	2.97
Java	171.9	40.5	3.01
Outer Islands	17.0	1.1	2.86
Indochina (1936)	38.8	3.9	3.82
British Malaya (1938)	100.1	12.5	36.06
Burma (1938)	45.2	3.4	3.69
Taiwan (1937)	94.4	43.3[b]	38.32
Korea (1938)	107.2	25.7	28.48

Sources: Philippines: Bureau of Census and Statistics 1947: 279, 304–307; Indonesia: Department of Economic Affairs 1947: 56, 97; Indochina: Robequain 1944: 94–97, 285; British Malaya: Depart-ment of Statistics 1939; Burma: Andrus 1948: 226, 237; Korea: Grajdanzev 1944: 72–74, 135, 185–192; Taiwan: Grajdanzev 1942: 118–119; Barclay 1954: 42.

[a] Data refer to installed capacity in kilowatts per thousand population for the following years: 1938 (Philippines), 1937 (British Malaya), and 1940 (Indonesia and Taiwan). For Burma, the data refer to the capacity of the large plants with an estimate for smaller plants.

[b] Data exclude 2,098 kilometers of special track for the transport of sugar.

1940 have been critical of at least three aspects of those policies: first, the regressive nature of colonial taxation systems; second, the failure to allocate expenditures to programs that enhanced the welfare of the indigenous populations; and third, the adverse macroeconomic effects of fiscal policy.

The regressive nature of colonial revenue policy has attracted considerable attention, especially in the context of British Malaya, including both the FMS and the Straits Settlements, where government revenues were relatively high in per capita terms. Critics have stressed the dependence on "vice" taxes, especially revenues raised from opium, liquor, and tobacco. It has already been pointed out that in the Straits Settlements, the opium monopoly alone accounted for almost half of the government revenues between 1900 and 1920, although its importance declined thereafter, and by 1938 it accounted for around 9 percent of total revenues (see Table 4.1). In the FMS, reliance on the opium levy also fell after 1920, but even as late as 1938, excises on the sale of opium and other items together with import duties on tobacco and spirits still accounted for around 20 percent of all government revenues (Department of Statistics 1939: 241). Given that low-income Chinese and Tamil workers together accounted for a high proportion of the opium, alcohol, and tobacco purchases, it is probable that these revenue sources were regressive in their impact.

In contrast, highly paid government officials and private sector employees paid no income tax, and there was (excepting a brief period during the First World War) no tax on corporate profits. Colonial officials in the FMS claimed that large estates were taxed through the export tax, but export tax rates were low, and revenues were not large. The export tax rate on rubber varied between 2.5 and 3 percent of the export value and fell on all exports whether produced by estates or by smallholders (Barlow and Drabble 1990: 206). Given the domestic supply and foreign demand elasticities, the incidence of the export tax must have fallen on the domestic producer rather than the foreign buyer, and increasingly the domestic producer was a smallholder (see Table 2.8). But total revenues remained quite small; at no time between 1912 and 1929 did revenues from the rubber export tax equal revenues from the opium levy, and they were also well below the tin export tax (Li 1982: 103; Lim 1967: appendix 9.1).

Elsewhere in Southeast Asia after 1900, governments did try to widen the tax net and reduce the burden on poorer groups by taxing wage and salary earners and corporate incomes, by increasing import duties on imported luxuries and removing duties on imported necessities such as rice, by assessing higher land taxes on those cultivators in possession of well-irrigated land, and by charging fees for government-provided services such as electricity, railways, and telecommunications, which were mainly used by the better-off. In Vietnam, where opium and other government monopolies accounted for almost half of government revenues in the early 1920s, the proportion did fall thereafter as the government tried, albeit with only limited success, to diversify the revenue by introducing new excises and charges for public services. Thompson argued that the attempt by Varenne to introduce an income tax in 1927 was "the first approach to real justice" (1937: 194), but the initiative failed, although in 1935 a tax on very high incomes was introduced. It did not bring in much revenue, but it did establish a principle; nonetheless the regressive head tax was not rescinded. Opinion differs about the incidence of the monopolies; Bassino suggested that the opium levy was less regressive in Vietnam than in British Malaya because the Chinese community was better off in relation to the indigenous population and the habit of opium smoking spread to wealthy Vietnamese and Europeans as well (2000b: 281). The same argument applied to the alcohol monopoly. In contrast, the salt monopoly was certainly regressive, as indeed were similar levies elsewhere in Asia (Murray 1980: 77).

In the Philippines, where opium revenues had been phased out by 1914, American policy was to diversify the revenue base by introducing a wider range of taxes and improving administration. But Luton argued that "the Americans showed a surprising lack of real commitment to equity in taxation" (1971: 136), in spite of their professed aim of reforming and modernizing what they saw as the inefficient, outdated, and unfair Spanish fiscal system. In order to encourage export agriculture, the government did not levy any export taxes, while the land tax (which accrued to provincial and municipal governments) was assessed on the capital value of the land and buildings. This system had the potential to be strongly progressive, but because of resistance on the part of large landowners, it was never properly implemented (ibid.: 137).

Pressure from lobbies representing both business and agricultural interests prevented the inclusion of either a tax on corporate income or an inheritance tax in the Revenue Law of 1904. The *cedula,* which was a roughly graduated head tax and accounted for over half of all revenues in the late Spanish period, was converted into a flat capitation tax, not a step in the direction of greater equity (Luton 1971: 14). In 1907, a law was passed that permitted provincial authorities to double the cedula in order to raise money for roads and bridges. While this did lead to considerable improvements in the road network, the funds were inadequate to cover other sectors where the American administration had ambitious plans, such as education (May 1980: 145). Only very modest progress was made in widening the tax base over the next thirty years; by the late 1930s, direct taxes and customs revenues accounted for a lower proportion of government revenues in the Philippines than in most other parts of the region (see Table 4.1). May concluded that lack of revenues was "one of the greatest obstacles to social engineering in the Philippines. Policy-makers could advance in one area only if they were willing to accept a regression in another" (ibid.: 146).

High dependence on direct taxes, including land taxes, did not mean that the taxation system was equitable in its impact, across regions or income classes. In Burma, two-thirds of government revenues were derived from customs revenues, land taxes, and income taxes in 1938–1939; the land tax alone accounted for one-third of total revenues in that year (Andrus 1948: table 37). The official view was that the assessment standard in Burma should be half the net profits from the land, but as Furnivall pointed out, it was in practice "impossible for any government to take so large a share of the proceeds of cultivation" (1957: 216). So in Lower Burma the formula was changed to one-quarter of net produce, although in Upper Burma one-half remained the standard. In practice neither formula was effectively applied; the result was an assessment procedure that varied both by region and by sector. Incomes in the urban sector, both personal and corporate, were not taxed at anything like the same rate as those in rural areas. The issue of intersectoral inequities in the burden of taxation was to become a major problem for governments in the postindependence era.

In his comparison of the implementation of land taxes in Burma and Java, Furnivall (1934a) argued that the Javanese system was less burdensome on the cultivator with rates varying between 8 and 20 percent of taxable yield, which was estimated with more generous deductions for costs of cultivation than was the case in Burma. In addition, by the 1930s, land taxes were a much lower proportion of total revenues in Indonesia than in Burma. By the late 1930s, taxes on wages and other forms of personal and corporate income brought in more than four times as much as the land tax. Revenues from import duties and excises on petroleum products were also far more important than land taxes (Central Bureau of Statistics 1947: 133). As the incidence of all these taxes would have weighed more heavily on the upper income groups, it is probable that tax incidence in Indonesia in the last years of the Dutch era was less inequitable than in other parts of colonial Asia. Certainly the Dutch were sensitive to the problem of tax burdens on the indigenous population; several reports were published in the 1920s that argued that, given the poverty of the natives, there was little scope for further tax increases (Booth 1998: 147). Apart from the land tax, the other tax that fell directly on cultivators was the export tax; in the mid-1930s, a special tax was levied on smallholder rubber producers that was highly inequitable, but it was rescinded after protests. It was replaced by quotas that attempted, with varying success, to achieve the same goal of restricting smallholder output (Bauer 1948: 142–153).

In Korea, revenues from the land tax also accounted for a diminishing proportion of total government revenues during the 1930s, while taxes on personal and corporate income increased. Kimura has argued that the land tax in Korea was in theory a proportional tax but in practice regressive (1989: 303), so its declining importance relative to income taxes could indicate greater progressivity in the system. But Korea in the late 1930s was less dependent on tax revenues than Indonesia; monopolies alone accounted for more than 16 percent of all revenues, excluding borrowings. Grajdanzev argued that taxes and other revenues that fell on the better-off sections of the population accounted for only around 30 percent of the total, while the remainder fell on the rest of

the population, many of whom were very poor (1944: 214). "We must therefore conclude that those who drew large incomes were treated with greater
consideration than the poorer sections of the population" (ibid.: 215). His
analysis of the revenue system in Taiwan found that an even lower proportion
of total revenues (10 to 20 percent) in the latter part of the 1930s fell on the
wealthiest, many of whom were Japanese. He pointed out that the government, under pressure to increase revenues further, preferred to borrow from
the rich rather than to tax them more (Grajdanzev 1942: 135).

Revenue policy is only half of the fiscal equation, and colonial governments did have the opportunity to effect some redistribution through government expenditures designed to improve incomes of the indigenous populations. This was most obviously the case in British Malaya, where expenditures
per capita were high by the 1920s in comparison not just with other parts of
Southeast Asia, but also with the Japanese colonies of Korea and Taiwan (see
Table 4.4). We have seen that expenditures on public works grew rapidly from
the 1890s onward. Even critics of British colonialism conceded that the heavy
expenditures on transport infrastructure in the three decades up to 1925
brought about a transformation in production possibilities that benefited
indigenous populations as well as large foreign companies (Li 1982: 26–27).

In addition, increased government expenditures on health led to a gradual improvement in modern medical facilities, and death rates declined. Educational enrollments also increased over the early part of the century. The
evidence on mortality rates, together with other social indicators, will be
reviewed further in Chapter 7. The expansion in public expenditures meant
that public sector employment grew rapidly in both the Straits Settlements
and the FMS, and with it spending on salaries, wages, and pensions. Debt
servicing charges also increased. Although in 1931 the FMS was still devoting a higher proportion of total expenditures to "developmental" activities
than any other colony except the Philippines (Schwulst 1932: 57), there was
growing unease in some quarters after 1930 about the "cost of swollen departments, at a time of revenue ebb" (Khor 1983: 62). Retrenchment followed, but
growing expenditures on defense during the 1930s meant that public works
never regained their pre-1925 share of total expenditures.

Elsewhere, colonial governments had fewer budgetary resources in per
capita terms than in British Malaya, and there was considerable variation, both
across the region and over time, in the allocation of expenditures. It has been
noted that the main pillars of the ethical policy in Indonesia were the development of improved irrigation facilities, increased access for the indigenous population to health and education facilities, and land settlement schemes outside
Java. There can be no doubt that, at least until the 1920s, more budgetary
resources were allocated to these purposes, and they did lead to some increase
in incomes for sections of the indigenous population, although most of the
irrigation expansion would have benefited the better-off households in rural
areas of Java. This was also true of the expenditures on irrigation and drainage

in southern Vietnam. In Burma, where expenditures per capita were comparatively low, expenditures on education, medical services, civil works, and agriculture accounted for less than one-fifth of total budgetary expenditures from
1937–1938 onward, as military outlays increased (Andrus 1948: 322).

Grajdanzev's analysis of government expenditures in Taiwan and Korea
during the 1930s concluded that most budgetary outlays were devoted to
maintaining the bureaucracy, pensions, police, prisons, and the army. In both
colonies, according to his argument, these expenditures were largely on Japanese staff and for the benefit of the Japanese population. In the case of Taiwan,
expenditures on research were not insignificant, but they were much less than
what was devoted to prisons and the police (Grajdanzev 1942: 137–138). The
judgment of Grajdanzev on Korea was that, while the government was "generous to its bureaucrats, police, prison, and army, it is miserly with respect to
social services for the native population" (1944: 220). While this may well
have been true, a more positive case regarding the impact of budgetary expenditures on the welfare of the Korean population has been made by Cha (1998).
He argues that the public health measures introduced by the Japanese led
to rapid population growth, and while the government did intensify the tax
burden on the Korean population, it also increased public investment. This
led to improvements in land productivity and also during the 1930s to rapid
growth of manufacturing output, which offset, to some extent at least, the
"Malthusian" consequences of sustained population growth. These arguments
are examined further in Chapter 7.

Budgetary Surpluses and Colonial "Drains"

Critics of colonial fiscal policies in Southeast Asia have also emphasized the
large surpluses of revenues over expenditures and the "drain" abroad of public
funds that these surpluses allegedly permitted (Golay 1976). In the nineteenth
century, the remittance abroad of budgetary surpluses was most pronounced
in Indonesia, where under the culture system unrequited transfers on government account to the home budget were substantial. These transfers were
brought to an end in the 1870s, and from 1881 onward the fiscal balance
in Indonesia was negative for all decades until 1940 (Booth 1998: 137–141).
Elsewhere, budget outturns were rather different. In both the Straits Settlements and the FMS, government budgets were in surplus for most quinquen-
nia between 1902 and 1937 (see Table 4.5). Because of the currency board
arrangement, it was considered essential to hold large balances in the metropolitan power, usually earning very low interest rates. In effect the colony was
extending soft loans to the metropolitan power (Khor 1983: 44–49). The fiscal
surpluses were even larger in Burma, where the gap between revenues appro-
priated by the government in New Delhi and the expenditures paid by that
government amounted to between 3.6 and 8.4 percent of net national product
between 1901–1902 and 1931–1932 (Booth 2007: table 9). The surpluses came

to an end only with the granting of complete financial autonomy to Burma in 1937. Postcolonial scholars have attributed the large export surpluses in Burma from 1900 onward to this fiscal drain to Delhi, although remittances on the part of Indian migrants also contributed (Shein, Myint, and Tin: 1969; Andrus 1948: 182).

The situation in Vietnam was very different from both British Malaya and Burma. The balance of payments estimates prepared by Bassino indicate that Indochina as a whole ran large current account deficits from 1899 to 1914, which reflected the heavy expenditures by both government and the private sector on imported capital goods (2000b: table 2). The budget was in surplus during the second decade of the twentieth century but swung into deficit again in the 1920s and early 1930s (see Table 4.5). In Indonesia, where the budget was in deficit for most years from 1900 through to 1940, the balance of payments surplus must have been due to a surplus of private savings over investment. Just why these private surpluses were so large and sustained over such a long period is still a matter of some controversy; the debates are examined further in the next chapter. In the Philippines, budgets were more or less in balance with the exception of the early 1920s and the early 1930s. As has already been noted, the early 1930s saw a tendency toward budget deficits in many parts of Southeast Asia as government revenues fell with declining export earnings; the exceptions were Burma and Thailand.

The evidence from the budget data for the various colonies in Southeast Asia over the first four decades of the twentieth century shows considerable differences between them in taxation and expenditure policies and in the size of budget surpluses and deficits. Generalizations about "fiscal exploitation" should thus be treated with caution. In the case of Indochina, it was argued by one foreign scholar that Indochina was "one of the most intensively exploited colonial areas" in the world (Mitchell 1942: 151). But the evidence from the government accounts and the balance of payments hardly bears this out. While the overall incidence of the fiscal system may have been regressive, it is not clear that it was any more regressive than those in several other colonies, including Korea. In Burma, where remittances on government account were much larger and more sustained than in other parts of the region, the beneficiary was the budget in New Delhi, rather than that in London. While there can be little doubt that colonial officials were always under pressure from home governments to balance the budget and curb foreign borrowing, in practice achieving balanced budgets was far from simple, especially in times of falling export revenues.

In both Taiwan and Korea, budgets were in surplus for most years from 1900 (1910 in the Korean case) to 1938 (see Table 4.5). In the case of Korea, it should be noted that part of the reason for these surpluses was that revenues were boosted by subventions from the Japanese budget, in effect a type of aid. In Taiwan, the large and sustained surpluses financed outward flows of capital; the balance of payments was consistently in surplus for most years from 1900 onward. We examine the links between the budget and the balance of payments for Taiwan and other Asian colonies in more detail in the next chapter. By the 1930s, the Japanese government was using Taiwan as a base for its penetration into Southeast Asia, and Taiwan was making considerable contributions to the Japanese budget for this purpose.

CHAPTER 5

International Trade, Balance of Payments, and Exchange Rate Policies: 1900–1940

The Open Dualistic Model and Its Implications

As we saw in Chapter 1, the open dualistic model developed by Paauw and Fei and others stressed that earning profits in and remitting them from the export enclave was an integral part of the operation of colonial economies in Asia and indeed elsewhere. One consequence was that large commodity export surpluses were sustained, often over long periods of time, that were only partly offset by deficits in services. Thus the current account of the balance of payments was expected to be in surplus. A further consequence of the model was that the colonial export enclaves were tightly tethered to the metropolitan economies, in that most exports were sent to markets either in the metropolitan economy or in other parts of the empire controlled by the metropolitan economy, and most imports originated from the same sources. These biases in trade flows were mirrored in investment flows; most investment, whether direct investment in productive enterprises such as plantations or mines, or portfolio investment, originated from the metropolitan power.

Thus bilateralism was alleged to be a crucial feature of colonial trade and investment flows in Asia. It was often argued that such bilateralism was enforced by a variety of controls, sometimes explicit and sometimes more subtle, on both trade flows and capital flows. By the beginning of the twentieth century there was evidence that such controls were being used to insulate colonial markets from imports and investment flows from more powerful economies. Both the Dutch and the French as well as the Japanese were concerned about British and American economic penetration in their colonies and took steps to limit it. By the 1920s, all the European colonial powers and the Americans were becoming more nervous about growing imports into their territories from Japan. These concerns grew as the impact of the world depression of the early 1930s on the Asian economies became more severe, although responses to the "Japanese threat" varied considerably across the region.

The 1930s also posed challenges for all the trading economies of Asia, whether they were independent states or colonial territories, regarding appropriate exchange rate policy. In 1930, when the Indochina piastre was given an exact value in gold equal to ten times that of the French franc, all the currencies in Southeast Asia together with that of Japan and the Japanese colonies were briefly on the gold standard. During the early part of the 1930s, the various Southeast Asian colonies followed their metropolitan masters in deciding whether to abandon or stay with the gold standard; the British colonies left with sterling in September 1931, while Indonesia stayed on gold with the Netherlands until 1936. Thailand stayed on the gold standard for several months after sterling was devalued while an intense policy debate raged about appropriate policy responses to the deepening world crisis (Batson 1984: chap. 7; see also Vichitvong 1978). Finally, in May 1932, the Thai cabinet agreed to relink the baht to sterling at the rate that prevailed before sterling went off gold, and this link was maintained until 1942. The Philippines had been pegged to the US dollar since the Philippine Gold Standard Act of 1903. The system broke down in 1918, and in 1922 a separate Gold Standard Fund and Treasury Certificate Fund were established. Thereafter, the overwhelming priority of successive Philippine administrations was to maintain the peg to the US dollar rather than to maintain a fixed parity with gold, and the peso went off the gold standard with the dollar in 1933. Japan, having pegged its currency to gold in 1929, left the gold standard in December 1931, with important consequences for its own traded goods industries and those of its colonies, which will be reviewed in more detail below.

Exchange rate policy was important for all the colonies in East and Southeast Asia because, by the third decade of the twentieth century, they had all developed considerable export sectors, and in several cases the main export industries were becoming more dependent on markets outside those controlled by the metropolitan power. Every colonial territory had experienced some growth in exports per capita between 1905 and 1920; in Taiwan and Korea as well as in Burma and British Malaya, this growth was sustained until 1929 (Table 5.1). By the late 1920s, exports had reached around 40 percent of GDP in Taiwan, and about 20 percent in Korea (Figure 5.1). They comprised between 35 and 40 percent of GDP in Burma for most years from 1906 to 1931 (Aye Hlaing 1964: 111). By 1926, exports comprised around 25 percent of GDP in both Indonesia and Vietnam and probably a higher ratio in the Philippines (Booth 2003c: table 2). In British Malaya, the estimates prepared by Benham (1951) for 1947 found that exports were 31 percent of GNP. Given that world trade had only begun to recover from the ravages of war in that year, it is probable that the ratio for the late 1920s was much higher.

The Evolution of Commodity Trade Flows: 1900–1940

The British Malayan case is important not just because exports per capita were so high (among the highest in the world at the time), but also because there had been, during the 1920s and 1930s, substantial diversification of markets

Table 5.1. Exports Per Capita, 1905–1938 (US dollars)

Colony	1905	1913	1920	1929	1934	1938
Taiwan	4	8	31	32	19	25
Korea	1	1	6	9	7	12
Indochina	1	3	7	4	2	3
Thailand	4	5	4	8	6	6
Burma	7	11	16	18	13	11
FMS	44	76	93	126	74	48
British Malaya	n.a.	n.a.	n.a.	126	58	63
Philippines	4	5	14	13	8	9
Indonesia	3	6	14	10	6	6

Sources: Taiwan and Korea: Mizoguchi and Umemura 1988: 247–248, 256; Philippines: Bureau of Census and Statistics 1947: 347; Indonesia: Korthals Altes 1991: tables 1B, 2B, 3B, 4B; van der Eng 2002: 171; Indochina: Doumer 1902: 296–297; French Indochina: Service de la Statistique Générale 1947: 290; Banens 2000; FMS: Fraser 1939: appendix A; British Malaya: Kratoska 2000: table 13.1; Department of Statistics 1939: 120; Burma: Saito and Lee 1999: 7, 177; Thailand: Ingram 1971: appendixes C and D; Manarungsan 1989: 32. Population data from sources given in Table 2.1; exchange rates taken from van Laanen 1980: table 8; Service de la Statistique Générale 1947: 288.

Note: n.a. = not available.

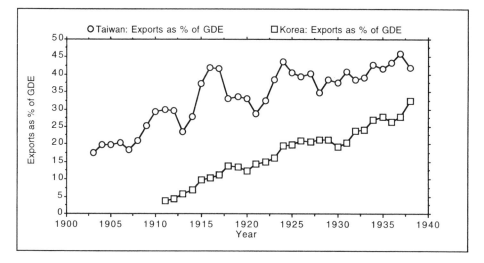

Figure 5.1. Exports as a proportion of gross domestic expenditure, Taiwan and Korea. (Source: Mizoguchi and Umemura 1988: part 3, tables 5, 14, 7, and 15)

away from Britain and the British empire. By the late 1930s, only about 14 percent of exports from British Malaya were going to the United Kingdom, and about 18 percent of total imports were sourced from there; 36 percent were sourced from the United Kingdom and all other British colonies and dominions (Table 5.2). On the export side, the demand in the British market for Malaya's main exports, rubber and tin, was limited compared with that in the United States, where the automobile and canned foods industries were growing rapidly. Only a small proportion of Burma's exports went to the United Kingdom, although the great majority went to British territories, mainly in British India. The share of Indonesian trade with the Netherlands also declined after 1900, and by 1939 only 14 percent of exports went there. As in British Malaya, Indonesia's main exports (rubber, tin, petroleum products) were in greater demand in the United States and in other parts of Asia than in the metropolitan economy. This was also the case with French Indochina, where only one-third of all exports were taken by France in 1939, although this was a higher ratio than earlier in the century.

While trading links between the European colonies and their metropoles had in most cases weakened by the 1930s, trade flows to and from Taiwan and Korea, and the Philippines were tightly tied to Japan and the United States respectively. In the case of Taiwan and the Philippines, the percentage of exports and imports sent to and sourced from Japan and the United States rose sharply after 1900; by 1939, more than 80 percent of exports from both colonies went to metropolitan markets. In Taiwan, trade with both Britain and America was larger than trade with Japan before 1895, and British banks, ship-

Table 5.2. Percentage of Exports and Imports to/from Metropolitan Power

| Country / Years | Early Twentieth Century | | C. 1939[a] | |
	Exports	Imports	Exports	Imports
Korea (1904–1906)	84.6	73.3	73.2	88.5
Taiwan (1896–1900)	19.6	27.0	86.0	87.6
Philippines (1902–1904)	40.1	13.5	82.0	68.3
Indochina (1897–1901)	20.6	44.6	32.3	55.4
Indonesia (1900–1904)	35.4	31.4	14.4	18.7
British Malaya (1938)	n.a.	n.a.	14.1 (31.6)	18.2 (36.1)
Burma (1904–1907, 1938–1939)	9.2	26.7	12.7 (67.0)	18.2 (72.1)

Sources: Korea: Bank of Chosen 1920: 166–168; Grajdanzev 1944: 227; Philippines: Bureau of Census and Statistics 1947: 347; Indonesia: Korthals Altes 1991: tables 1B, 2B, 3B, 4B; Indochina: Doumer 1902: 296–297; Bassino and Huong 2000: 305–323; Taiwan: Grajdanzev 1942: 144; British Malaya: Department of Statistics 1939: 114; Burma: Office of the Prime Minister 1958; Andrus 1948: 167–176.

[a] Figures in parentheses refer to all exports and imports from both the United Kingdom and British dominions and colonies.

ping, and trading companies based in Hong Kong dominated trade and commerce. But all foreign companies were gradually ousted after 1900 in favor of those from Japan (Grajdanzev 1942: 146–147). In Korea, exports per capita were still very low in 1905, and such trade as there was took place largely with Japan, although around one-quarter of imports came from elsewhere. Exports from Korea grew rapidly after 1913, and most of the growth was with Japan and other parts of the Japanese empire, especially Manchuria. By 1939, Korean exports to non–yen bloc countries amounted to only 3 percent of the total (Grajdanzev 1944: 228).

A frequent argument made by critics of colonial trade policies, especially those associated with nationalist movements in Asia, was that metropolitan governments protected the markets of their colonial territories from foreign competition in order to provide home producers of goods such as textiles and other manufactures with captive consumers. A study of colonial trade patterns of the main European imperial powers at the end of the nineteenth century found that one-third of total British exports in 1892–1896 went to colonial possessions, about 24 percent of Spanish exports, almost 10 percent of French exports, and 5 percent of exports from the Netherlands (Flux 1899: 491). While to some extent this pattern reflected the fact that the British empire was considerably larger than any of the others, it is also true that British colonial policy stressed the importance of colonial markets as outlets for British manufactures to create employment at home. This emphasis continued into the twentieth century (Meredith 1996: 38–39). And yet by the 1930s, the British share of both Burmese and British Malayan imports was under 20 percent. In France, where Jules Ferry pronounced his well-known dictum that "la politique coloniale est fille de la politique industrielle" (colonial policy is the daughter of industrial policy) in the early twentieth century, exports to the colonies, while not a large share of total exports, were important in some industries, especially cotton textiles, and this importance grew rapidly after 1900 (Marseille 1984: 54).

In spite of the rapid growth of trade of both Taiwan and Korea with Japan after 1900, colonial trade represented only a minor part, at most around 20 percent, of total Japanese trade until the late 1920s (Moulton 1931: 211). But during the 1930s, the share of total Japanese exports going to markets outside the Japanese empire fell sharply (Figure 5.2). Imports sourced from foreign countries also fell as a percentage of all imports. On the export side, this fall was due to the sharp increase in exports to both Taiwan and Korea as well as to Kwantung province in southern Manchuria. The increased exports to colonial territories in the 1930s were dominated by producer goods and were the result of the rapid development of industry and infrastructure. Increased imports of consumer products such as cotton textiles, which were flooding into other Asian markets from Japan in the 1930s, only accounted for a minor part of the growth in Japan's trade with its own colonies.

The obvious lesson from even a cursory examination of the evidence on

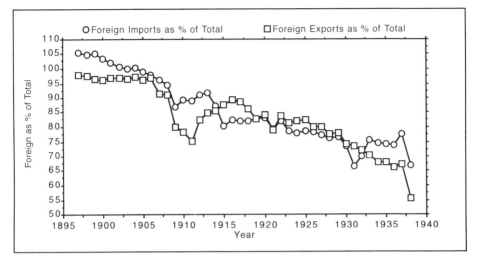

Figure 5.2. Japanese trade outside the Japanese empire as a proportion of total Japanese trade. (Source: Mizoguchi and Umemura 1988: part 3, tables 13 and 17)

trade flows between colonies and metropole in East and Southeast Asia after 1900 is that generalizations are impossible. While the two Japanese colonies and the Philippines appear to conform to the open dualistic model in that both exports and imports became more tightly linked to the metropolitan power after 1900, that was much less the case in the other Southeast Asian colonies. In order to explain these divergent outcomes, we need to examine both trade and exchange rate policy in more detail.

Evolving Trade Regimes and Structures of Protection

Already by the early 1900s, there were considerable differences across Southeast Asia in trade regimes and structures of protection, and these differences became more pronounced during the next four decades. In order to explain the differences in outcomes shown in Table 5.2, I begin with an analysis of trade policy in the Philippines and French Indochina, which were the two colonies of Southeast Asia most tightly tied to their metropoles by the 1930s, before examining policies in Indonesia, British Malaya, and Burma, which, while not very closely linked to the metropole, had very close ties to British India. I then look at trade policies in the two Japanese colonies.

Acts passed by the US Congress in 1909 established free trade between the United States and the Philippines, although some quantitative restrictions remained on Philippine exports to the United States (Espino 1933: 8). These were largely removed by the Underwood Tariff Act of 1913, which permitted all Philippine products containing no more than 20 percent by value of foreign materials to enter the United States duty free. Essentially the Under-wood Act remained in force until the mid-1930s, when the Philippines was granted self-government. Owen has argued that in fact the Underwood Act removed many tariffs on all imports into the United States, so those from the Philippines received no special treatment (1972: 53). Important exports such as coconut oil and cordage remained on the free list until the 1930s. The main product to enjoy preferential tariffs was sugar, together with some minor exports such as tobacco and embroideries, even though these were the prod-ucts that competed in the American market with home production.

Whether because of preferential treatment or because the United States was a natural market for Philippine exports, as it increasingly was for exports from other parts of Southeast Asia, there was a rapid shift in trade flows toward the United States after 1910. By the end of the First World War, almost two-thirds of Philippine imports originated from the United States. In 1929–1933, the American share of Philippine imports was four times its share of world exports (Table 5.3). An even higher proportion of Philippine exports went to the United States. This reliance led some Filipinos to argue for political independence on the grounds that they must regain tariff autonomy in order to foster their own industries (Espino 1933; see also Owen 1972: 52). But agricultural interests, especially the sugar growers, were far from enthusias-tic about independence, as they realized they would lose preferential access to the American market (Friend 1963; Friend 1965: 116–121; Corpuz 1997: 251–262).

French attitudes were rather different. As we have seen, after 1900 French policy became more consciously directed toward securing colonial markets for French products, which was never an important concern in the United States. Until 1928, trade between metropolitan France and the French colo-nies was governed by tariff laws that provided extensive protection for French products in colonial markets, and leading French politicians made little secret of the fact that a key role of colonies was to provide protected markets for French industries. But the tariff provisions were not reciprocal in that colonial products did not automatically enjoy duty-free entry into France. This ineq-uity gave rise to great resentment in Indochina and was finally removed in 1928, when a regime of reciprocal free trade was established within the French empire. As a result of this protectionism, Indochina conducted little of its trade with neighboring countries, while the share of metropolitan France in Indochina's imports was nine times France's share of world exports in 1929–1933 (see Table 5.3).

The discriminatory trade regimes imposed by both the United States and France on their Southeast Asian colonies was sometimes contrasted with the more liberal approach of the Dutch. Not only was there virtually no tariff or nontariff discrimination against imports from any source after the reforms of the 1860s and 1870s, but there was also an open capital account facilitating the inflow of capital and the repatriation of profits. Although both specific and ad valorem import taxes were levied, Dutch and foreign commentators emphasized that tariffs were purely for revenue purposes, and the idea of protection was totally foreign (Paulus 1909: 124; Fowler 1923: 399; Kuitenbrouwer 1991: 67). But in spite of the apparently nondiscriminatory trade regime, the Netherlands continued to account for a much greater share of imports into Indonesia than its share of total world trade would have justified. Import enforcement ratios fell between 1880 and 1900, but by 1929–1933, the Dutch share of imports into Indonesia was still almost eight times its share of world exports (see Table 5.3). It is likely that various forms of subtle discrimination against British and other importers persisted after 1870 through the dominance of Dutch trading houses in the export-import sector and through a Dutch commercial and legal system that would have advantaged Dutch merchants.

It has already been noted that the share of imports sourced from the

Table 5.3. Metropolitan Shares of World Export Trade and Colonial Import Trade, 1929–1933

	Metropolitan Share of Imports (%)	Metropolitan Share of World Exports (%)	Ratio
Taiwan	74.7	2.9	26.1
Korea	76.7	2.9	26.8
Indochina	55.3	6.2	9.0
Thailand[a]	15.5	10.3	1.5
Burma[b]	22.7 (45.4)	10.3 (3.3)	2.2
British Malaya[c]	14.8 (32.9)	10.3	1.4
Philippines	63.8	13.8	4.6
Indonesia	17.0	2.6	7.8

	Japanese Share of Imports (%)	Japanese Share of World Exports (%)	Ratio
Indochina	2.8	2.9	1.0
Thailand	11.4	2.9	4.0
Burma	9.3	2.9	3.3
British Malaya	3.9	2.9	1.4
Philippines	9.2	2.9	3.2
Indonesia	14.3	2.9	5.0

Source: Thailand: Swan 1988: 76; French Indochina: Service de la Statistique Générale 1947; Philippines: Bureau of Census and Statistics 1941; Indonesia: Korthals Altes 1991; Burma: National Planning Commission 1960b: Statistical Appendix; British Malaya: *Annual Departmental Reports of the Straits Settlements* (Singapore: Government Printing Office, 1930–1934); Taiwan and Korea: Mizoguchi and Umemura 1988: 246–251. Data on metropolitan countries' share of world exports from Clark 1936: 62–63.

[a] Metropolitan power is the United Kingdom.

[b] Figures in parentheses are for the rest of British India.

[c] Figures in parentheses include all countries in the British Empire.

United Kingdom in British Malaya was quite low by the 1930s; the share was little more than would be expected given the British share of world exports (see Table 5.3). It would appear that British exporters did not see the Malayan market as having the same strategic importance as that of British India. In addition, there were vested interests in Singapore in particular that supported the free port policy, although as will be seen below, this was tested by the rise of Japanese imports after 1930. The situation in Burma was complicated by the fact that Burma was just a small part of Britain's vast colonial possessions in the Indian subcontinent and until the latter part of the 1930s had no autonomy in economic or indeed other matters. The constitutional reforms of the early 1920s gave India considerable autonomy in setting tariffs, and during the 1920s some tariff protection was accorded Indian producers of iron and steel products and textiles (National Planning Commission 1960b: 84–90).

But these tariffs had no protective function in Burma, which did not possess such industries; their only effect was to increase prices of imported textile and steel products. After the Ottawa Agreement of 1932, India shifted to a system of tariff preferences for products from other parts of the British empire, and during the next two years very high tariffs were levied on imports from countries outside the imperial system, most notably textile products from Japan (Chaudhuri 1983: 869). The impact of these policies on Burma will be examined in more detail in the next section. In the early 1930s, almost 45 percent of Burmese imports came from India and a further 22 percent from Britain (see Table 5.3). The very high reliance on imports from India did not change much after the formal separation of Burma from India in 1937 (Andrus 1948: 187–192).

Although Thailand was not a colony, the influence of British financial advisers in the kingdom was considerable up to 1932, and as late as 1929–1933, the proportion of total imports from Britain was higher than the British share of world exports (see Table 5.3). The Bowring Treaty and similar treaties signed with other powers in the latter part of the nineteenth century had deprived Thailand of any capacity to use tariffs for protective purposes, but by 1926 these treaties had been revoked and tariff autonomy was substantially restored (Ingram 1971: 147). Thereafter, only very limited use was made of tariffs as a means of fostering domestic industry. As will be shown below, Thailand's liberal trade regime and reasonably buoyant agricultural economy through the 1930s led to considerable growth in imports from various sources, especially Japan.

It is clear from Table 5.3 that, by the early 1930s, the two Japanese colonies were more tightly tied to Japan than was the case with any of the Southeast Asian colonies, even the Philippines. Japanese exports to Taiwan and Korea comprised around 75 percent of all imports; this ratio increased further in the latter part of the 1930s as Japanese export trade became more concentrated on its colonial possessions rather than on the wider world (see Figure 5.2). Some foreign scholars supported the Japanese view that the high degree of reliance of both colonies on Japanese imports was due to geographical proximity and comparative advantage. Given their different factor endowments and levels of development, it was inevitable that Taiwan and Korea would supply agricultural products and other raw materials to the Japanese economy and receive manufactured goods back in return (Vinacke 1928: 366). Critics such as Grajdanzev viewed the Japanese domination of Korean trade in a rather different light:

> The influence of Japanese political control on Korean trade was exercised not only through the tariff wall which guarded Korea against the intrusion of non-Japanese goods (goods from Japan entered duty-free), but through the control of the country's entire economic life. Industry, banks, communications and the government machinery were in Japanese hands. Under these conditions it was inevitable that the decisions as to what to import or what and where to export were taken by Japanese import and export firms, and that these decisions were influenced by official Japanese policy. (Grajdanzev 1944: 229)

In the context of Taiwan, it was argued by Japanese scholars that it was inevitable that Japanese merchants would displace traditional trade with China, as they possessed a far stronger capital base and were supported by Japanese subsidies and the powerful presence of Japanese trading firms, shipping firms, and banks. But as Grajdanzev pointed out, there was little evidence that much of the capital invested in Taiwan was brought from Japan; most was generated within Taiwan itself (1942: 147). It does seem clear that, increasingly during the 1930s, Japanese firms in Taiwan played an important role in the Japanese government's strategic aims of extending commercial penetration into both southern China and Southeast Asia (Schneider 1998; Howe 1996: 359–360). Government assistance to firms to achieve these aims took a variety of forms, including the granting of monopoly rights, subsidies, tariff protection, and tax benefits.

As a result of these policies, the export industries that Japan established in both Taiwan and Korea were high-cost and uncompetitive in regional markets. Rice prices in Korea were well above those in Southeast Asian markets from 1915 onward (Figure 5.3). This imposed a considerable burden on Korean consumers, who might, under freer trade, have preferred to consume cheaper Indica varieties of rice rather than the barley and pearl millet that many were forced to substitute for rice. In Taiwan also, consumers might have preferred to eat more rice rather than sweet potatoes had relative prices been different (Anderson and Tyers 1992: 119). Taiwanese sugar could not compete on international markets with low-cost sugar from Java or from Hawai'i and Cuba (Howe 1996: 359). It could only be sold in mainland Japan because of

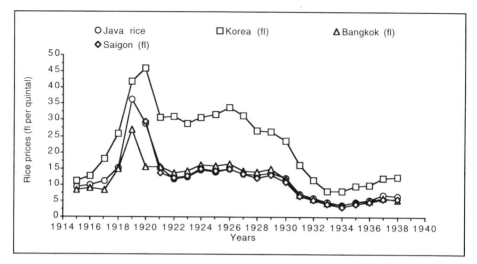

Figure 5.3. Rice prices in Korea and Southeast Asia (Indonesia guilders [fl.] per quintal). Rice variet-ies: Bangkok: Straits quality; Saigon: No. I quality; Java: Saigon quality. (Sources: Korea: Rose 1985: 90; Bangkok: Central Service of Statistics 1940: 515; Saigon: Direction des Services Économiques 1947: 299; Java: Department of Economic Affairs 1938: 5)

high tariffs on imports from outside the empire. Japanese consumers were thus subsidizing not just producers in Taiwan and Korea, but also the long-run strategic aims of their government in other parts of Asia.

Responses to Growing World Protectionism and the Japanese "Threat"

One of the most striking aspects of the development of intra-Asian trade in the interwar years was the growth of Japanese exports. After 1920, Japan, as a "newly industrializing nation," embarked on the kind of export strategy that the erstwhile Japanese colonies, South Korea and Taiwan, were to adopt in the 1960s and many other Asian countries after 1980. Labor-intensive indus-tries in such goods as textiles and garments, footwear, bicycles, and house-hold utensils that had been produced largely for the domestic market began to penetrate export markets in other parts of Asia. Because industrial labor was much cheaper in Japan than in the more mature industrial economies of Western Europe and North America, Japanese products could be priced very competitively, and they found a ready market among millions of consum-ers who were more concerned about price than about quality. In 1920, over half of total Japanese exports were going to Asia, and this percentage did not change greatly until the latter part of the 1930s. A growing proportion of the Asian share of Japanese exports went to parts of Asia that were under the con-trol of the British, Dutch, and Americans; by 1935, British India, the Straits

Settlements, and Indonesia accounted for about 40 percent of exports to Asia outside the Japanese empire (Booth 2000: table 14.3).

That it suited the interests of powerful lobbies in British Malaya, Indonesia, and the Philippines to have cheap Japanese wage goods flooding into these colonies in the early 1930s cannot be doubted. Large estate companies were desperate to hold down labor costs as prices for primary products slumped after 1930 and world markets contracted. In addition, there was resentment, especially in the British colonies, that quotas on Japanese textile products would amount to a tax on "poor peasants" in order to assist high-cost Lancashire producers. Meredith quotes an article from *The Economist* in May 1934 pointing out that "the cheapness of Japanese cotton exports has been doing the world a considerable service by helping the consumer in tropical countries to maintain his purchases" (1996: 43). In Singapore, the Chamber of Commerce appeared to agree with this; its members voiced considerable opposition to the decision of the British government in 1934 to impose quotas on imports from Japan of cotton and rayon piece goods on the grounds that the Malay peasant would suffer, and it was far from clear that the Lancashire producers would derive much benefit anyway (Brown 1994: 116–123). The quotas were nonetheless imposed, and the Japanese share of total imports to British Malaya fell after 1934 (Table 5.4).

In Indonesia, the competitive position of key export industries such as rubber and sugar was eroded relative to those in other parts of the tropical world by the Dutch decision to stay on the gold standard after 1931. Because Indonesia was a more open and less protected economy than the Philippines

Table 5.4. Percentage of Total Imports from Japan

Year	Thailand	Philippines	French Indochina	Indonesia	Burma	British Malaya
1928	2.8	9.6	2.1	9.1	6.5	2.0
1929	8.1	8.1	1.8	10.4	8.4	2.6
1930	11.2	10.5	1.1	10.9	8.9	3.5
1931	8.4	11.1	1.6	15.2	8.9	3.9
1932	14.4	7.8	1.1	19.1	11.6	4.5
1933	19.2	8.4	2.2	29.8	9.4	7.4
1934	25.3	12.4	2.2	31.9	9.3	8.0
1935	29.1	14.2	3.3	29.5	10.9	6.4
1936	28.3	13.1	3.1	26.2	10.6	6.3
1937	21.5	14.8	3.2	24.2	8.3	5.8
1938	15.6	9.6	3.1	14.5	6.6	n.a.
1939	9.6	6.2	1.7	16.1	7.1	n.a.

Sources: Thailand: Swan 1988: 76; French Indochina: Service de la Statistique Générale 1947; Philippines: Bureau of Census and Statistics 1941; Indonesia: Korthals Altes 1991; Burma: National Planning Commission 1960a–b: statistical appendixes; British Malaya: *Annual Departmental Reports of the Straits Settlements* (Singapore: Government Printing Office, 1930–1938).

Note: n.a. = not available.

or French Indochina as well as being a much larger market, it is not surprising that Japanese exports were much larger in absolute terms than those to the other colonies (Booth 2003c: table 9). They also comprised a greater share of total imports, especially after 1930 (see Table 5.4). Given the increasing power of the militarist factions in the Japanese government during the 1930s, it was inevitable that the Dutch colonial authorities began to worry about the political and strategic motives behind the rapid growth of Japanese exports. Japanese government agencies were deeply involved in the export expansion into Southeast Asia, and the huge Indonesian archipelago was, in the eyes of the Dutch colonial establishment, especially vulnerable to Japanese "subversion by trade" (van Gelderen 1939: 21).

The first years of the world slump were especially damaging to Indonesia not just because of falling prices for key export staples, but also because of contracting markets. As both the British and French empires retreated into greater protectionism, it became increasingly difficult to sell products such as sugar into either British or French territory. Given that the metropolitan market in the Netherlands for tropical products was small and the Dutch possessed few other colonial territories, there was little option but to cut back production. In 1929–1930, when Java sugar production was at its peak, it was more than three times that of the Philippines. By 1935–1936, Javanese production had fallen to only about 20 percent of the 1929–1930 level, while that in the Philippines had surpassed Javanese production by almost 50 percent (Booth 2000: table 14.4).

Facing such problems in leading export industries, it was hardly surprising that Dutch free-trade principles were tested beyond their limits, and "the idea rapidly spread that the unlimited free trade and open-door policy, which governed the whole foreign trade of the Netherlands, including its inter-imperial relations, had to be reconsidered in the light of post-crisis conditions" (van Gelderen 1939: 30). The new policies took two main forms. First, trading links between the metropolitan economy and Indonesia were strengthened by policies designed to reserve a large share of the Dutch metropolitan market for colonial imports of sugar, corn, and vegetable oils. In the case of sugar, the Netherlands guaranteed a quota in the home market of 85,000 tons annually, in spite of protests from Dutch sugar beet producers. But this was only about 16 percent of the very reduced level to which production had fallen by 1935. The rest still had to be sold into those markets that were unregulated for whatever price could be negotiated.

Van Gelderen pointed out that these quota allocations were granted in part as a compensation for the implementation of the second class of policies, which involved imposing quotas on imports into Indonesia for a range of imports. Some goods were subject to general quotas, which enabled colonial importers to purchase from the cheapest source (usually Japan), but other goods were subject to specific country quotas. Typically cheap cotton goods and some household utensils were subject to general quotas, while superior textile products, paper products, rubber tires, chemical manures, light bulbs, and so forth, were subject to country quotas. The purpose of this system was to reserve a share of the colonial market for Dutch and to a lesser extent other European producers. It led to a marked downturn in the percentage share of Japanese imports in total imports from the peak reached in 1934, although in absolute terms Japanese exports reached a peak in 1937 and fell thereafter. In spite of the quota restrictions, Indonesia remained a very large market for Japanese cotton textile exports; in 1937, the value of these exports to Indonesia was higher than anywhere else in Asia (Sugiyama 1994: table 2.5).

In the Philippines, commercial interests in the United States were also putting the colonial administration under strong pressure to place tariffs or quantitative restrictions on Japanese imports, especially of cotton textiles. Mindful of the approach of self-government and also concerned about the impact of trade restrictions on prices of important consumer goods, the Bureau of Insular Affairs, the main agency responsible for economic policy, took a cautious approach to the imposition of import controls in 1934–1935. The Japanese for their part were pointing out to Filipinos the benefits that would accrue after independence from diversifying markets for their exports and imports, and establishing closer economic and technical links with neighboring countries. Japan financed lobbyists to stress the importance of cheap wage goods to low-income workers (Goodman 1983: 48–50).

But American congressional pressure grew, and senators such as Millard Tydings began to suggest that if restrictions on Japanese imports were not imposed, the United States would take a much tougher approach to the granting of duty-free access into the US market for Philippine agricultural imports. Negotiations dragged on through 1935 between the American and Japanese governments; the upshot was that, in October 1935, Japanese yarn and textile producers agreed to a system of voluntary export restrictions to the Philippine market (Goodman 1983: 53; Guerrero 1994: 175–179). Japanese exports to the Philippines were never especially large in relation to total Japanese exports, and the Japanese government no doubt reasoned that it was more prudent to appease the US Congress than to increase commercial penetration of the Philippine market. After 1937, the absolute value of Japanese exports fell, as did the share of Japan in total Philippine imports (see Table 5.4). As in other parts of Southeast Asia, this decline reflected, in part at least, the increasing reluctance of Chinese shopkeepers and traders to handle Japanese goods, given the violent behavior of the Japanese army in China.

In French Indochina, by contrast, Japan was never able to get more than a tiny share of the total import market, and the absolute value of Japanese exports into Indochina was minuscule. Indeed the balance of trade between Japan and Indochina ran in favor of Indochina throughout the 1930s (Rahm 1952: table 17). What explains this outcome? Exchange rate policy is unlikely to have accounted for the persistent trade surpluses, as the piastre appreciated against the yen in real terms for much of the decade. We must seek the explanation in terms of trade policy. Norlund presents a clear analysis of the tangle of vested interests, both in the colony and in metropolitan France, which affected trade policy decisions in French Indochina as the world crisis deepened:

> Agricultural interests in France wanted the French market to be protected from colonial imports; French industrialists wanted protection for their goods in the colonial market; colonial agricultural interests wanted the abolition of restrictions on the import of their production into France and opposed the protection of French goods in the colonial market. The *Comite de l'Indochine* lobbied effectively for protection for Indochinese crops. Its greatest achievement was to secure a free loan of 100 million francs in 1932 for French rubber plantations. (Norlund 2000: 216)

Faced with this barrage of contradictory demands, the French colonial administration decided to restrict imports from other parts of Asia and especially from Japan and China. As far as the Japanese were concerned, there is some evidence that they viewed the Indochina market in a rather different light than markets in other parts of colonial Asia, such as British India or Indonesia. No doubt French tariff policies accounted for much of the Japanese hesitation. Touzet quoted a former Japanese consul general in Hanoi as stating in 1930 that "Japan has much to ask of Indochina but nothing to offer her" (1934: 151). This was certainly not the Japanese view regarding Dutch and British colonies. It appears that the robust nature of the French response to any sign of interest in the Indochina market on the part of Japanese exporters after 1930 served as a potent deterrent or at least persuaded Japanese textile exporters, to take one example, to target other parts of Asia where colonial governments were more laissez-faire in their trade regimes.

After the tariff changes of 1928–1929, French textile interests lobbied hard to prevent any imports into Indochina from Japan, and in 1932 (at least two years before either the Dutch or the Americans were stirred into action), the Japanese and French governments signed a trade accord that regulated trade between Japan and Indochina. A list of products that the Japanese could export to Indochina with an agreed reduction in the general tariff was drawn up; in Touzet's words, the list was *"sans doute un peu limité"* (1934: 153), but that was all that the French were prepared to offer. It appears that the main lobby groups acting on behalf of the French estates were less concerned about the availability of cheap wage goods than in other parts of Southeast Asia. Their main concern was to persuade the government to increase tariff protection for colonial products in France and give interest-free loans to rubber producers (Schweitzer 1971: 238–239).

Even a senior colonial official like Touzet was somewhat ambivalent about the impact of this aggressive protectionism; he acknowledged that the level of trade between Indochina and Japan was "derisory" and expressed the view that it could and should expand. But he also pointed out that Japan engaged in trade practices that were potentially dangerous to Indochina; these included not only "currency dumping" through the depreciation of the yen, but also dumping of manufactures at prices made possible by *"salaries derisoires, longues heures de travail"* (Touzet 1934: 156). Touzet noted the export offensive that the Japanese mounted against both British India and Indonesia, and pointed out that Indochina had been spared most probably because of the relatively small size of its market. But the nature of French protectionism was almost certainly the most important explanation, and Japanese exports to Indochina were to expand rapidly after 1941, when the disruption of trade links with France made it a far more open and attractive market for Japanese manufactures.

The robust nature of the French protectionist response in Indochina can be contrasted with the situation in Burma, where a form of "double colonialism" prevailed. Given that Burma in the early 1930s was simply a province of British India with no autonomy in economic policy, trade policy was determined in New Delhi and London. Japanese exports to British India as a whole almost trebled in terms of nominal yen between 1931 and 1937 in spite of the imposition of imperial preference in 1932 and high tariffs on Japanese textile imports in 1933. Japanese imports into Burma reached 11.6 percent of total imports in 1932, and although the percentage declined slightly during the next two years, Japanese imports still comprised almost 11 percent of total exports in 1935–1936, suggesting that the effect of the protectionist measures adopted in 1932–1933 was at best transitory (see Table 5.4). There was no large-scale domestic textile industry in Burma to protect from foreign competition, either from the rest of India, Britain, or Japan. The desire to keep the price of wage goods cheap must have been an important factor weighing on the minds of British administrators in Burma, and as Brown (2000) argued, there is little evidence that textile imports declined on a per capita basis after 1931.

In Thailand, where the government was not under the same pressure from metropolitan vested interests in determining tariff policies, the share of Japan in total imports increased sharply after 1931 and by 1935 was as high as in Indonesia (see Table 5.4). The Thai government that had come to power after the 1932 coup against the absolute monarchy did not share the fears of the Dutch or the British about Japanese intentions in Southeast Asia. The decline in imports from Japan as a percentage of total Thai imports after 1936–1937 was mainly due to Chinese merchants boycotting Japanese goods and replacing them with goods from other countries (Swan 1988: 95–96). But the boycott eventually crumbled, and after the European war made it increasingly difficult to obtain imports from the United Kingdom and elsewhere, the Japanese share increased again.

Exchange Rate Policies

It is impossible fully to understand changing trade relationships between Japan and other parts of Asia without considering exchange rate policies. In relation to one another and to other important currencies such as the yen and (except in the Philippines) the dollar, nominal exchange rates in the colonies followed the movements of the metropolitan currencies during the 1930s. Relative to the dollar, the piastre first appreciated, along with the franc, and then depreciated after 1936 (Bassino 1998: fig. 1). This was also the path followed by the sterling-based currencies, the straits dollar, the baht, and the rupee. The Indonesian guilder underwent a sharp appreciation against the dollar until 1936, when the Netherlands finally decided to go off the gold standard. The yen by contrast left the gold standard in December 1931, after the Japanese had lost 675 million yen in gold in a vain attempt to defeat speculators, and thereafter depreciated rapidly against both the dollar and sterling, and the other currencies pegged to them (Kindleberger 1987: 163–164). By 1935, the yen had lost more than half its value against the various Southeast Asian currencies; the nominal devaluation was especially steep against the Indies guilder.

In Indonesia, there was a sharp deflation during the years from 1929 to 1936; by 1936, the cost of living for low-income indigenous families in Batavia (Jakarta) was only half what it had been in 1929 (Booth 2000: table 14.5). But given the magnitude of the nominal appreciation, the deflation was insufficient to restore the real value of the guilder against the yen (Booth 1994: table 6.8). In Indochina, where the rate of deflation was far more modest, the piastre appreciated sharply against the yen between 1931 and 1935; indeed the real exchange rate of the piastre against the yen only returned to its 1931 value in 1937 (Booth 2000: table 14.6). Given the extent of the appreciation against the yen, why did Japanese imports not flood into Indochina? The answer lay in the ever more stringent controls applied by the French against all imports originating from outside the French empire. It has already been pointed out that the French administration faced a complicated set of demands from diverse vested interests in both the colony and metropolitan France as the crisis deepened. But ultimately, considerations of imperial preference weighed more heavily in the minds of the French than those of consumer welfare in the colony.

The departure from gold made Thai rice exports more competitive, although the price advantage was offset in several key markets by the import controls that many rice-importing countries in Asia and elsewhere imposed after 1932 (Manarungsan 2000: 192). In addition, Thai rice exports were of higher quality than those from Vietnam and Burma, and consumers in important markets such as neighboring Malaya switched to less expensive rice as their incomes fell. But in spite of these problems, Thai rice exports recovered in volume terms quite rapidly from the low point reached in 1930, and the average annual tonnage exported in 1936–1938 was some 13 percent higher than the average for 1928–1930. The Thai government was sensitive to the problems of rural producers and realized that exchange rate policy alone was insufficient to boost rural incomes. After 1932, both the tax on rice fields and the poll tax were reduced, and many agricultural debts were written off (ibid.: 194–195).

Balance of Payments Surpluses, Investment Flows, and the Colonial "Drain"

The open dualistic model assumed that the main economic goal of colonialism was to create an export surplus, which was then used to finance remittances abroad on both government and (more often by the early twentieth century) private account. In other words, the commodity trade surpluses were not balanced by deficits on services, so that the current account was usually in surplus even in years of slow or negative economic growth. These surpluses were frequently cited by nationalists in various parts of Asia, both during the colonial era and more recently, as evidence of colonial exploitation. In fact, when we examine the data on export surpluses in Korea, Taiwan, and Southeast Asia in the first four decades of the twentieth century, we see very different outcomes in different colonies. These outcomes were in turn the result of different macroeconomic and sectoral policies pursued by the different colonial regimes.

In one colony, Korea, commodity exports were always below imports (Table 5.5). The current account was always in deficit (Figure 5.4), and by the late 1930s, these deficits amounted to around 10 percent of gross domestic expenditure (GDE). The situation in Taiwan was very different; in the early

Table 5.5. Export Earnings as a Percentage of Import Earnings, 1897–1938, in Taiwan, Korea, the Philippines, and French Indochina (averages for years shown)

Year	Taiwan	Korea	Philippines	French Indochina
1896–1900	80.6	93.7	85.9[a]	107.5
1901–1905	94.7	62.7	94.4	69.4
1906–1910	107.8	54.8	104.2	95.8
1911–1915	105.0	49.4	95.8	114.0
1916–1920	133.4	82.3	118.2	148.0
1921–1925	150.3	97.3	115.1	122.7
1926–1930	134.9	86.8	116.4	114.0
1931–1935	140.1	90.1	128.4	111.3
1936–1938	130.9	80.5	134.7	160.4

Sources: Taiwan and Korea: Mizoguchi 1974: table 3; additional data for Korea from 1896 to 1910 from Bank of Chosen 1920: 166–167; Philippines: Bureau of Census and Statistics 1947: 347; French Indochina: Bassino and Huong 2000: table 1.

[a] 1899–1900 only.

phase of the Japanese occupation, commodity exports were below imports, and until 1915 the current account balance was mostly in deficit (Table 5.5 and Figure 5.5). But after 1915, exports exceeded imports by a margin of at least 30 percent; although there was a deficit on service transactions, it was much less than the commodity surplus (Mizoguchi and Umemura 1988: 295).

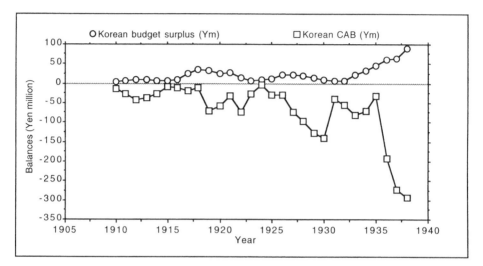

Figure 5.4. Korea: budget and current account balances. (Source: Mizoguchi and Umemura 1988: part 3, tables 57 and 63)

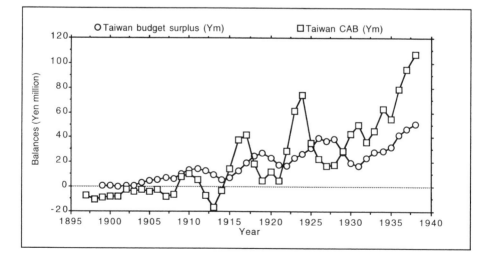

Figure 5.5. Taiwan: budget and current account balances. (Source: Mizoguchi and Umemura 1988: part 3, tables 54 and 60)

The current account surpluses increased steadily until the late 1930s, when they amounted to 9 percent of GDE. If the balance of payments outcomes in the two Japanese colonies were very different by the 1930s, that was also the case in the two British colonies in Southeast Asia. In Burma, export earnings were already more than 30 percent above imports by 1900, and the margin widened rapidly thereafter (Table 5.6). There are no balance of payments figures for colonial Burma, but there can be little doubt that the current account surplus was substantial and that it financed outward remittances of Indian workers and subventions by Burma to the British Indian government in Delhi. It was pointed out in the previous chapter that the fiscal surpluses in Burma were large and amounted to as much as 8 percent of NDP by the 1930s. Even after the system was terminated in the mid-1930s, the export surplus remained very large and must have reflected outward remittances on private account by individuals and companies. In the Federated Malay States, large export surpluses were also recorded for most years after 1900, but they were to a considerable extent offset by deficits in other parts of British Malaya. When consolidated export and import data for all of British Malaya were published in the 1920s, they showed a much lower export surplus (Table 5.6). It is probable that the current balance was in deficit in the decade from 1926 to 1935, given that the commodity trade was almost balanced and that there would have been a deficit on services.

In the Philippines and French Indochina until 1915, the trade balance was frequently in deficit or showed only a small surplus (see Table 5.5). In Indochina, there were large inflows of capital in the late nineteenth and early twentieth centuries on both government and private account, mainly to develop infrastructure and to support the growing French bureaucratic pres-

Table 5.6. Export Earnings as a Percentage of Import Earnings, 1897–1938, in Indonesia, Burma, Thailand, and the Federated Malay States

Year	Indonesia	Burma	Thailand	Federated Malay States [a]
1896–1900	124.1	134.8	126.1	144.4
1901–1905	134.0	130.1	136.5	161.5
1906–1910	149.1	144.6	139.7	161.8
1911–1915	151.0	148.7	124.3	195.1
1916–1920	186.7	156.0	115.2	252.9
1921–1925	167.3	181.5	127.1	217.1 (123.5)
1926–1930	153.3	180.3	121.1	178.6 (106.5)
1931–1935	155.6	246.5	154.8	171.6 (101.5)
1936–1938	171.8	228.3	158.8	221.8 (120.6)

Sources: Indonesia: Korthals Altes 1991; Burma: Saito and Lee 1999: 177–178; Thailand: Ingram 1971: appendix C; Federated Malay States: Fraser 1939: appendix A: British Malaya: Kratoska 2000: table 13.1 and Department of Statistics 1939.

[a] Figures in parentheses refer to the consolidated data for British Malaya from 1924 onward.

ence (Bassino 2000a: tables 2 and 3a). Bassino's estimates show that current account surpluses were consistently positive and large only for the years from 1936 to 1944. It is probable that during these years outward remittances by the Chinese were an important factor driving the large surpluses (ibid.: 335). The surpluses on the trade account recorded in the Philippines after 1915 were not as large as in Taiwan and were probably largely offset by negative balances on services. Balance of payments estimates prepared by the American government for the decade from 1925 to 1934 indicate that for most years the deficit on services together with interest and dividend movements offset the positive balance of trade to a considerable extent, although there was still a positive outflow over the decade (United States Tariff Commission 1937: table 8; Golay 1976: 375–376).

In Indonesia, for most years from the late 1890s to 1940, exports earnings exceeded imports by a large margin; Golay estimated that in the 1920s the Indonesian surplus accounted for more than half that of Southeast Asia as a whole (1976: 375). The large trade surplus was not offset by a deficit on services, and the current account balance was positive for much of the period from 1901 to 1939 (Korthals Altes 1987: table 1; Booth 1998: table 5.5). In Thailand, the commodity surplus was also substantial, especially during the 1930s (see Table 5.6). We do not have balance of payments estimates for this period, but it is probable that there was a positive current account balance for much of the period from 1900 to 1940.

It seems clear that there is no single explanation that fits all these outcomes. Arguments in terms of "colonial drains" and "exploitation through trade" seem inadequate, given the divergent empirical evidence. Rather we must seek reasons for the very different outcomes in each colony. Let us start with Korea, where imports often exceeded exports by 15 percent or more. Given that the balance of trade in services was also negative, Korea was running current account deficits for most years from 1911 to 1938 (see Figure 5.4). These deficits were funded by transfers from the Japanese government and after 1927 by increasing long-term capital inflows (Mizoguchi and Umemura 1988: 298). Given that the Korean budget was usually balanced or showed a slight surplus, the trade and current account deficits had their origins in private sector transactions. The large investments by Japanese corporations, especially in the 1930s, were undoubtedly an important factor; in addition, there were large numbers of Koreans living in Japan and Manchuria, and they were remitting more than 100 million yen annually back to Korea (Grajdanzev 1944: 237). At least part of these remittances would have been spent on imported goods. Imports from Japan by Japanese residents, many of them earning higher salaries than their counterparts in Japan, and the wealthiest groups among the Korean population would also have been substantial.

In Taiwan and in most parts of Southeast Asia, explanations must be sought for persistent and in several cases high trade and current account surpluses. A number of reasons have been put forward. Golay argues that an understanding of the colonial drain

> is to be found in the processes of capitalist development which flourished in the colonial world. There, the savings of a rentier class of foreign investors and the capital and enterprise of aliens resident in Southeast Asia who participated actively in colonial economic development—predominantly Western, Chinese and Indian—were combined with indigenous labor and readily exploitable natural resources to produce tropical foodstuffs and industrial raw materials in strong demand outside the area. Relatively modest initial injections of alien/foreign-owned capital and alien entrepreneurship initiated a process of economic growth which became self-sustaining and increasingly independent of further geographic inflows of capital and entrepreneurial resources from the outside world. (1976: 371–372)

Golay stresses the importance of reinvested profits in the development of large-scale enterprises in Southeast Asia, as did Drake (1972: 953–954), who pointed out that many forms of export expansion are relatively "undemanding of capital goods, particularly imported capital equipment." It was possible for many estate and mining companies to get started in Southeast Asia with only modest amounts of investment from abroad; sometimes loans from local trading houses, usually located in the port cities, were sufficient. Once they began to make profits, the tendency was to plow back profits into further expansion, especially if the world price for the particular commodity was buoyant. Even where the crops were grown not by large-scale estates but by smallholder producers, Drake suggested that large profits were reaped by traders who exploited imperfections in the marketing system. Ultimately profits made by foreign traders, whether Asian or European, were remitted abroad, and it was these remittances, which were not offset by inward investment flows, that accounted for the balance of payments surpluses.

The idea that the profits accruing to foreign enterprises in Southeast Asia were attributable to monopolistic and monopsonistic exploitation of indigenous consumers and producers was widespread in the colonial and postcolonial literature. Even some commentators from the metropolitan powers supported it (see, for example, Gonggrijp 1931). Investors from the metropolitan power were undoubtedly dominant in their own colonies, whether British, French, Dutch, or American, even if they had only a minor share of global investment flows (Lindblad 1998: 14). In this sense, the skewed distribution of investment flows mirrored the trade data (Svedberg 1981). In the British context, there is some evidence that the discrimination in favor of British firms in British colonies led to larger profits being earned in colonial territories than in other parts of the world (Svedberg 1982). Marseille has suggested that French firms operating in French colonies in the early part of the twentieth century, including Indochina, also made large profits in comparison with firms operating at home and in other parts of the world (1984: 109–115). Lindblad has argued that Dutch firms in Indonesia also paid out high dividends to overseas shareholders, in comparison with local and Chinese firms (1998: 80–81). Oil and mining companies and some estate companies (cinchona and tobacco) were particularly profitable.

But profit remittances were only one factor in the outflow of funds on the capital account of the balance of payments. In the Indonesian context, outward flows of life insurance premiums and pensions were also significant by the 1920s, as were "increases in private floating balances abroad" (Korthals Altes 1987: table 1). These would have included remittances of Chinese as well as European expatriates. In addition, there were outflows on government account to redeem both short- and long-term government debt. As the Indonesian budget was either balanced or in deficit for much of the period from 1915 to 1940, most of the outflow over these twenty-five years were on private account.

In Taiwan, imports exceeded exports in the first phase of the Japanese colonial era, and the current account balance was almost always in deficit until 1915 (see Figure 5.5). These deficits were funded by transfers from the Japanese budget and also by private flows of portfolio capital and direct investment (Mizoguchi and Yamamoto 1984: 408). After 1915, the balance of payments was always in surplus, and there were considerable capital flows back to Japan. These consisted of loans from the Taiwanese central bank, the Bank of Taiwan, to firms in Japan and also a substantial buildup in reserve funds held in Japan. Thus, in contrast to Korea, Taiwan by the 1930s was a net creditor to Japan (ibid.: 411).

Other colonies with currency board arrangements that pegged their currencies to the metropolitan currency, including British Malaya and the Philippines, also built up substantial reserves in the United Kingdom and the United States respectively. These reserves have been much criticized by postindependence economic analysts, who claim that the funds should have been used for investment in the colony itself (Khor 1983: 49–64). The traditional colonial defense of currency boards was that they guaranteed a stable exchange rate and thus reduced risk for foreign investors. While there may have been some truth in this, it has also been argued that the fixed exchange rates were often overvalued, and this overvaluation made investment in traded goods industries (producing both exports and imports) increasingly unattractive, especially after 1920, when the terms of trade turned against most of the Southeast Asian colonies.

Hooley has argued in the context of the Philippines that the two peso to the dollar exchange rate was overvalued even in 1904, when it was originally fixed (1996: 296); after 1920, the consequences of the dollar peg were increasingly serious for all traded goods producers. But the response was to seek preferential access to the American market via quotas rather than to devalue the currency. If internal prices were flexible, then a real depreciation could have been achieved in the Philippines and elsewhere through a fall in the internal price of nontraded goods and services relative to traded goods. But the evidence suggests that this did not happen in the main Southeast Asian economies. In both Indonesia and British Malaya, the evidence indicates that prices of nontraded goods and also wages remained sufficiently high relative to the price of manufactures to deter investment in industry (Huff 2002: 1102–1107). In Malaya, even the imposition of quotas on Japanese textile imports did not attract investment into the domestic manufacture of textiles, although, as was argued in Chapter 2, in Indonesia and Vietnam there was some growth in domestic production during the 1930s.

CHAPTER 6

Growth and Diversification
of the Market Economy

The Precolonial Economy of Southeast Asia

Since the 1960s, many observers have pointed to the apparent ease with which a successful indigenous entrepreneurial class emerged in both Taiwan and South Korea, which was, in only a few decades, able to build up successful firms that rapidly made inroads into world markets for a range of manufactured products. This success has been contrasted with the apparent failure of indigenous entrepreneurship in Southeast Asia, where it has been argued that much of the industrial growth since the 1960s has been the result of foreign investment. Where local industrialists have emerged in Thailand, Malaysia, Indonesia, and the Philippines, they have almost all been of Chinese descent. Surely this striking contrast must have been been the result of different colonial policies?

The argument that colonial policies stifled indigenous entrepreneurs in Southeast Asia receives some support from the work of historians, who have found that, in the fifteenth and sixteenth centuries, there was a considerable increase in trade between Southeast Asia and other parts of Asia, and also with the developing economies of Europe. Reid (1993) has called the years from 1450 to 1680 the "age of commerce" in Southeast Asia, a period characterized not just by increased international trading links, but also by the growth of cities throughout both mainland and insular Southeast Asia and a considerable expansion of domestic entrepreneurial and trading activity. By the middle of the sixteenth century, Reid argues, there were at least six trading cities with populations in excess of 20,000 people; several almost certainly had populations of well over one hundred thousand (ibid.: 69).

By the middle decades of the seventeenth century, that number had expanded. These cities were not just trading centers, but also the conduits through which both religious and secular ideas from many countries filtered into domestic societies. Populations were mixed, with indigenous people associating freely with traders from the Middle East, South Asia, and China. Several of these cities, including Aceh, Banten, and Brunei, contained at least one-fifth of the total population under the control of the states where they were located. In Southeast Asia as a whole, at least 5 percent of the population was living in large urban trading centers. This was a larger proportion than in contemporary northern Europe, although probably not larger than in Mughal India or China at that time (Reid 1993: 75).

In spite of the relatively high level of urban development in Southeast Asia in the seventeenth century, there were several areas where the region was still well behind other parts of Asia as well as Europe. Banking in its modern form, as distinct from traditional moneylending, was unknown; in addition, the impersonal institutions to safeguard capital and property that were developing in Europe were "totally absent in Southeast Asia" (Reid 1993: 129). Reid goes on to argue that the close links between rulers and the marketplace that characterized much of precolonial Southeast Asia made the evolution of individual property rights difficult throughout the region, in contrast to late medieval Europe and Tokugawa Japan. On the one hand, many members of the political elite were involved in trade and commerce, which made them more sympathetic to such activities than their counterparts in other parts of Asia or indeed in parts of Europe might have been (ibid.: 270). But on the other hand, a robust independent class of indigenous traders and entrepreneurs, protected by an impartial legal system, was unable to emerge. By the eighteenth century, European observers in many parts of Asia were blaming the rapacity of native rulers for this failure, but the activities of the Europeans themselves were hardly helpful.

To blame the collapse of most of the powerful Southeast Asian trading and maritime cities on the increasing power of European, especially Dutch, commercial penetration alone is clearly an oversimplification. The Dutch would not have been able to destroy centers such as Banten and Makassar if there had been more trust and greater willingness to form durable alliances between the various indigenous kingdoms in different parts of the Indonesian archipelago. Aceh and several trading cities in mainland Southeast Asia did not fall under Dutch control, but they disengaged from the regional and global trading system because they no longer found such activities profitable or because their rulers wanted their populations to concentrate on food-crop cultivation (Reid 1993: 299–301). This was even more the case for the increasingly powerful inland states that were hostile to the coastal trading states. Other factors such as climate change may also have contributed toward the demise of the age of commerce in the region by the end of the seventeenth century. By 1700 the main Asian-ruled trading cities had "lost their place both in world trade and within their societies" (ibid.: 328). Not only did regional and global trading links become attenuated, but the outward-looking, cosmopolitan, urban centers underwent a steady decline.

The Emergence of the Plural Economy

The eighteenth century saw the growth of several port cities, such as Batavia (now Jakarta) and Manila, that were under the control of European powers and from which the tentacles of foreign domination stretched out to the hinterlands. But the total urban population almost certainly declined, and this century saw a retreat from the market into the subsistence agricultural economy in many parts of Southeast Asia. In addition, it also witnessed the beginnings of what was, by the early twentieth century, characterized as the plural economy, where ethnicity and economic role were tightly linked. In most parts of Southeast Asia, the emergence of the plural economy was inextricably linked to the growth of resident Chinese populations. During the "age of commerce," the Chinese were just one of several trading minorities active in the larger port cities, and they mixed with both indigenous and other trading groups without appearing to dominate. But by the eighteenth century their numbers had grown, mainly because economic and demographic pressures in China itself were pushing more Chinese into trading and commercial ventures in Southeast Asia (Reid 2001: 50). The European-controlled port cities held several attractions for Chinese traders in the eighteenth century. They were important sources of valuable commodities and precious metals, especially silver, which were much in demand in China, and they provided a "stable environment in which Chinese could grow wealthy and even influential without ceasing to be Chinese" (Reid 1993: 317).

Reid argued that the single most important development that led to the sharp functional separation of economic activity by ethnic group was the introduction of tax farming, which was initiated by the Dutch in Batavia in the seventeenth century and spread to various native states in Java, Thailand, and Cambodia over the next century (1993: 318–319). These developments on the one hand permitted rulers to withdraw from commercial concerns, while on the other, they gave the Chinese considerable economic power and social prestige without threatening the position of the rulers. Reid suggests that it was perhaps no accident that those ethnic groups in Southeast Asia where the entrepreneurial spirit best survived into the twentieth century were located in remote regions where Chinese tax farming did not penetrate or where religious and cultural hostility to the practice made local rulers reluctant to adopt it.

The nineteenth century saw further growth of European-controlled port cities, and by the 1890s, there were a number of port cities in mainland and island Southeast Asia with populations in excess of 50,000 including Rangoon and Moulmein, Bangkok, Singapore, Batavia, Semarang, Surabaya, Palembang, Saigon-Cholon, and Manila. In addition, some inland cities, including Mandalay, Yogyakarta, Surakarta, and Hanoi had become important centers of administration and trade by the turn of the twentieth century. But the nineteenth century was a period of rapid population growth in much of Southeast Asia, and several scholars have pointed out that it is probable that urban populations actually declined relative to total populations in some parts of the region.

The European colonial powers were not in favor of rapid in-migration of indigenous populations to urban areas, and neither was the governing elite in Thailand, where it has been claimed that the "court helped to develop urban Siam as a Chinese preserve" (Phongpaichit and Baker 1995: 174). As was pointed out in Chapter 2, it would be an exaggeration to claim that urban populations were always overwhelmingly European and Chinese or Indian. In the Javanese cities, indigenous Indonesians were in the majority by 1890, and this continued to be the case until 1942 (Boomgaard and Gooszen 1991: 220–221). But in Bangkok, it has been estimated that, by the 1850s, Chinese outnumbered indigenous Thai by two to one, and Chinese in-migration accelerated from the 1860s onward, as the demand for urban labor increased. The government was also an important source of employment for Chinese workers, especially on railway construction, while the port of Bangkok became "virtually a Chinese preserve" (Phongpaichit and Baker 1995: 174–175). In Rangoon, where Indian in-migration accelerated between the late nineteenth century and 1930, the 1931 census found that Indians comprised 53 percent of the population. They were almost 11 percent of the population in Lower Burma as a whole. Only 32 percent of the population of Rangoon comprised indigenous Burmans (Baxter 1941: 9–21).

After the turn of the century, the division between the newly arrived Chinese and the established families became more pronounced, not just in Java but in other parts of Southeast Asia as well. Many children from the "old migrant" families began to assimilate; they ceased speaking Chinese dialects, learned Dutch, English, or French, and wherever possible gravitated toward salaried jobs. As educational opportunities increased for Chinese, especially in Indonesia and British Malaya, they were, as Rush (1991: 24) and Mackie (1991: 89) have pointed out, attracted to the genteel professions rather than the hurly-burly of commerce. It was the new arrivals from China, mainly single men, who became coolie laborers, itinerant peddlers and moneylenders, and artisans. By the 1930s, the Chinese in Indonesia, the Straits Settlements, the Federated Malay States, and Thailand were spread across a variety of occupations; in all these territories, the majority were in nonagricultural occupations, although more than 40 percent were in agriculture in the Outer Islands of Indonesia and in the FMS, mainly as plantation laborers (Table 6.1).

The lack of interest in commercial careers on the part of the assimilated, Dutch-speaking Chinese (known as *peranakan*) in late colonial Indonesia led Williams to argue that "the Chinese in Indonesia did not achieve entrepreneurship" (1952: 34). His thorough survey of the evidence from the interwar years led him to the conclusion that the Indonesian Chinese were unable or at least unwilling to extend their commercial and industrial enterprises beyond the "limits imposed largely by tradition" (ibid.: 55). There were exceptions, the most famous of whom was the "sugar king" Oei Tiong Ham, who built up a large conglomerate based mainly on plantations in the early part of the twentieth century (Panglaykim and Palmer 1970; Yoshihara 1989). In an official handbook listing all firms operating in the colony in 1940, the Oei Tiong Ham concern, including both sugar and banking interests, was the

Table 6.1. Percentage Distribution of the Chinese in the Labor Force by Sector, 1930s

Sector	Java 1930	Outer Islands 1930	Straits Settlements 1931	FMS 1931	Thailand 1937	Philippines 1939
Agriculture	9.1	44.7	17.2	41.5	25.4	1.8
Manufacture	20.8	19.5	17.6	27.3	20.3	14.3
Transport	2.8	2.6	12.5	3.4	3.9	1.3
Commerce	57.7	23.2	23.3	12.2	34.9	53.7
Public service	0.5	0.7	0.2	0.1	1.2	0.2
Professions[a]	2.1	1.2	2.3	1.2	1.2	3.6
Other services	6.9	8.2	26.8	14.4	14.2	25.1
Total	100.0	100.0	100.0	100.0	100.0	100.0

Sources: Indonesia: Department of Economic Affairs 1936: vol. 8, table 18; Thailand: Central Service of Statistics c. 1946: 75; Straits Settlements and FMS: Vlieland 1932: tables 126, 134; Philippines: Commonwealth of the Philippines 1941: 505–521.

[a] Includes clerical workers.

only Indonesian Chinese business with assets in excess of 40 million guilders (Twang 1998: 32).

Based on official data and interviews, Twang has assembled a list of the large Chinese firms operating in Java and Sumatra in 1940 (1998: table 2.3). Most were either in agrobusiness or in trade and banking. Few were in manufacturing, apart from agricultural processing. Several large Chinese companies were still exploiting the so-called private lands *(particuliere landerijen),* mainly in West Java, that had been in Chinese hands for many decades in spite of Dutch attempts to expropriate the Chinese owners in the early twentieth century (ibid.: 33). There were many medium- and small-scale enterprises, some of which were in manufacturing and by no means all of which were Chinese-owned. In the 1920s, a government survey showed that there were almost 1,700 Chinese-owned industrial firms employing more than five people, compared with 2,800 European firms and 870 owned by indigenous Indonesians (Fernando and Bulbeck 1992: 254–259). But all these numbers pale into insignificance when compared with developments in other parts of Asia (especially Japan) at the same time. Prominent though the Chinese might have appeared in the commercial life of Indonesia and other Southeast Asian cities in the 1920s and 1930s, they were hardly laying the foundations for an industrial take-off.

Nonetheless, by the 1920s, the contours of the "plural society" were plain to see:

The western superstructure is only one aspect of a distinctive character, common to all tropical dependencies, that cannot fail to impress even the most casual observer; the many coloured pattern of the population. In Burma, as in Java, probably the first thing that strikes the visitor is the medley of peoples—European, Chinese, Indian and native. It is in the strictest sense a medley, for they mix but do not combine. Each group holds by its own religion, its own culture and language, its own ideas and ways. As individuals they meet, but only in the market place, in buying and selling. There is a plural society, with different sections of the community living side by side, but separately, within the same political unit. Even in the economic sphere there is a division of labor along racial lines. Natives, Chinese, Indians and Europeans all have different functions, and within each major group subsections have particular occupations. (Furnivall 1948: 304–305)

Furnivall admitted that traces of a plural society were evident in several societies outside the tropical world, including Canada, the United States, and South Africa. He pointed out that, in these countries and in Australia and New Zealand, "when the influx of alien elements threatened national life," restrictions were placed on in-migration (1948: 305). By the second decade of the twentieth century, some colonial regimes in Southeast Asia, especially the Dutch, were also seeking to control in-migration from China in particular, although British policy in both Malaya and Burma was more laissez-faire with respect to both Chinese and Indians. By the 1930s, when the severe economic downturn reduced in-migration in many parts of Southeast Asia, the plural society and economy were well entrenched. Especially in Indonesia, official concern about its consequences intensified in the last phase of Dutch colonial rule.

The "Problem" of Indigenous Entrepreneurship

Like many other colonial administrators in different parts of Asia, Furnivall recognized that the "development of native enterprise must be a chief object of policy in any dependency which is valued as a market for the products of the colonial power" (1948: 293). He argued that subsistence producers should be brought into the market economy, if necessary by imposing taxes that had to be paid in money, and was in favor of inducements to encourage indigenous cultivators to grow export crops and of expanded credit to native producers, even where this meant borrowing on the security of crops. Again like the views of other colonial administrators, Furnivall's views were at least partly motivated by a desire to create larger and more dynamic markets for metropolitan manufactures in the colonies. But at the same time, he was well aware of the debates in the various colonial regimes in Southeast Asia concerning the desirability of exposing indigenous producers to the full blasts of global capitalism. The great majority of colonial officials would have been unaware of the precolonial economic history of the regions they were controlling, and even if they had realized that there had been an "age of commerce" several centuries earlier, they would no doubt have argued that the world economy in the early twentieth century was very different from that four centuries earlier, and while the rewards of involvement in international commerce were great, so were the dangers.

The Dutch in particular debated endlessly the extent to which indigenous Indonesians were being incorporated into the "Western sphere" of economic influence, the factors that promoted or inhibited such incorporation, and its effects on the economic and social welfare of the population The views of Boeke on these issues were well known in the English speaking world and were much criticized in the postindependence period by writers such as Higgins (1956) and Sadli (1971). But Boeke's views underwent considerable change in the course of his long career and cannot be considered typical of the Dutch colonial establishment as a whole, as de Vries, among others, has pointed out (van der Eng 1991: 42–43). Indeed it is far from clear whether, by the early twentieth century, there was an "official view" on the part of the Dutch regarding the entrepreneurial capacities of the indigenous population, although a number of Dutch officials working in Indonesia had strong views on the subject.

In his study of the formation of occidental stereotypes of the "Malay character," Alatas pointed out that "the general negative image was not the result of scholarship" (1977: 112). Most of those who proclaimed the indigenous peoples of Southeast Asia to be indolent, dull, treacherous, childish, and lacking any talent for or interest in trade and commerce were either colonial officials, planters, military people, or casual tourists. And yet, as Alatas concedes, even at the high noon of Western imperialism, there were some who were prepared to admit that these alleged features of the "Malay character" were by no means universal and where they were widely found had quite rational economic foundations. By the early twentieth century, most colonial scholars and policy makers in Indonesia, and in other parts of the region as well, would doubtless have concurred with van Gelderen that "the inhabitant of the tropics is further removed from the classical *homo oeconomicus* than the Westerner" (1927: 144), but at the same time the reasons for the apparent lack of "rational economic behavior" on the part of the indigenous population in Indonesia were much disputed.

Some colonial officials were content to ascribe this perceived lack to culture, religion, and the climate, but others thought differently. In 1941, van der Kolff published a remarkable paper that argued that, to the extent that Indonesians, especially Javanese, adopted short time horizons and were unwilling to invest in risky operations that would yield results only in the longer term, this was because they were ignorant, poor, and insecure. It was, according to van der Kolff, poverty and insecurity that led to practices such as *ijon* (selling the crop while still immature), and such behavior was perfectly rational given the constraints within which many Javanese had to make decisions on consumption, saving, and investment (1941: 247). Other writers also stressed the economic rationality of farmer behavior in the more land-abundant parts of the region, such as British Malaya. It was argued that the Malay reluctance to work for wages did not reflect an aversion to effort or a lack of desire for a cash income, but rather that with relatively abundant supplies of land they could earn more in agriculture than as unskilled workers in the city. As Richard Winstedt pointed out, "because he is an independent farmer with no need to work for hire, the Malay has got an undeserved reputation for idleness, which his Asiatic competitors take care to foster" (Alatas 1977: 50).

Such views would not have been universally held, although there would have been greater agreement on a further assertion of van Gelderen's that the indigenous cultivator was likely to be exploited in his or her dealings with the market economy because of the "great difference in bargaining power between the buyer on the one hand and the seller on the other" (1927: 147).

> The buyer usually has both superior knowledge of the market situation and greater possibilities to reach and make use of more than one local market. This preponderance is even greater if the buyer is the only one, or one of a very small group of competitors, as against a larger number of persons offering the commodity for sale. In such a case it is very easy for a monopoly or semi-monopoly situation to develop, so that the local price of a commodity is forced downwards. Another factor producing the same effect is the vast difference in the value of the same unit of money for the two parties to the transaction. . . . In many cases, in fact, the normal situation is one in which the necessity to sell is so urgent that what takes place is actually a forced sale. (van Gelderen 1927: 147)

The underlying implication was that the monopsonistic middlemen were almost always Chinese, and it was their superior knowledge and bargaining power that led to the exploitation of the indigenous producer. Regardless of whether these assertions were true, they were held by many Dutch colonial administrators as well as many indigenous Indonesians. Indeed Kahin argued that the rapid growth of the Sarekat Dagang Islam, formed by Raden Mas Tirtoadisoerjo in 1909, into a political-nationalist movement was in large part due to "sharp Chinese trading practices" on the part of "aggressively competitive Chinese entrepreneurs" whose commercial power had increased as a result of the lifting of travel restrictions on Chinese between 1904 and 1911 (1952: 67). The Sarekat Islam attracted "an avalanche of members" and galvanized anti-Chinese feelings to the point where, in 1912, there were anti-Chinese riots in both Surakarta and Surabaya.

Outside Java, although the Chinese presence was larger relative to the indigenous population, some indigenous business groups did emerge in the last phase of the Dutch colonial era. Post has described the rise of a group of Sumatran traders who were able to establish themselves in Java and built up quite extensive trading links with other parts of Asia, especially Japan (1997: 93–103). Several had close ties to leaders of the independence struggle, particularly Hatta, and accompanied him on a trip to Japan in 1933. The Japanese were keen to build up a network of indigenous traders in Indonesia for products such as textiles, especially as Japanese products were increasingly subject to boycotts by Chinese merchants. These links were strengthened during the Japanese occupation, and some of the Sumatran traders survived to play an important role in the early postindependence era.

Paradoxically, in spite of the Dutch concern about the ability of the Javanese to participate in the "modern economy," native Javanese accounted for a higher proportion of the nonagricultural labor force than was the case in most other parts of the region (Table 6.2). Although it may have been true that many jobs in the nonagricultural labor force occupied by Javanese in the 1930s were in petty trade and cottage industry, they also outnumbered both Chinese and Europeans in professional occupations and in the civil service. Even in trade, where the Chinese were certainly important, their numbers were only around 12 percent of indigenous workers in Java and 37 percent in the Outer Islands (Table 6.3). By the 1930s, it would appear that many indigenous Indonesians were availing themselves of a greater range of economic opportunities than were other Southeast Asians or indeed the indigenous populations of Taiwan and Korea. It is arguable that many were forced into nonagricultural occupa-

Table 6.2. Indigenous Labor Force as a Percentage of the Total Labor Force, c. 1930

	Indigenous Workers as Percentage of		
	Total Labor Force	Agricultural Workers	Nonagricultural Workers
Java (1930)	98.2	99.7	95.5
Outer Islands of Indonesia (1930)	94.7	97.1	85.2
Straits Settlements (1931)	16.9	38.8	7.8
FMS (1931)	19.9	27.5	7.4
Burma (1931)	87.9	94.7	72.4
Philippines (1939)	98.6	99.7	97.9
Thailand (1937)	94.5	98.1	66.7
Korea (1930)	96.9	99.6	87.2
Taiwan (1930)[a]	92.3	99.5	80.1

Sources: Indonesia: Department of Economic Affairs 1936: vol. 8, table 18; Thailand: Central Service of Statistics c. 1946: 75; Straits Settlements and FMS: Vlieland 1932: tables 121–141; Burma: Baxter 1941: 25; Philippines: Commonwealth of the Philippines 1941: 505–521; Korea: Chang 1966: table 2; Taiwan: Barclay 1954: 71.

[a] Refers to male labor force only.

tions by the growing scarcity of agricultural land. But whether out of choice or through desperation, indigenous Indonesians were moving into new occupations and accepting new challenges, both as employees and as self-employed businesspeople.

It is instructive to compare developments in Indonesia with those in the Philippines. Although the Chinese were not in fact a much smaller proportion of the total population in the Philippines than in Java (see Table 2.2), the American administration did not seem to be nearly as anxious about their economic role as were the Dutch. The Americans were keen to build up a robust indigenous entrepreneurial class in the Philippines and viewed education as a key policy in achieving this goal. As will be shown in the following chapter, they facilitated the development of both secondary and tertiary education to a much greater extent than administrators in any other Asian colony. But other aspects of American policy were less conducive to the development of indigenous entrepreneurs. Owen pointed out that when the Americans arrived, there was very little large-scale Filipino manufacturing (1972: 52). The advent of a free trade regime with the United States together with an overvalued peso made investment in Philippine industry unprofitable except in a few export-processing sectors. Because several of the key politicians who emerged in the period immediately preceding self-government were connected to and dependent on the sugar sector, there were few advocates for rapid industrialization. Much of the large-scale manufacturing industry that did emerge was controlled by foreign interests, either American, Chinese, or Spanish. This was also true of commercial banking.

Table 6.3. Indigenous and Chinese Labor Force by Sector, Indonesia 1930

Sector	Indigenous Labor Force by Sector		Indigenous as Percentage of Total Labor Force		Chinese as Percentage of Indigenous Labor Force	
	J	OI	J	OI	J	OI
Agriculture	65.3	81.6	99.7	97.1	0.2	2.7
Industry	11.5	7.7	97.4	88.2	2.3	12.4
Transport	1.4	1.4	93.2	89.0	2.5	9.1
Trade	6.3	3.1	87.9	70.1	11.6	36.6
Professions	0.7	0.7	89.1	87.4	3.6	7.9
Government	2.6	2.0	95.5	94.6	0.3	1.8
Other	12.1	3.5	98.9	89.0	0.7	11.5
Total	100.0	100.0	98.2	94.7	1.3	4.9

Sources: Department of Economic Affairs 1936: vol. 8, table 18.

Note: Agriculture includes hunting, fishing, forestry, mining, and salt manufacture. Government service includes police, army, and navy. J = Java, OI = Outer Islands.

The Chinese dominated internal trade, especially retailing, and also participated in wholesaling and importing, as indeed was the case in other parts of Southeast Asia. Foreign observers such as Kurihara emphasized the lack of involvement of indigenous Filipinos in large-scale manufacturing and argued that the "Philippine experience was no different from that in European dependencies or in independent countries which, economically, occupy a semi-colonial status" (1945: 11). His analysis of the 1939 census data on employment showed that most workers engaged in manufacturing were employed in traditional labor-intensive industries such as embroidery, dress-making and tailoring, hat making, carpentry, native textiles, shoe and slipper manufacture, mat making, and cigarette manufacture (ibid.: 16–17). Many women were employed as home workers on a subcontracting basis. Few workers were learning new skills in factories using modern technologies, and even fewer were learning how to manage large-scale enterprises, whether in manufacturing or in other sectors of industry and commerce.

While Kurihara's criticisms were broadly correct, there is evidence that Filipinos were, by the late 1930s, controlling a higher proportion of nonagricultural assets in the economy than the populations of other Asian colonies. Golay used the 1939 census data to estimate that Philippine citizens owned 45 percent of all nonagricultural assets; in manufacturing industry the figure was higher (55 percent) (1969b: table 1). Chinese controlled around 14 percent of assets and Americans 25 percent. It is probable that many Filipinos of mixed Chinese or Spanish descent were classified as indigenous Filippinos in the census data, but even allowing for this, Golay's figures do suggest that, on the eve of the Pacific War, Philippine citizens already exercised considerable control over the nonagricultural sectors of the economy. The consequences of this for postindependence development are explored in subsequent chapters.

Thailand, although never a colony, also had to face the problem of considerable foreign control over important sectors of the economy. Ayal pointed out that the leaders of the 1932 coup "were imbued with Western ideas of exclusive nationalism and were therefore more sensitive to the presence and activities of unassimilated aliens in their country" (1969: 338). The notion of "Thaification" gained support, and from 1935 onward, laws were passed to reserve certain urban occupations for Thais and to give preference to firms owned by indigenous Thais in allocating government contracts (Phongpaichit and Baker 1995: 179; Yoshihara 1994: 32–35). The Business Registration Act of 1936 was designed to facilitate the compilation of information on business ownership, and in 1938 a government-controlled Thai Rice Company was formed by the purchase of ten Chinese rice mills. The Liquid Fuel Act of 1939 attempted to establish government control over oil imports and distribution (Ayal 1969: 300–301). Some of these policies were reversed later, but the measures of the 1930s set a precedent for "persistent, if erratic" policies to indigenize the economy that continued after 1945 (ibid.: 338).

The Development of Markets for Land, Labor, and Capital: Indonesia and British Malaya Compared

It would be wrong to assume that the attitude of all colonial officials in Southeast Asia was one of purely paternalistic concern that the commercially incompetent indigenous population be protected from the rapacity of the clever Chinese. By the beginning of the twentieth century, it was becoming clear to at least some Dutch and French administrators, concerned about what was perceived as overpopulation in Java and Tonkin, that the living standards of the indigenous populations would only improve to the extent that they could participate more fully in the modern, nonagricultural economy. In Java, two facts were widely acknowledged by most scholars and administrators who had studied the empirical evidence: the proportion of agricultural output, including foodstuffs, that was sold on the market had increased to almost 50 percent in many parts of the island, and most rural households were diversifying their sources of income away from purely agricultural pursuits to manufacturing, transport, trade, and wage labor (van Laanen 1990: 265; Boomgaard 1991: 34–36). More broadly, Burger, who discussed the "government's native economic policy" in a thesis defended in 1939, quoted several officials including van Gelderen, Meijer Ranneft, and Boeke to support his argument that the indigenous economy was becoming ever more monetized and commercialized, and as a result a native business class was slowly emerging (p. 329).

The slow speed of development of this business class was a source of frustration to many Dutch observers as well as to Indonesians themselves. Burger was no doubt correct when he argued that "if a vigorous group of native entrepreneurs had arisen, the authorities would almost certainly not have gone so far with their welfare policies as they have done" (1939: 329). Boeke (1927), in a lecture delivered in the late 1920s, in fact called for a different type of government policy that put less emphasis on improving the general level of welfare and more on encouraging the emergence of outstanding individuals with genuine entrepreneurial ability, a policy later characterized by Wertheim as "betting on the strong" (1964: 264–265). Only the emergence of such individuals could, according to Boeke, pose an effective challenge to European and Chinese domination of the economy. But the 1930s were hardly a propitious time for such a new breed of entrepreneurs to emerge and consolidate their position within the colonial economy. By the late 1940s, when Boeke's best-known works were published, "the gradualistic approach to rural society, via well-to-do advanced farmers" no longer occupied a central place in his thinking (ibid.: 266).

While the debate was continuing about the entrepreneurial capacities of indigenous populations, their involvement with market institutions was steadily increasing. By the dawn of the twentieth century, thousands of Javanese were moving to Sumatra to work as wage laborers, and many more were seeking opportunities as wage laborers at home. These numbers increased steadily until the onset of the depression of the 1930s. The increased willingness of the Javanese to move in search of better economic prospects contradicted the stereotype of the indolent native who was unwilling to seek opportunities for economic self-improvement. And the involvement with market institutions was not limited to the labor market. As was argued in Chapter 3, land also was becoming a marketed commodity, both in Java and in other parts of the archipelago. In addition, the colonial authorities were experimenting with several credit programs, which attracted attention and admiration from both English and French colonial officials (Henry 1926; Angoulvant 1926: 282–283; Furnivall 1934b, 1934c).

Furnivall was at pains to emphasize that even in the depths of the depression, the entire credit system was solvent and required no state subsidies (1934b: 26). He argued strongly against the assertion that the government-operated institutions simply displaced private ones, especially those run by the Chinese. It appears that the government pawnshop service was operated more efficiently than the nineteenth-century Chinese pawnshops, and while the relaxation of the laws on Chinese residence might have led to greater Chinese activity in rural areas in the twentieth century, it cannot be argued that taxpayers' money was used to subsidize financial institutions that the private sector would have provided more efficiently. The private system did continue to expand alongside the state one, although in the absence of data, it is impossible to tell how important privately supplied credit was compared with state provision.

Given that the people's credit system did develop so rapidly in the interwar years, what was its impact on the indigenous economy in Java? Scholars seem very divided in their opinions. Alexander and Alexander have argued that there is little evidence that the various rural credit institutions served to stimulate economic diversification, and the main effect of the government-sponsored initiatives was to institutionalize the two-tier credit market in the rural economy (1991: 386–387). The relatively wealthy could get access to credit at lower rates of interest, which they could then lend at higher rates to the relatively poor, making large profits in the process. While no doubt correct, this argument ignores the basic economic point that credit markets always reflect a degree of dualism in the sense that some people will always be seen as more creditworthy than others.

If the government initiatives did greatly increase the supply of loanable funds to rural areas in Java, were these funds used for productive investment or for consumption purposes? Alexander and Alexander argue that most went toward consumption, ceremonial expenditures, and for tiding people over in emergencies such as ill health, unusually long dry seasons, and so on. Other authors have argued that the credit available from both pawnshops and other credit institutions was at least partly used for productive purposes; Furnivall pointed out that "a man may pawn his wife's bangles and use the proceeds as the first installment towards buying a motor bus on the hire purchase system" (1934c: 11). Both Furnivall and van Laanen (1990) have suggested that the pawnshops were not the last resort of the desperate (as they tended to be in Europe) but rather a convenient source of credit to many people who were far from destitute but who kept their savings in commodities rather than in cash or bank deposits. The fact that the real value of credit advanced through government institutions dropped so sharply after 1930 indicates that borrowings were related to investment opportunities rather than to financial pressures, and when the investment climate deteriorated as a result of the depression, the demand for loans fell.

In comparison with developments in Indonesia, the indigenous population of the Malayan peninsula was drawn more slowly into the cash economy in the nineteenth and early twentieth centuries. Indeed Indonesian migrants began arriving in British Malaya in large numbers from the 1870s to take advantage of trading opportunities and the growing demand for wage labor, which the indigenous Malays were reluctant to avail themselves of (Roff 1974: 37). According to Roff, the greater part of the Malay merchant community in Kuala Lumpur in the 1890s was said to originate from the Minangkabau region of West Sumatra, while Javanese began to arrive in considerable numbers in the Straits Settlements to work as laborers. Most Malays preferred to stay in their traditional occupations as farmers and fishermen, and the British did not encourage them to move out of these roles. By the end of the nineteenth century, seeds were sown that were to develop into ever more bitter ethnic hostilities over the next century. Roff has quoted articles that appeared in a Straits Chinese newspaper in 1894, which drew attention to Malay educational and economic backwardness and attributed it to "their slavish adherence to outmoded custom, the dissoluteness of their traditional leaders . . . their lack of industry and ambition, their hostility toward anyone who showed exceptional talents, and their inability to practice mutual self-help" (ibid.: 54). Roff comments that, however unfair these accusations were, "they came for many Malays uncomfortably near the truth."

In the second decade of the twentieth century, the British colonial authorities became more obsessed with rice self-sufficiency and more frustrated that production was not growing fast enough to keep up with rising domestic demand. The 1913 Malay Reservations Enactment gave Residents in the Federated Malay States the power to set aside land (mainly but not only rice land) for exclusive Malay ownership. The land could not be mortgaged, leased, or sold to non-Malays. Although in passing this legislation the British claimed to have been influenced by the earlier land legislation in Indonesia, in fact, the Malay enactment was more stringent in that it prevented even the leasing of land to non-Malay parties. In 1917, following mounting anxiety about food shortages, more legislation was passed that empowered Residents to regulate cropping patterns on Malay land, in effect preventing the cultivation of nonrice crops (Roff 1974: 123; Lim 1977: 121).

These draconian interventions in markets for both land and crops went well beyond Dutch measures in Indonesia and indeed beyond what the British did in other parts of Asia under their direct control. While one motivation was a genuine concern on the part of the colonial establishment that the growth of foreign estates could lead the Malay cultivator to become landless in his own country, it was clear that it was the official intention to keep the Malay away from the cultivation of crops other than rice. In particular, colonial officials showed themselves to be increasingly hostile to the idea that Malays should be involved in the cultivation of rubber (Lim 1977: 116). After 1917, Malay smallholders were not permitted to obtain non-Malay land for rubber cultivation, and indeed land already alienated to Malays that was found to be used for growing rubber was withdrawn.

Colonial officials appeared impervious to the fact that growing rubber afforded a better return on land and labor than growing rice, even at the increased rice prices prevailing in 1918–1920. The Stevenson Scheme, implemented in both Malaya and Ceylon in the 1920s to restrict the growth of rubber output and maintain its price, affected smallholder cultivation more severely than that of the estates (Sundaram 1988: 69). The main beneficiaries of this scheme were in fact smallholders in Indonesia, whose production really took off at this time. Although the Dutch colonial establishment gave the Indonesian smallholder little positive encouragement, they were not discriminated against, and their ready access to land meant that they could increase output with little official harassment.

Paddy cultivation was to remain, in the words of one economic historian, "the least profitable of all major occupations in Malaya" right up to the 1950s (Lim 1967: 176; see also Sundaram 1988: table 3.1). This did not prevent the British from continuing to deter the rural Malays from doing anything else. Their zeal to keep the Malays in traditional occupations also affected educational policy. Winstedt, an influential official, argued that the provision of English-language schools should be restricted lest it make rural Malays restless and eager to leave the kampong for the wider world (Lim 1967: 176). Roff quotes a director of agriculture in 1934 who warned against the dangers of inducing the rural Malay to "forsake the life of their fathers for the glamour of new ways which put money in their pockets today but leave them empty tomorrow, and to abandon their rice-fields for new crops which they cannot themselves utilize and the market for which depends on outside world conditions beyond their orbit" (1974: 125). The result was that the Malay vernacular schools had quite a different aim from the English-medium schools. They were not intended to train clerks and office workers (Wyndham 1933: 210). But many Malay parents could not see the point of education that did not lead to social mobility (Snodgrass 1980: 237–243; Rudner 1994: 289–290). Although enrollments in Malay vernacular schools increased rapidly, by the late 1930s only about 20 percent of eligible children were attending school.

It is probable that many Dutch administrators in Indonesia in the interwar years had similar feelings to those of British officials about the dangers of exposing indigenous cultivators to the full blast of national and world market forces. But Dutch colonial thinking had, by the 1920s, been forced to recognize reality. As we have seen, the great majority of the population in Java and other parts of the archipelago were involved in the cash economy not just as producers of cash crops, but also as suppliers of wage labor. Given the increasing density of population on restricted supplies of land, they had little option but to avail themselves of whatever nonagricultural opportunities for earning money were available. The purpose of the ethical policy and the interventions adopted in the 1930s was not so much to protect peasants from capitalism as to facilitate their gradual absorption into the market economy. In Malaysia, by contrast, the aim of colonial policy appeared to be to build ever higher fences between the kampong Malay and the market economy.

According to the 1931 census, Malays comprised less than 10 percent of the nonagricultural labor force in both the Straits Settlements and the FMS (see Table 6.2). This was a much lower percentage than in Java or the Outer Islands of Indonesia, or in Burma, the Philippines, and Thailand, although the Thai census data used a "nationality" criterion that probably underestimated the actual number of ethnic Chinese in the labor force. It was also much lower than in Taiwan and Korea. Indigenous Malays were a very low proportion of both manufacturing workers and those engaged in trade and commerce compared with Burma, the Philippines, and Indonesia, as well as Taiwan and Korea (Table 6.4). In the FMS, they comprised only 3 percent of the manufacturing labor force and less than 3 percent of those engaged in commerce and trade. To some extent, the very low proportion of indigenous

Table 6.4. Indigenous Workers as a Percentage of the Labor Force in Manufacturing, Commerce, Professions, and Government Service

	Manufacturing	Commerce / Trade	Government and Professions
Indonesia (1930)	95.3	84.3	93.6
Straits Settlements (1931)	7.2	3.9	20.5
FMS (1931)	3.0	2.4	32.9
Burma (1931)	80.8	73.3	86.7
Philippines (1939)	97.6	82.7	96.5
Thailand (1937)	55.2	60.6	95.2
Korea (1930)	89.7	85.1	59.8
Taiwan (1930)[a]	78.5	86.9	49.2

Sources: Indonesia: Department of Economic Affairs 1936: vol. 8, table 18; Thailand: Central Service of Statistics c. 1946: 75; Straits Settlements and FMS: Vlieland 1932: tables 121–141; Burma: Baxter 1941: 25; Philippines: Commonwealth of the Philippines 1941: 505–514; Korea: Chang 1966: table 2; Taiwan: Barclay 1954: 71.

[a] Male workers only.

Malays in the nonagricultural labor force reflected the fact that Malays were a much lower proportion of the total labor force than the indigenous population in other parts of East and Southeast Asia. But there can be little doubt that the large influx of migrant workers into British Malaya together with British policy aimed at keeping the indigenous population in rural areas created a more extreme example of the plural economy than in other colonies in East and Southeast Asia. It was a legacy that postcolonial governments struggled with for the last four decades of the twentieth century.

Indigenous Entrepreneurship and Economic Opportunity in Colonial Korea and Taiwan

The plural economy that attracted such attention throughout Southeast Asia in the last phase of European colonial rule did not exist in the Japanese colonies. There was very little in-migration from China or any other Asian country, except Japan, into either Taiwan or Korea, although the percentage of the population from the mainland in Taiwan was estimated at around 1 percent, which was higher than the percentage of Chinese nationals in the Philippines and only slightly lower than the percentage in Burma and Java (see Table 2.2). What did stand out in both Korea and Taiwan by the 1930s was the Japanese presence; Japanese citizens comprised over 5 percent of the total population in Taiwan and just under 3 percent in Korea (see Table 2.2).

The vast majority of Japanese workers in both colonies were in nonagricultural occupations; in Taiwan, the largest number of employed males in 1930 were in the professions and government, followed by commerce and manufacturing (Barclay 1954: table 16). Many indigenous Taiwanese were in these occupations as well; in 1930, indigenous Taiwanese comprised slightly less than half of male workers employed in government and the professions. In Korea, the proportion was around 60 percent. These were higher proportions than in British Malaya, although much lower than in Burma and Indonesia, where indigenous races accounted for the great majority of employed workers in the professions and government service by 1930. In Indonesia, indigenous workers accounted for a higher proportion of the manufacturing labor force than in either Taiwan or Korea and a roughly similar proportion of the labor force in trade and commerce (see Table 6.4).

There is little evidence that the Japanese colonial regimes in either Taiwan or Korea were much concerned with the development of entrepreneurial capacity among the indigenous populations. In the context of Taiwan, Ho argued:

> During the colonial period, the government relied primarily on its own savings and the savings of the Japanese corporate business structures it helped create to provide the capital for industry. It never encouraged the emergence of an indigenous industrialist class; in fact, its whole policy

was directed toward preventing the emergence of such as class. Until 1924 Taiwanese were not allowed to organize or operate corporations unless there was Japanese participation. Thus the modern sector became a monopoly of the Japanese capitalists. Even after this restrictive rule against Taiwanese participation was rescinded, Taiwanese were reluctant to seek entry to the modern sector because of its domination by Japanese capitalists. Through its power to regulate, and license, and by granting exclusive privileges to Japanese capitalists, the government successfully kept the Taiwanese from acquiring any economic power. (1971: 323)

Ho's argument is that Japanese policy in Taiwan was trapped in an image of its own creation. Taiwan was to be developed as an agricultural appendage of Japan, and it was only in the 1930s, when the Japanese government became more preoccupied with war preparations, that these views changed. In Korea in the 1930s, Juhn pointed out, when the Japanese authorities were trying to attract the *zaibatsu* to invest in Korean industry, some officials did argue for a strategy that also encouraged Koreans to establish small and medium enterprises (1977: 48). But few policies were implemented, and Korean businesses received little assistance, compared with that granted to Japanese firms, who remained in a dominant position in virtually all sectors of industry and trade. Juhn argued that the activities of the industrial cooperatives that were established in Korea after 1910 were "insignificant and ineffective" compared with small producers' cooperatives in Japan (1973: 128).

A figure frequently quoted for Korea is that Japanese investors accounted for around 90 percent of all paid-up capital in industry by the late 1930s (Kim 1973: 110–111; Haggard, Kang, and Moon 1997: 871; Chung 2006: 123). These authors have emphasized that Japanese investors dominated light as well as heavy manufacturing and that most skilled workers and almost all managers were Japanese. The figure of 90 percent has been challenged by Eckert, who claimed that it ignores joint Japanese-Korean companies that "may well have garnered the lion's share of Korean capital" (1991: 54). Eckert also argued that such statistics did not capture the full extent of the transition, although often incomplete, by Korean merchants and landlords into the ranks of the industrial bourgeoisie (ibid.: 55). He cites the examples of the men who would go on to found the *chaebol* that became famous in the post-1960 era, including Samsung, LG, and Hyundai. Most were sons of landlords who became small-scale businessmen in the 1930s and 1940s in sectors such as brewing, rice milling, textiles, and vehicle repair.

A few Koreans did rise to control substantial business empires during the Japanese era. The outstanding example of an indigenous Korean industrial family that rose to wealth and power in the Japanese era were the Kim brothers, who founded the Kyongsong Spinning Company. They came from a family that had accumulated substantial holdings of rice land in the southern part of the country, and after education in Japan, the two sons moved into industry in the 1920s. The move was fraught with difficulties, not the least being the stiff competition from better-funded Japanese firms (McNamara 1988: 174–175). But by the 1930s they had managed to consolidate their position in Korea and move into southern Manchuria, where they established a spinning plant in 1937. The textile venture survived the war and liberation, and prospered under the First Republic (McNamara 1990: 117; Juhn 1977: 49–50).

The Kim success story was exceptional, although other large-scale Korean businesses were able to emerge and compete with Japanese firms in banking and trade. Examples of successful entrepreneurs that are often cited include Pak Hung-sik, who established a substantial wholesale and retail business, and the aristocratic Min clan, who moved into banking during the Japanese era (Juhn 1973: 126; McNamara 1990: chaps. 5 and 6; Chung 2006: 263–264). After the establishment of formal Japanese rule, there were few positions available to Koreans in the upper ranks of the civil service or the military, so banking and finance became a socially acceptable occupation for men from families that had previously occupied senior bureaucratic posts. Chung has estimated that there were some sectors of light industry, such as brewing and pharmaceuticals, where Korean capital comprised at least 40 percent of the total by 1938 (2006: table 5.1). But as McNamara argued, all Korean business people "had to carefully align their investments to find a niche in the development plans of the colonial administration" (1990: 49). Few were able to exploit such niches and build up substantial enterprises, and most businesses remained small-scale, as indeed was the case in other parts of colonial Asia.

However limited the development of an indigenous entrepreneurial and managerial class in Korea before 1945, it is arguable that more was achieved there than in most other colonies in Asia, outside India and possibly the Philippines. One would search in vain for successful industrial ventures similar in size to the Kyongsong Textile Company owned and managed by indigenous families in Thailand, British Malaya, or Indonesia before 1942. And as Eckert has pointed out, some indigenous Koreans did own stock in both Korean and Japanese companies (1991: 55). This hardly ever happened in Indonesia, Thailand, or British Malaya. Here the combination of foreign capital and local Chinese and Indian domination made it almost impossible for indigenous entrepreneurs to move beyond small-scale trading and manufacturing. Lack of access to credit was one factor; in addition, very few indigenous Thais, Indonesians, or Malays received the sort of education, either at home, in the colonial motherland, or elsewhere, that gave the Kim brothers the knowledge and confidence to establish new industrial ventures. The small number who did receive such education usually went into the civil service or the military. This tradition was to continue after the advent of political independence.

CHAPTER 7

Changing Living Standards and Human Development

Economic Growth and Living Standards

It is widely recognized by economic historians that trends in per capita GDP are not by themselves reliable guides to changes in living standards. It is indeed possible for economies to grow in per capita terms over a period of years or even decades with very little evidence of an improvement in living standards on the part of the majority of the population, especially those in the lower income groups. There are several reasons for this. First, economic growth often confers much greater benefits on some groups in society compared with others; in particular in the early stages of capitalism, profits are likely to increase more rapidly than wages, and thus there will be a widening gap in income and wealth between those who earn profits and those who earn wages. Second, and related to the first point, it is possible that much of the increase in income accruing to capitalists will not be consumed at all but saved and invested in expansion of productive capacity. In some economies, governments may appropriate a large share of the increase in taxes and invest these revenues in infrastructure and public services, including defense, which may not benefit a large part of the population.

A third reason is that in open economies a large part of the profits accruing to capitalists may be repatriated to other parts of the world; thus a rapid growth in gross domestic product may be accompanied by a sharp increase in surpluses in the balance of payments. This is a key feature of the open dualistic model of Paauw and Fei, among others, and, as argued in Chapter 5, several colonies in Asia did indeed experience sustained export surpluses in the late nineteenth and early twentieth centuries. In addition, a rapid growth in exports could show up as a rapid growth in gross domestic product, measured in constant prices, but if the terms of trade are declining, the impact on domestic consumption and investment expenditures may be much reduced.

Recent work on the impact of economic growth on living standards in Asia has tried to explore these issues. Williamson (1998, 2000) has examined trends in real wages in various parts of Asia and drawn from them conclusions regarding trends in living standards and inequality. His work is reviewed below. But first it will be useful to look at the evidence on several indicators of living standards in various parts of colonial East and Southeast Asia in the early part of the twentieth century, including consumption of food staples, food shares in household budgets, education, and mortality rates. Such evidence is not difficult to assemble because, during the first part of the twentieth century, colonial governments were themselves increasingly concerned with the problem of "native welfare" and indeed were under pressure from various forces, both in the colony and at home, to justify their regimes in terms of broadly based improvements in living standards and purchasing power. Thus official data-gathering exercises became more oriented to compiling evidence on indigenous living standards and how they were changing over time.

Debates and Evidence about Trends in Living Standards in Colonial Asia

In the postcolonial literature, a frequent criticism made of many colonial economic systems in Asia and elsewhere is that the economic growth that occurred did not benefit the great majority of the population. While exports may have boomed and government revenues expanded, nutritional intakes for the mass of the population did not improve, access to health care and secular education was severely limited, and as a result mortality rates were high and many adults were illiterate. Wage labor opportunities were limited, and wage rates were low. In Korea, where criticism of the impact of colonial policies on popular welfare by postcolonial scholars has been especially strong, it has been argued that by the 1930s, "pauperization among Korean farmers was becoming increasingly a pressing problem even for the colonial policy makers" (Chang 1971: 176).

There is considerable evidence to support the critics' case. In spite of some progress in the adoption of new production technologies, rice consumption per capita in Korea fell steadily from 1912 to 1930, forcing the great majority of the population to eat more inferior foods such as millet (Lee 1936: 275). Although there was some improvement in rice availability toward the end of the 1930s, total grain availability per capita was still, in 1937–1941, below the average for 1912–1916 (Johnston 1953: 55). Per capita rice availability in the late 1930s was also below the level of 1915–1919 (Table 7.1). The fall in domestic rice availability in Korea after 1910 has been explained by the increase in the proportion of arable land controlled by large-scale commercial owners, many of them Japanese. Rents were often paid in kind, so that a high percentage of the rice crop passed to landlords and then into the export market (ibid.: 55; Chang 1977: 58–59). By 1938, more than half of all farmers in Korea were tenants who did not own any land (Grajdanzev 1944: 109: Myers and Yamada 1984: 451–452). By the 1940s, even semi-official Japanese publications acknowledged that the majority of Korean farmers formed a "poverty-stricken community" controlling very small plots of land and earning very low incomes (Foreign Affairs Association 1944: 909).

Myers and Yamada have argued that the "dysfunctions" in Korean agriculture (especially regarding access to land) were much greater than in Taiwan, where rural living standards appear to have been higher by the late 1930s than in Korea (1984: 451). Certainly rice availability per capita was higher (see Table 2.6). Ka argues that rural living standards in the 1930s in Taiwan underwent "substantive growth" (1995: 144); he cites the estimates of Mizoguchi on rising real wages (1972: table 3) in both manufacturing and agriculture. Yet Chang's analysis of farm household surveys during the 1930s indicates some decline in rice consumption per capita between 1931 and 1937, although there was a sharp increase in intake of sweet potatoes (Chang 1969: table 14). He explains this switch in terms of movements in relative prices; real per capita expenditures of farm families between 1931 and 1937 increased by around 12 percent.

Several authors have used anthropometric evidence to examine trends in living standards in both Korea and Taiwan during the colonial period. In Korea, Gill found that the Korean population became shorter beginning with the birth cohorts of the late 1920s, and a secular growth in height only began with birth cohorts from the early 1950s (1998: 124–126). He argues that reduced grain consumption explained at least part of the decline in the colonial period. In Taiwan, by contrast, Morgan and Liu (2005) argue that rural food intake and per capita incomes improved from the 1910s to the 1940s, and this in turn led to an increase in male heights. This supports the

Table 7.1. Index of Rice Consumption Per Capita, 1915–1919 to 1935–1939 (1925–1929 = 100)

	Korea	Taiwan	Java	British Malaya
1915–1919	138	98	n.a.	93
1920–1924	123	100	99	91
1925–1929	100	100	100	100
1930–1934	87	88	96	94
1935–1939	125	70	94	99

	Philippines	French Indochina	Burma
1915–1919	87	91	139
1920–1924	99	99	105
1925–1929	100	100	100
1930–1934	84	107	91
1935–1939	80	109	100

Sources: Korea: Chang 1977: 58; Taiwan: Ho 1978: table 6.2; Java: Mears 1961: 248; British Malaya: Grist 1941: table 32; Philippines: Mears et al. 1974: appendix 4.1; French Indochina: Rose 1985: 110; population data from Banens 2000; Burma: Saito and Lee 1999: 80–81; conversion ratios as given in Richter 1976: table 3.

Note: n.a. = not available.

argument made by Ka that living standards did improve in Taiwan during the first decade of the twentieth century; as will be argued below, demographic evidence also confirms this view.

Turning to Southeast Asia, debates about living standards became increasingly prominent in several parts of the region after 1900. In Indonesia, the perception that living standards in Java had been falling during the nineteenth century led to the introduction of the ethical policy, with its emphasis on agricultural improvement, improved rural infrastructure, better access to education, and accelerated migration of poor people in the densely settled inner islands to less densely settled regions of the archipelago. The concern about declining welfare also led to a series of government investigations on indigenous living standards, access to land, tax burdens, and other economic and social issues that continued until the end of the 1930s, culminating in the so-called coolie budget surveys carried out in Batavia and among estate workers in Java. How much impact all this data collection actually had on policy is questionable. Husken has suggested that it was all "too little, and too late" (1994: 222). For budgetary reasons, expenditures on infrastructure and transmigration were cut back from the early 1920s, even before the full impact of the depression of the 1930s was felt in Indonesia. After 1929, expenditures on capital works were cut more severely than those on salaries and other perquisites of the civil service (Booth 1998: 145).

In British Malaya, there was also growing concern about indigenous welfare in the 1920s, although this concern was more clearly articulated by Malay writers than by the colonial establishment. It is perhaps ironic that, although rural Malays in fact enjoyed one of the highest living standards in rural Southeast Asia in the interwar years and certainly higher than in most parts of Indonesia, the small Malay intelligentsia became increasingly obsessed with what they saw as "Malay poverty." In 1923 the Malay writer and translator Zainul Abidin wrote that "the Malays, as a whole, are a particularly poor people. Poverty is their most outstanding characteristic and their greatest handicap in the race of progress. Poor in money, poor in education, poor in intellectual equipment and moral qualities, they cannot be otherwise but left behind in the march of nations" (quoted in Roff 1974: 151). Roff pointed out that this gloomy picture had its counterpart in many other articles appearing at the same time, but the debate showed "a real confusion about underlying causes and ultimate remedies" (1974: 151–152). Much of the discussion was fatalistic in tone, with participants apparently accepting the fact that little could be done to promote the economic advancement of the Malay in an economy where foreigners—European, Indian, and Chinese—were in effective control and dominated most types of nonagricultural employment. It was only in the 1950s, with political independence almost achieved, that a new generation of Malay intellectuals began to ask what government could do to increase the participation of ethnic Malays in the market economy. Aziz (1964) saw the poverty of the rural Malay as being due to governmental neglect in colonial times (he was especially critical of Winstedt's education policies), low agricultural productivity, and exploitation of rural Malays by monopsonistic middlemen. These ideas gained widespread support in the latter part of the 1960s and were very influential in the Second Malaysia Plan (1971–1975).

In other parts of Southeast Asia, debates about rural poverty were, as in Malaya, conducted less at the official level and more within higher education circles and in parts of the press controlled or influenced by indigenous nationalists. Trade unions were suppressed by the British, Dutch, and French authorities; in British Malaya, a wave of strikes in mines and estates in the late 1930s provoked a harsh response, and many hundreds of workers were forcibly repatriated to China (Bayly and Harper 2004: 42). In the Philippines, the freer political climate permitted more open militancy, which led to hundreds of incidents of agrarian unrest in the latter part of the 1930s (Larkin 1993: 218–236). There was mounting evidence that the growth that had occurred during the period of American control had not benefited all parts of the population, although the worst unrest was not in the poorest parts of the country. From 1929 onward, several studies of living conditions among different groups of the population were carried out; probably the most comprehensive was the survey in the Tondo district of Manila in 1933, sponsored by the local chapter of the American Red Cross. Although there was disagreement on what constituted a minimum income, in one estimate 44 percent of families lived below the income threshold necessary for a "decent standard" (Lava 1938: 19).

A study of living standards in the Ilocos region of northern Luzon by Lava found that families of five (three adults and two children) were subsisting on 5,700 calories per day (1938: 24). This was considerably below the calorific intake of prisoners, who also had regular supplies of drinks such as tea, coffee, and ginger root, which the Ilocano peasant regarded as a luxury. Most of the families surveyed ate meat only once or twice a month. More than 62 percent of the average household budget went toward food (Table 7.2). Another study by Runes of living standards among sugar workers found that the food share of household budgets was over 80 percent and that the typical family "spends almost the entire income for food and clothing of the lowest quality and quantity" (1939: 30; see also Larkin 1993: 220–221). Although Lava conceded that "actual stark starvation does not exist in the Philippines except in isolated cases" and that living standards in the Philippines might have been higher than in parts of Japan (1938: 81), both his study and that of Runes caution against any casual assumption that the population of the Philippines shared equally in the fruits of the economic growth that occurred in the American era. Indeed Kurihara quoted several authors who argued that, for many Filipinos, living standards in the late 1930s were little better than in the last phase of Spanish rule (1945: 40).

Other household budget studies carried out in the 1930s in both Vietnam and Java found that the food share of household budgets was high, especially for poorer groups in rural areas. Gourou reported survey results that showed

Table 7.2. Budget Studies in Vietnam, the Philippines, and Java, 1930s

	Percentage of Household Expenditures on	
	Rice	Food
Cochinchina: 1937		
Landless coolies	49	71
Small tenants	43	60
Middle tenants	39	60
Large tenants	29	43
Landowners	22	36
Tonkin delta: 1938		
Poor peasants	c. 55	79
Small proprietors	n.a.	63
Luzon		
Cavite / Tarlac (1929/1930)	n.a.	54
Ilocos (1937)	n.a.	62
Sugar workers (1938)	n.a.	82
Java: Batavia		
Poor coolies	44	61
Better-off coolies	26	52
Java: plantations		
Field workers	n.a.	73
Factory workers	n.a.	73
Senior workers	n.a.	58
Java: Farmers	n.a.	71

Sources: Vietnam: Gourou 1945a: 531–540; Philippines: Lava 1938: 13–21; Runes 1939: 93; Java (Batavia): Central Bureau of Statistics 1939: tables 39–41; Java (plantations): van Niel 1956: 77.
Note: n.a. = not available.

that the majority of the population in rural Cochinchina was spending 60 percent or more of budgets on food (1945a: 531), about the same share Lava reported from Ilocos (see Table 7.2). Poor peasants in Tonkin, who comprised the majority of the rural population, were spending almost 80 percent on food. In Java, the survey of coolie laborers in Batavia carried out in 1938 found that most were spending around 60 percent of the household budget on food, while in rural areas, the proportion among estate laborers varied from 58 to 75 percent. For plantation and factory laborers and the sample of farmers in Java surveyed at the same time, food shares were above 70 percent, which was about the same as for landless coolies in Cochinchina (see Table 7.2)

The comparison of household budgets can be supplemented with data on per capita rice availability, which was a widely used indicator of living standards in a region where rice has always been the preferred food staple (see Table 2.6). In Java, per capita availability of rice was only 85 kilograms by 1937–1939 and in the Philippines 97 kilograms, which was slightly higher than in Korea. This contrasts with around 140 kilograms in Thailand in the 1930s (Manarungsan 1989: 44–45). Gourou states that rice consumption per capita in Tonkin was 400 grams per day, or 146 kilograms per annum, which was about the same as in Thailand; he argues that it would have been rather higher in the south (1945a: 548). Everywhere in East and Southeast Asia, calorie intake was augmented by other foods including corn, cassava, and sweet potatoes; this was especially the case in the Philippines and Java. The time series produced by Mears on rice availability in Java shows some fluctuation between 1921 and 1941 but no discernible upward trend (1961: 248); by the latter part of the 1930s, average per capita availability was still below the 1925–1929 level (see Table 7.1). Nor was there any upward trend in estimates of total calorie supply per capita after 1920 (van der Eng 1993: figure 4).

In the Philippines, the series on rice and corn availability produced by Mears et al. showed increases in both rice and corn availability in per capita terms until the mid-1920s, and then some decline, especially during the 1930s (Table 7.3) (Mears et al. 1974: 355–357). By the latter part of the 1930s, annual per capita availability of both rice and corn was well below that of a decade earlier, although still higher than in 1910–1914. In British Malaya and in Burma, there was a fall in per capita rice availability in the early part of the 1930s, although in both these colonies consumption had recovered to 1925–1929 levels by the late 1930s (see Table 7.1). This would suggest that household budgets did come under pressure in the depression years virtually everywhere in Southeast Asia, although there was some recovery in the later 1930s in parts of the region. The main exception appears to have been Indochina, where per capita availability increased slightly during the 1930s.

Demographic Indicators and Access to Education

In addition to data on food availability and food shares of household budgets, changes in demographic indicators are used by many scholars as a guide to

Table 7.3. Rice and Corn Consumption Per Capita in the Philippines (annual average)

	Rice Consumption (kg.)	Corn Consumption (kg.)
1910–1914	67.3	18.3
1915–1919	100.1	21.7
1920–1924	113.5	22.6
1925–1929	114.9	20.0
1930–1934	96.4	15.4
1935–1939	92.2	17.4

Source: Mears et al. 1974: appendix 4.1.

changes in living standards; they are sometimes more accurate than indicators derived from household income and expenditure surveys. During the 1990s, both monetary and other indicators have been used by United Nations statisticians to compute a composite index of human development (UNDP 2003: 340–342). We do not have longtime series on, for example, infant mortality rates for all parts of East and Southeast Asia from 1900 onward, but we do have some estimates for most countries by the 1930s. It seems clear that infant mortality rates were lower in Taiwan, the Philippines, and British Malaya than in Indonesia, Indochina, and Burma (Table 7.4). The data on crude death rates (which are probably less reliable) tell a similar story. A comparison of life expectancies for Taiwan and Korea in the late 1930s indicates that they were very similar, which suggests that infant mortality in Korea was also about the same as in Taiwan (Chang 1966: table 7.3; Barclay 1954: table 37).

Figures on trends over time are more difficult to assemble. It is clear that infant mortality rates and crude death rates fell in Taiwan during the Japanese period (Barclay 1954: tables 36 and 39). Kimura has argued that there was also a decline in death rates in Korea after 1920 (1993: 643); this is supported by Chang's estimates (1966: 268). In the Philippines, there was also some decline in both indicators over the American period (Zablan 1978: tables 79 and 90). Banens's estimates found a decline in infant mortality rates among the Viet-

Table 7.4. Development Indicators: East and Southeast Asia, Late 1930s

Country	Per Capita GDP, 1938 (1990 international dollars)	Infant Mortality Rates	Crude Death Rates	Educational Enrollments as Percentage of Total Population
Philippines	1,522	139	23	11.5
Korea	1,459	n.a.	23	5.8
British Malaya[a]	1,361	147	21	7.8
Taiwan	1,302	142	21	11.4
Indonesia	1,175	225–250	28	4.0
Thailand	826	n.a.	22	10.7
Burma	749	232	30	5.4
Indochina	n.a.	190	24	2.5

Sources: GDP data: Maddison 2003: 182–183. Educational enrollments: Furnivall 1943: 111, with additional data on Korea from Grajdanzev 1944: 264. Data on infant mortality rates and crude death rates for Indonesia: Nitisastro 1970: 113, table 39, and refer to Java only; Korea: Chang 1966: 268; Philippines: Zablan 1978: 100–105; Taiwan: Barclay 1954: 146, 161; Thailand: Manarungsan 1989: 35; Vietnam: Banens 2000: 36–37; crude death rates refer to Cochinchina; infant mortality rates refer to Hanoi only. Burma: Sundrum 1957: 20, 52. British Malaya: Evans 1939: table 15; crude death rates: Palmore, Chander, and Fernandez 1975: table 4.1.

Note: n.a. = not available.

[a] GDP and crude death rate data refer to the area covered by the modern state of Malaysia and exclude Singapore. Infant mortality rates refer to the Federated Malay States only. Educational enrollments refer to British Malaya including Singapore.

namese population in Hanoi between 1925 and 1938, admittedly from a very high level of over four hundred per thousand (2000: table 7). In the Straits Settlements, there was a steady fall in infant mortality rates between 1914 and 1934, although the decline was much less for Malays than for the other ethnic groups (Manderson 1996: table 2.11).

In all these cases, no doubt, colonial governments would have attributed the declines to better access to modern health facilities and greater professional supervision of deliveries and provision of postnatal care. Especially in urban areas, improved provision of sanitation and clean drinking water would also have been important. But it was not true that infant mortality was always lower in urban areas; estimates for the Philippines in the early 1920s found that they were higher in Manila than in the provinces (Wood 1926: 48). The 1931 census data for British Malaya showed that infant mortality rates in the Federated Malay States were lower than in urban Singapore (Vlieland 1932: 110). These differences would have reflected the greater overcrowding in slum housing in Singapore and Manila compared with the rural areas.

A further set of indicators relate to education. Both literacy and years of schooling are used in the Human Development Index, published annually by the United Nations in their *Human Development Report.* But literacy can be a misleading indicator in the Asian context. In Indonesia, for example, where a question on literacy was included in the 1920 population census, only those who could read in the Roman script were deemed literate, although many thousands had learned to read Malay written in the Arabic script, and newspapers and books appeared in this format. Such people were not considered literate by the colonial statisticians. In the Japanese colonies, literacy was often equated with an ability to read and write Japanese. Comparisons of census and other official data on literacy are thus unreliable, and it is safer to look at the evidence on school enrollments.

Here the differences between colonies were quite stark by the 1930s. In spite of the assertions of authors such as Maddison that the Japanese were more successful in increasing access to education than the other colonial powers (1990: 365), the evidence indicates that neither in Taiwan nor in Korea did the Japanese achieve what the Americans accomplished in the Philippines. By 1940–1941, it was estimated that just over two million students were enrolled in public schools in the Philippines and a further 180,000 in private schools. Of these a remarkable 40,000 were in tertiary institutions, a much larger figure than in Korea, Taiwan, or any European colony (Bureau of Census and Statistics 1960: 21–29). Some of these institutions were Catholic foundations established in the Spanish period, but the government also became more involved in tertiary education during the American era. The University of the Philippines was established early in the American era on the model of the state university systems in America and by the 1930s was enrolling thousands of students across a number of faculties and campuses.

The American achievement was hardly an unqualified success; in spite of the rapid growth in school attendance, many children either did not enter school at all or dropped out before finishing sixth grade (Hunt 1988: 363). Lava found that, among the rural Ilocano families he surveyed, many parents had ambitions of higher education for their children (1938: 53–54). But financial pressures forced the great majority to drop out before completing fourth grade. The Monroe Commission of 1925 (named after Paul Monroe of Columbia Teachers College, who chaired it) found that many classes were badly taught by teachers with little command of English (May 1980: 124). Those who did manage to finish high school had not, on average, reached the same standard as their counterparts in the United States. Nevertheless, compared with other parts of the region, the results at all levels were substantial, and many bright young people from relatively humble backgrounds were able to get a college education and move into professional and administrative occupations.

In Korea by 1943, fewer than 10,000 students were in higher education (both government and private); in the government institutions, around 70 percent of the students were Japanese (Kim 1985: 168). The basic attitude of the Japanese authorities to higher education in Korea was that it was both unnecessary and potentially dangerous in that it would foster nationalist dreams of independence. In Taiwan, the Taihoku Imperial University was established largely for research purposes, and few Taiwanese students were accepted. The ten specialized middle schools, which were located in the cities and in the larger towns, were open to all Japanese boys but only a small number of carefully selected Taiwanese (Kerr 1942: 53; Barclay 1954: 68). In 1931, Japanese students were in the majority in the middle schools and also in the high schools for girls (Wyndham 1933: 154). Some children from wealthy homes in both Taiwan and Korea were sent to Japan for higher education, but they faced considerable discrimination in employment if they returned home.

In both Taiwan and Korea, the government did much more in developing primary education, especially in the 1930s. In Korea, an attempt was made to enroll children in remote rural areas by establishing "short course elementary schools" with a two-year teaching cycle (Foreign Affairs Association 1944: 914). But even with these initiatives, many Korean children had either no education at all or at most very brief schooling in poorly equipped rural facilities. More success was achieved in Taiwan, where by 1943 it was claimed that 70 percent of all children of legal school age were attending some sort of school (Barclay 1954: 68). But even in Taiwan, it was never the intention to achieve parity with Japan in educational standards. Tsurumi claimed that the goal of the Japanese educational system was only to "fashion the lower track of the two-track Meiji education system" (1984: 308).

Apart from the Philippines, educational access in most parts of Southeast Asia was even more restricted than in Korea, especially at the secondary and tertiary levels. Many children in Burma and Thailand learned basic literacy in monastic schools, but beyond that there were few facilities outside the large towns. In Indonesia and Indochina, official policy on education was to limit it to at most a very basic curriculum of short duration, although in Indonesia the Islamic schools also provided some instruction, especially in rural areas. In addition, a system of Chinese schools was established in the early part of the twentieth century that gave Chinese children tuition in Dutch (Suryadinata 1972). In British Malaya, Chinese children also had better access to schools, especially in urban areas, and by the interwar years, a considerable gap had opened up between Malays and other races in access to education and especially education in English.

The comparative data assembled by Furnivall showed that Taiwan and the Philippines were well ahead of most other parts of East and Southeast Asia in terms of the ratio of educational enrollments to total population by the end of the 1930s (see Table 7.3) (1943: 111). At the other end of the scale was Indochina. In British Malaya, the ratio was above that of Korea, although a disproportionate number of students were Chinese and Indian rather than Malay. The "plural society" that had been created by large-scale in-migration from China and India to Malaya, Burma, and Indonesia had led to a skewed access to education by race. Correcting this bias proved to be a major challenge for postindependence governments.

What Do Trends in Wages Tell Us about Living Standards?

In recent years, a number of scholars have constructed long-term series on wages for various parts of the world and used these series to draw conclusions about trends in living standards. In a paper purporting to examine living standards in various parts of Asia before 1940, Williamson has claimed that "living standards of ordinary workers as captured by real wages are a better indicator of the economic well-being of the vast majority in any society" than per capita GDP (2000: 19). While this may be true for some economies, there are several reasons why the use of real wages may produce misleading results regarding trends in living standards in many parts of Asia before 1940 and indeed in more recent times.

First, in most parts of East and Southeast Asia in the early part of the twentieth century, only a small part of the labor force was in full-time wage employment. Even in the 1970s, census data for most parts of the region showed that wage and salary earners were less than a quarter of all employed workers, and the figure would probably have been lower in the early decades of the twentieth century. Only a minority of families would have been deriving all, or even as much as half, of the household income from wages in most parts of Asia. In the more land-abundant parts of the region, most households made their living from cultivation, with some additional income from raising livestock and poultry, and handicrafts. Young males in particular may have taken up wage work if it was available for a few weeks or months, but this would not have composed the main part of the household's income. Even in the more land-scarce regions, it is unlikely that wage earnings made up a large share of household earnings for the majority, although they may have been important for households controlling little or no land. Thus wage trends are by themselves not a good indicator of trends in household incomes.

A second point relates to the way labor markets functioned. Williamson and others who have argued that trends in real wages can be a good proxy for trends in living standards appear to assume that most labor markets in Asia functioned according to the simple supply-demand model, with wages quickly adjusting to changes in either demand or supply. But in fact a number of distortions led to segmentation by region and to considerable nominal wage rigidity, especially in times of economic depression. Although trade unions were weak and minimum wage legislation not widely imposed, there were exceptions, such as the Philippines in the 1930s. Here a minimum wage was introduced for workers in government employment, although it was not universally implemented (Kurihara 1945: 42–43). It is probable that such legislation aggravated the gap between urban and rural wages, which was already significant in earlier decades (Doeppers 1984: 39–41).

A more important problem was that of nominal wage rigidity, which seems to have been a feature of some labor markets in Asia by the early twentieth century. Several authors have pointed out that in labor markets in Java and Vietnam, nominal wages did not decline in the early 1930s as rapidly as prices declined so that the real wage actually increased even though wage employment opportunities were declining. By 1934, when the full impact of the world depression was transmitted to markets in Southeast Asia, real wages in Java, Sumatra, Hanoi, Saigon, and Bangkok were all above 1929 levels (Table 7.5). The data for workers in the Java sugar industry illustrate the problem very clearly; by 1935, numbers employed as factory and field workers had fallen to less than 20 percent of the 1929 level, but average daily wages in 1929 prices for both male and female workers were still well above those prevailing in the late 1920s (Table 7.6).

Several explanations have been suggested for these apparently paradoxical trends. First, as usually happens in periods of business downturns, it is likely that many employers dismissed the most junior and least experienced workers first. Thus the average wage might appear to rise, because those receiving the lowest wages had been dismissed, although those more experienced workers remaining in employment could well have been getting a lower nominal wage (Goudal 1938: 145). Second, employers would have been uncertain as to how long the bad conditions were going to last and thus continued to pay their best workers enough to retain their loyalty because they would be needed again when conditions improved. Third, conditions of work probably deteriorated for many workers who remained in employment; they might have been expected to work longer hours per day and could have lost some fringe benefits (Ingleson 1988: 309). Fourth, for many workers hired on a daily or weekly basis, fewer days or weeks of employment were available, so total earnings on a monthly or annual basis probably dropped sharply. Even if they were lucky enough to keep some wage employment, many millions of workers across the region had lower annual incomes and lower purchasing power, which in turn affected many small enterprises in manufacturing, trade, and transport.

For all these reasons, it would be unwise to interpret apparent increases in real wages as indicative of broad-based improvements in living standards. Williamson argued that living standards in the Philippines doubled under the American occupation because a series on real wages that he compiled showed

Table 7.5. Index of Real Wages: Java, Sumatra, Hanoi, Saigon, and Bangkok, (1925 = 100)

Year	Java (a)	Java (b)	Sumatra	Hanoi	Saigon	Bangkok
1921	98.7	94.7	n.a.	80.9	n.a.	107.1
1922	109.4	108.4	n.a.	95.5	n.a.	121.4
1923	105.7	106.7	n.a.	93.3	n.a.	107.1
1924	99.1	99.4	97.2	94.9	n.a.	114.3
1925	100.0	100.0	100.0	100.0	100.0	100.0
1926	96.3	94.8	105.6	107.7	102.6	92.9
1927	105.0	104.4	116.1	104.6	103.2	100.0
1928	111.6	111.5	126.7	105.9	100.2	100.0
1929	105.5	105.1	118.7	99.0	103.7	100.0
1930	109.9	108.6	121.5	97.0	102.0	121.4
1931	148.5	158.2	167.9	95.6	110.1	164.3
1932	157.1	174.6	195.4	92.0	115.5	171.4
1933	159.8	179.3	218.8	101.7	114.0	192.9
1934	145.7	158.8	229.1	104.6	110.2	200.0
1935	133.3	140.1	231.2	108.5	108.2	157.1
1936	128.7	137.5	247.4	106.4	104.8	157.1
1937	119.7	126.6	227.1	89.0	101.4	142.9
1938	131.8	138.4	222.3	79.2	92.0	150.0
1939	139.2	146.7	n.a.	87.0	95.2	n.a.
1940	140.2	147.7	n.a.	81.5	86.7	n.a.

Sources: Java: *Statistisch Jaaroverzicht van Nederlandsch-Indie* (Batavia: Department of Economic Affairs, annual publication, 1922–1940); deflators from Polak 1943: 80 and Central Bureau of Statistics 1947; 125. Sumatra: Dros 1992: 116; deflators from Polak 1943: 80. Hanoi and Saigon: Giacometti 2000b: 204–205; deflators from Direction des Services Économiques 1947: 301. Bangkok: Ingram 1964: 115.

Note: Java (a) refers to wages of male factory coolies on the Java sugar estates deflated by the price index given in Polak 1943: 80; Java (b) refers to the same wage data deflated by the Java food price index given in Department of Economic Affairs 1947: 125. Data for Sumatra refer to wages of tobacco estate workers excluding supplements, deflated by the Polak index. Data for Hanoi and Saigon refer to wages of unskilled male workers. Bangkok data refer to unskilled rice-mill workers.

n.a. = not available.

Table 7.6. Trends in Total Wage Bill, Numbers of Workers, and Real Wages, Java Sugar Industry, 1921–1940

Year	Total Wage Bill (fl. millions: 1929 prices)	Total Workers (thousands)	Daily Wages (cents: 1929 prices)	
			Male	Female
1921	77	98	41	34
1922	90	101	47	37
1923	90	109	46	36
1924	87	114	43	34
1925	88	115	47	34
1926	86	116	41	32
1927	97	120	45	36
1928	112	129	49	39
1929	102	132	46	37
1930	101	130	48	38
1931	128	119	68	55
1932	109	97	79	62
1933	56	55	84	63
1934	26	29	72	57
1935	17	25	64	52
1936	24	28	60	55
1937	48	54	55	48
1938	54	56	61	52
1939	64	59	64	55
1940	n.a.	62	62	53

Sources: Daily wages of factory coolies: *Statistisch Jaaroverzicht van Nederlandsch-Indie* (Batavia: Department of Economic Affairs, annual publication, 1922–1940). Java food price deflator from Central Bureau of Statistics 1947: 125. Total wage bill from Polak 1943: 46.

Note: n.a. = not available.

that real wages more than doubled between 1895–1899 and 1935–1939 (Williamson 2000: 23, table 1.2). He found that real wages in the Philippines were 80 percent higher than those in Japan in 1920–1924 and more or less the same as in Japan by 1935–1939, although he cautioned that the deflators he used might not be reliable. After 1910, he argued, real wages in the Philippines were higher than in either Korea or Taiwan, or in Thailand and Indonesia. But other data from the Philippines throw some doubt on these assertions.

It was true that wages for laborers in Manila in the late 1930s were high in comparison with most other parts of Asia (see Table 3.11). But this was a market where minimum wage laws would have been applied, albeit weakly, by the late 1930s. The data from Runes' survey shows that wages for sugar workers in rural areas were much lower than the urban unskilled wage and indeed lower than the wage for estate workers in Sumatra (see Table 3.11). As we have already seen, data from the surveys conducted by Runes, Lava, and others indicate that many Filipinos in rural areas were living at a very low level in the late 1930s. While there was an improvement in per capita food availability between 1910–1914 and 1925–1929, by the latter part of the 1930s, rice availability was quite low in comparison with many other parts of the region. This would suggest that living standards were not as high, relative to other parts of the region, as the urban wage data alone might indicate.

Who Did Have the Highest Living Standards?

One obvious conclusion suggests itself from the preceding discussion. It is very unwise to draw conclusions from a single indicator about differences in living standards across countries or regions at a point in time or about trends over time. While there is now widespread agreement that per capita gross domestic product or per capita national income are not always reliable indicators, either for cross-country comparisons or for trends over time, other indicators can also be misleading. This strengthens the case for composite indicators, such as the Human Development Index, although even these do not yield unambiguous results. In the context of East and Southeast Asia, the data in Table 7.4 would suggest that Taiwan and the Philippines enjoyed the highest standards of human development in the latter part of the 1930s, especially if we allow for the probable underestimation of Taiwan's GDP in the Maddison figures. There can be no doubt that these two colonies were well ahead of the others in terms of educational enrollments, although Taiwan was behind the Philippines in the development of tertiary facilities.

Computing a Human Development Index for most countries before 1940 is very difficult, as data are usually lacking for one or more of the components. The attempt by Metzer ranked thirty-six countries in the late 1930s and placed the Philippines at 22, which was above Thailand (at 26) and India (bottom at 36) (1998: 57). No other Asian country was included in Metzer's sample, but the Philippines was ranked above all the Latin American countries except Chile. The Human Development Index can be criticized for ignoring consumption indicators (such as intakes of calories and proteins), for neglecting infrastructure endowments, and for failing to include any indicator of inequality in the distribution of income or assets. As we have seen, rice consumption in the Philippines was relatively low by Asian standards in the late 1930s, although calorie intake was boosted by consumption of corn, as it was boosted by millet in Korea. Taiwan did rather better, at least in part because of Japanese efforts to raise productivity, although the focus of the "agricultural revolution" in colonial Taiwan was very much toward producing more rice and sugar for export to Japan. The highest rice consumption per capita in Asia in the 1930s was in the surplus regions of Thailand and southern Vietnam, although they ranked lower in terms of educational indicators.

The Philippines had a poorer infrastructure endowment than Taiwan by

the 1930s, whether one looks at roads, railways, irrigation, or power generation facilities. Yet infrastructure was highly developed in regions such as Java,
which scored lower in terms of both per capita GDP and indicators such as
infant mortality rates and educational enrollments. Indicators of inequality
are more difficult to compile, as large-scale income and expenditure surveys,
which could be used to estimate income or expenditure inequalities, are not
available. Even data on land distribution are scarce for many parts of the
region before 1940 and often of doubtful accuracy. Williamson has estimated
ratios of real wages to real per capita GDP for a number of Asian economies
in the latter part of the nineteenth and the early twentieth centuries (2000:
table 1.7). He argued that this gives at least a rough guide to trends in factor
shares; if real wages are stagnating while per capita GDP is rising, this suggests
that most of the additional income is accruing to owners of land and capital,
who are assumed to be richer than most wage workers. Thus trends in the ratio
should "approximate changes in the economic distance between the working poor near the bottom of the distribution, and the average citizen in the
middle of the distribution" (ibid.: 35).

Williamson's series tend to show a V-shaped result for most of Southeast Asia; the wage to per capita GDP ratio fell through the latter part of the
nineteenth century and rose again after 1920. He suggested that these trends
could represent an improvement in the incomes of the poor relative to others,
although the estimates seem vulnerable to the same criticisms as those already
made of the real wage series. Unsurprisingly, given the evidence of considerable nominal wage rigidity on the one hand and falling per capita GDP on
the other, the wage per capita GDP ratio rose sharply in the early 1930s in
Indonesia, compared with the previous decade. A similar trend occurred in
Thailand and to a lesser extent in the Philippines. But does this really indicate
that the poor as a group were doing better than the rich in Indonesia in the
early 1930s? Or simply that a small number of privileged workers had enjoyed
an increase in real wages while the great majority were losing what meager
wage-earning opportunities they may have possessed before the crisis hit? The
Java sugar data would suggest the latter was the case.

Williamson also found that the wage to per capita GDP ratio fell in Taiwan
between 1900–1904 and 1915–1919, although it rose thereafter. The Korean
series was shorter but showed the same trend. Perhaps more revealing is the
series on wage/land rental ratios for both Taiwan and Korea, both of which
showed a consistent increase over the early decades of the twentieth century,
almost doubling in both cases (Williamson 2000: table 1.8). This would seem
to cast some doubt on the argument that Japanese landlords consistently
gained relative to native workers in both Japanese colonies, although once
again one must exercise some caution over the wage data. Many wage earners
in both economies, especially outside agriculture, were Japanese, not native
Koreans or Taiwanese. And most of the very poor in Korea and probably in
Taiwan as well were tenant farmers rather than wage workers. This was prob-

ably the case in the Philippines and parts of Vietnam, Indonesia, Thailand, and Burma as well. How they fared relative to both landlords and wage earners during the colonial era is far from clear.

Taken together, the evidence on inequality is too fragmentary to allow any definite conclusions to be drawn, either from Southeast Asia or for Korea and Taiwan. On balance, taking all the available indicators together, it is probably true that Taiwan enjoyed the highest living standards in colonial Asia by the late 1930s, followed by the Philippines. It is quite possible that the majority of the population in both colonies enjoyed living standards that were higher than the poorest decile in Japan. Populations in land-abundant Thailand and Malaya also seem to have enjoyed relatively high living standards; per capita availability of rice was high, death rates were lower than in other parts of the region, and most boys had some access to schooling, even if it was in poorly equipped rural facilities. Living conditions in both countries were probably better for the majority than they were for indigenous Koreans. Life was grimmest for the landless and near landless in the densely settled parts of Tonkin and Java. Here many families faced a constant struggle even to get enough food; decent housing, education, and medical treatment were unattainable luxuries.

Reflecting on the problems of the Tonkinese peasant in 1945, Gourou argued that one remedy was accelerated out-migration, while another was industrialization (1945b: 15–17). But he thought that both these options had limited potential; he also emphasized that there would have to be greater efforts to improve agricultural yields through better irrigation, more use of fertilizers, and improved flood control systems. He also advocated tenure reform, gradual abolition of the great estates, and better rural credit facilities. These were all policy measures that, with the exception of land reform, had been implemented by the Dutch in Java four decades earlier. Their impact on living standards had been, to many Dutch and Indonesians, disappointing. By the 1930s, nationalists in many parts of Southeast Asia had more radical ideas for improving living standards, which involved the end of colonialism and the creation of independent states. Left-wing nationalists envisaged the implementation of sweeping programs of asset redistribution and expropriation of all foreign-controlled enterprises. Debates over these policies were to continue after 1945, sometimes with violent consequences.

CHAPTER 8

The Greater Asian
Co-Prosperity Sphere:
1942–1945

Emergence of the Greater Asian Co-Prosperity Sphere

During the 1930s, both Korea and Taiwan experienced faster economic growth than the Southeast Asian colonies, whose economies were subject to the full force of the world slump of the early 1930s. But even allowing for the growth slowdown in much of Southeast Asia, the evidence does not support the argument that living standards in either Taiwan or Korea were markedly higher than in the Philippines, British Malaya, or even Thailand in the latter part of the 1930s. By then, the economies of both Taiwan and Korea were tightly integrated into the Japanese military-industrial complex, and after Pearl Harbor and the beginning of the Pacific War, this integration intensified. In 1942, Korea ceased to be regarded as a colony and became an integral part of Japan, governed through the Home Ministry (Brudnoy 1970: 189). Northern Korea, like Manchuria, underwent rapid industrial development based on exploitation of its mineral resources and hydroelectric potential, but these changes were "externally induced and served Japanese, not Korean, interests" (Cumings 1997: 175).

In 1936, the Japanese navy had already initiated plans for a "southern advance," which involved, among other initiatives, the seizure of oil fields in Sumatra and Borneo (Tsunoda 1980: 241). The outbreak of the war in Europe in 1939 and the rapid capitulation of both the Netherlands and France to the German army together with what seemed to be the imminent collapse of Britain gave Japan its chance to intensify demands on the European colonial territories in Southeast Asia. Beasley argued that Japanese military planners viewed the advance to the south as part of the broader strategy of national defense (1987: 224), but the economic role allotted to Southeast Asia was quite different from that given to China, Korea, and Manchuria. In Northeast Asia, Japan planned to build an integrated industrial complex; the role of territories in the south was to supply raw materials and also provide a market for Japanese exports.

This role was in fact not very different from what had happened in the 1930s, except that under the new order controlled by Japan, the European and American colonial governments would no longer be in a position to frustrate Japanese demands for greater market access, as they had done during the 1930s. As we have seen in Chapter 5, by the early 1930s, Japanese consumer goods were flooding into markets in Indonesia, British Malaya, Thailand, the Philippines, and Burma. But in the mid-1930s, all the colonial governments had imposed restrictions on Japanese imports and in some cases on exports to Japan as well. Even with these controls, Japan still relied on imports of strategic raw materials such as iron ore, rubber, tin, coal, and above all petroleum from British Malaya, the Philippines, French Indochina, and Indonesia. Indonesia supplied around 25 percent of Japan's oil imports in 1936, making it the second largest supplier after the United States (Beasley 1987: 223). By 1941, the United States no longer appeared a reliable trading partner. It was essential for the Japanese war economy to secure supplies from elsewhere in Asia, preferably from a territory firmly under Japanese control.

The Japanese took advantage of the German occupation of the Netherlands in 1940 to demand guaranteed supplies of oil, bauxite, nickel, and rubber from the government in what was still the Netherlands Indies (Beasley 1987: 228–229). Negotiations dragged on into 1941, but the Dutch were not cooperative, especially on the vital issue of oil supplies. The leader of the Netherlands Indies delegation, van Mook, was given credit for standing up to Japanese demands (Kemperman 2002: 30). But this intransigence strengthened the hawks in Japan who argued that nothing short of military force would suffice to secure supplies of vital raw materials from the south. In Indochina, the pro-Vichy regime was more cooperative with Japanese demands. An economic settlement negotiated in 1941 gave Japan the kind of privileges it had failed to get from the Dutch; supplies of rice, rubber, coal, and other metals were guaranteed, and Japanese manufactures were given unrestricted access to the markets of Indochina. In addition, Japanese citizens were free to establish businesses and undertake mining operations (Beasley 1987: 231). Japan also secured the right to station troops in Indochina and to make use of existing naval bases and airfields (Kemperman 2002: 30–31).

By December 1941, the Japanese government had come to the conclusion that diplomacy would not achieve its aims in Southeast Asia. It was essential to secure direct control over the region and also ensure that no power was in a position to threaten shipping links between Japan and Southeast Asia. The American navy posed the greatest threat, and on December 7, a surprise raid on Pearl Harbor in Hawai'i destroyed most of the American Pacific fleet. This immediately provoked a declaration of war by the United States, Great Britain, and its allies. A strategy document adopted by the Liaison Conference on December 12, 1941, stated clearly that, in the short run, the primary objective of the Japanese in the south must be to "fulfill the demand for resources vital to the prosecution of the present war" (Lebra 1975: 116). A few weeks earlier, the principles for administration of the southern areas had stated that in order to secure vital raw materials, economic hardships would have to be endured by the indigenous populations. The armed forces would have to be locally provisioned, even if that meant depriving indigenous populations of part of their food supplies. The minister of finance went so far as to state that "it will not be possible for us to be concerned with the livelihood of the peoples in these areas" (Lebra 1975: 115; Tarling 2001: 219).

In December 1941 and early 1942, the Japanese armed forces swept down through Hong Kong, the Philippines, Malaya, Burma, Indonesia, the Solomon Islands, New Guinea, and other parts of the southwest Pacific. By the end of April 1942, the colonial regimes had all been forced into humiliating surrenders, and large numbers of prisoners were taken. The Japanese themselves seem to have been surprised by the speed and success of their blitzkrieg and by the abject failure of the colonial powers to put up any effective resistance. By mid-1942, Japanese military and economic control stretched from the southwest Pacific to the eastern borders of British India and from Manchuria to the Indonesian archipelago. Northern Australia was under threat. The power of imperial Japan seemed unstoppable. But the Japanese administrative machinery was ill prepared to deal with the problems of governing the vast areas that their armed forces had conquered in Southeast Asia.

To many indigenous people in Southeast Asia, the Japanese army appeared to be liberators rather than occupiers. In Indonesia, nationalists formed "freedom committees" in many towns in Java and Sumatra and offered their assistance to the Japanese armed forces in maintaining law and order (Kemperman 2002: 42). The Chinese were more fearful, mindful of the atrocities that had already taken place in China. The worst fears of the Chinese population in Singapore were soon realized when, in February 1942, thousands of young men were rounded up and executed on suspicion of being sympathetic to the Chinese Nationalist Party (KMT) or to the communists. It was estimated after the war that between 50,000 and 100,000 were executed during the so-called *sook ching* (Lee 1998: 58).

The policy of the Japanese army, which was in control in the densely settled parts of Southeast Asia, was to govern through local leaders where possible. The Japanese redrew the colonial boundaries and established new regions of control; Sumatra, the Federated Malay States, Johore, and the Straits Settlements were all governed from Singapore. The northern Malay states were handed back to the Thai government, whose leadership was pro-Japanese. Thailand and French Indochina, by then controlled by a pro-Vichy group of officers, were placed in "Area B" and given greater administrative autonomy. Elsewhere, cooperating native officials were selected to run local government and essential services. In the Philippines, a largely compliant native bureaucracy, already in place, continued with most of its routine administrative tasks (Goodman 1988: 101). In many parts of Indonesia, low-ranking Indonesian officials were promoted into senior posts after their Dutch bosses left or were imprisoned.

Benda has pointed out that the aim of the Japanese occupiers was "to erase Western legacies" and impose a new system of values on all the former colonies and a new orientation, cultural as well as economic, toward Japan (1967: 69–71). The over-arching goals of the Greater East Asian Co-Prosperity Sphere were economic autarchy and tight political control from Japan. The policies already imposed on Taiwan and Korea, and on Manchuria were to be extended to Southeast Asia, the South Pacific, and eventually to India, Australia, and New Zealand. The goal of the Japanese government was to create "an economic and strategic organism centered on Japan with each part having a defined place and function" (Swan 1996: 145). Although lip service was paid to national liberation and to preserving the "honor of Thailand as an independent state," the Japanese regimes in Southeast Asia were hardly anticolonial. Rather, the government wished to replace European and American colonialism with a much more tightly regulated version that served the strategic aims of imperial Japan.

On the cultural front, few in Southeast Asia understood the Japanese language, so one important consequence of the new policies was a much greater emphasis on indigenous languages. Dutch and English were officially forbidden, although used in practice for some government programs. Burmese, Malay, and Tagalog were all given official status in education and government. The Japanese deliberately encouraged the formation of youth groups; school and college students were organized into a number of different associations, some of which were in effect paramilitary combat forces. As Mortimer put it in the context of Indonesia, "the Japanese for the first time provided Indonesian youth with a political role and an organizational identity" (1974: 31–32). The members of Japanese-sponsored groups were not always uncritical admirers of their sponsors, but they imbibed the same fierce nationalism the Japanese themselves exhibited, albeit directed to their own situations. It was these groups that constituted the "potentially most revolutionary legacy that Japanese rule was to bequeath to the de-colonization process in many parts of Southeast Asia" (Benda 1967: 780).

The Economic Consequences of Japanese Control: Falling Production and Rising Prices

If the immediate goals of Japanese economic policies in Southeast Asia were to secure supplies of key raw materials and to use local markets as outlets for their own manufactures, it rapidly became clear that neither aim would be easily achieved. The American navy recovered far more quickly from the devastation of Pearl Harbor than the Japanese had expected. From early 1942, the entire American economy was placed on a war footing, and the building of new warships and fighter planes was accorded top priority. In mid-1942, the Americans inflicted a heavy defeat on the Japanese navy at the Battle of Midway, viewed by most historians as the key turning point in the Pacific arena. From then on, American and Allied forces fought their way from island to island; once strategic islands were liberated, they could be used as air and naval bases to support the next stage of the war.

Johnston argued that the Japanese government had been, from the beginning of the Pacific War, too optimistic about the country's shipping capacity, and destruction of merchant shipping by Allied forces was far greater than the war planners had allowed for (1953: 140–141). Between December 1941 and mid-1943, over one million tons of shipping was lost; this figure more than doubled in 1943–1944, and in 1944–1945 it was estimated that over 3 million tons were destroyed, the majority by American submarines. By mid-1944, the Allies were within bombing range of the Japanese mainland, and shipping services within Japan and between Japan and Taiwan, Korea, and Manchuria were badly disrupted. Supplies of rice and other foods from Taiwan and Korea fell sharply, and the food situation in Japan itself became grave.

But before Japanese shipping losses had removed any possibility of effectively integrating Southeast Asia into the Co-Prosperity Sphere based on Japan, the occupying forces made it clear that the economies throughout the region would have to be drastically restructured. The Japanese had little interest in encouraging the production of traditional export staples such as sugar, coffee, tea, and spices. Japan was already supplied with sugar from Taiwan, and precious shipping space could not be wasted on transporting luxury foodstuffs that the metropolitan economy did not need. In both Java and the Philippines, sugar factories, on the one hand, were either closed or converted (almost always unsuccessfully) into plants that produced alcohol from molasses, which could then be used for fuel (Larkin 1993: 237; de Jong 2002: 254). On the other hand, the Japanese armed forces in Indonesia did establish or expand factories for the production of explosives and other military supplies as well as cement, medicines, shipping parts, and textiles (Siaahan 1996: 115). Such factories were probably constructed in other parts of Southeast Asia as well.

Throughout Southeast Asia, Japanese officials insisted that large tracts of agricultural land be switched to growing crops that were in short supply in the region or in Japan. Of particular concern was the shortage of food, vegetable oils, and fibers such as cotton and jute. In Java, some land used for sugar cultivation reverted to food crops, and some to cotton. Tea and coffee estates were either neglected or used for food-crop cultivation; it was estimated that, by 1945, over half the tea plantations on Java and 28 percent of the coffee gardens had been dug up (de Jong 2002: 253). In South Vietnam, rubber estates were switched to cotton cultivation, although most land under rice in the south was not converted to other crops. In Tonkin, however, the Japanese insisted that agricultural land under rice and maize be used for cultivation of jute, cotton, and hemp, as well as peanuts and castor oil plants (Dung 1995: table 1; Anh 1998: table 9.4). This enforced conversion of food-crop land was to have grave consequences for food supplies in the final stages of the war.

Rubber was needed by Japanese industry, but as transport became more difficult, some rubber plantations in Sumatra and Java were dug up and converted to other uses. Instructions on land use were often countermanded when new priorities emerged or simply because of bureaucratic bungling. In Malaya, the military authorities announced in 1942 that rubber acreage was to be reduced in favor of food crops but reversed this ruling in the following year. By 1943, production was less than one-quarter of the average for 1935–1941, and there was only a modest recovery the following year (Kratoska 1998: 227). Tin output also fell sharply in both Malaya and Indonesia. Petroleum output, which was crucial to the Japanese war machine, also declined. The departing Dutch had inflicted considerable damage on the Indonesian installations in early 1942, and output in 1942 was less than half that of 1938. Japanese engineers were successful in repairing the damage, and in 1943 output was 90 percent of the 1938 level. De Jong estimated that between April 1942 and March 1943 around 40 percent of oil production reached Japan (2002: 236). The proportion fell the following year, as shipping became scarcer. Output fell rapidly in 1944 and 1945 (Hunter 1966: 257). In 1945, the Sumatran installations were subject to heavy Allied bombardment, but by then the transport of oil to Japan, and even within Southeast Asia, had become virtually impossible.

But it was food supplies even more than strategic raw materials that preoccupied the Japanese from 1942 onward. By the 1930s, Indonesia, the Philippines, and British Malaya were all net importers of rice. British Malaya depended on imports for around 60 percent of domestic consumption during the 1930s (Grist 1941: table 32). The estate regions of eastern Sumatra were also very dependent on imports, as were large parts of the Philippines and northern and central Vietnam. After 1942, there was a sizable Japanese military population to feed and also growing numbers of Southeast Asian workers who had been forcibly conscripted into various public works projects and had to be supplied with food and other basic necessities. Furthermore, all this had to be done in the context of disintegrating transport facilities. Shipping even in coastal waters was becoming vulnerable to Allied air attacks, and road transport was made more difficult because of gasoline shortages and lack of spare parts for lorries. It is far from clear whether the Japanese administrators realized the extent of the integration of regional rice markets within Southeast Asia before 1942, but even if they had done so, there was little they could do to preserve the prewar trading networks as hostilities continued. All they could do was encourage regional self-sufficiency in food and other basic needs.

It had been expected by wartime planners that Japan would supply a range of consumer goods, including textiles, clothing, household utensils, bicycles, and so forth, to Southeast Asia, as indeed it had done in the 1930s. But as the Japanese economy moved to a total war footing, production of "nonessential" goods was curtailed, and there was little to spare for export (Pluvier 1974: 274). The Japanese shipped a large number of idle spindles to various parts of Southeast Asia, and it was expected that the cotton and other fibers produced locally would be used to produce yarn and cloth, gunny bags, and other products (Kratoska 1998: 195). The success of this policy was modest, and the shortage of textiles grew more acute through 1944 and 1945. Many people resorted to old rice sacks or even tree bark to make clothing. Women in particular displayed great ingenuity in producing a range of household products, including textiles, soap, vegetable oils, and mats, both for their own use and for sale or barter.

The increasing shortages inevitably led to smuggling and black marketeering. Officially such activities were strongly discouraged, and penalties were severe. In practice, lower-ranking Japanese soldiers took bribes in order to turn a blind eye or became actively involved themselves (Kratoska 1998: 171; de Jong 2002: 470–472). The shortages of food and other basic needs added to inflationary pressures, which were fueled by the increased supply of currency under the Japanese. The Singapore cost of living index, which stood at 100 in December 1941, had reached 10,980 in May 1945 (Kratoska 1998: 203), and by late 1944, prices were also spiraling out of control in Indonesia, the Philippines, Vietnam, and Burma. In Manila, the open market price of rice (per sack) was between eight and twelve pesos in early 1942. By December 1944, it had reached 11,000 pesos (Jose 1998: table 4.6). In Hanoi, the cost of living index for workers increased more than fivefold between 1940 and 1944, and increased almost four times more in the first nine months of 1945 (Direction des Services Économiques 1947: 301). These massive increases in prices were to lead to enormous suffering for many millions in the closing phase of the Pacific War.

While shortages contributed to the accelerating inflation, the fundamental reason was the rapid growth in money supply engineered by the Japanese authorities. Throughout the Japanese occupation of Southeast Asia, the Japanese continued to issue their own "scrip" or campaign money. Although the stated intention of the Japanese government was to use local currency as much as possible in the occupied areas, it was conceded that existing stocks of coin and banknotes would have to be supplemented with Japanese scrip in order to obtain essential war materials (Lebra 1975: 115). As Swan has pointed out, it was not the law that gave military scrip its legitimacy "but rather the ability of the military to maintain its authority over a territory and the large amount of business transacted between the military and the local population" (1989: 315). As more and more Japanese money, denominated in local currencies, flooded the Southeast Asian economies (often with no serial numbers so that it was easy to forge), many people hoarded the old colonial money, which by 1945 could often be exchanged for more than twice as much Japanese scrip with the same face value.

In April 1942, a Southern Region Development Treasury was established in order to exercise some control over the release of scrip into the economies of Southeast Asia. But it lacked the power to veto the military, who continued to issue paper money in order to secure resources. In Indonesia, it was estimated that, by the end of the occupation, the amount of paper money in circulation had increased almost sevenfold compared with March 1942 (de Jong 2002: 235). In British Malaya, the Japanese used various methods to reduce the money in circulation, including enforced "gifts" from wealthy Chinese and lotteries. But these ploys were rendered ineffective by the continued printing of more banknotes by the Japanese until the final months of the war (Kratoska 1998: 213). Only in Thailand, where economic relations with Japan were conducted on a government-to-government basis, did the administration manage to keep some control over economic policy and currency issues (Swan 1989: 346).

The Welfare Consequences of Japanese Control: Forced Labor, Starvation, and Premature Death

As is always the case, the impact of rapid inflation was especially severe on those with fixed money incomes and little or no ability to earn extra, either in cash or in kind. The plight of many pensioners was exacerbated by the refusal of the Japanese to honor colonial pension payments; many retired civil servants found they had nothing to live on. By 1945, poverty was so widespread in Malaya that the charitable institutions could not cope (Kratoska 1998: 205). The Japanese were alarmed at the increasing number of vagrants and destitute people, but there was little they could do. If the situation was bad in Malaya, which had been comparatively affluent in the interwar years, it was much worse in other parts of the region. In Java, many small farmers were forced to sell whatever meager amounts of land they owned, and it was these people who were vulnerable to the inflation and shortages of the final phase of the Japanese occupation (Sato 1994: 230).

The plight of those forced to survive on fixed incomes in a time of growing inflation or to sell their assets, although severe, was probably not as bad as that of the conscripted workers. The exact number of those forced to work on Japanese construction projects *(romusha)* has almost certainly been underestimated by many historians, who have tended to count only those who were forced to move from one part of Southeast Asia to another. In the Indonesian context, Sato has pointed out that labor mobilization to repair damaged infrastructure was initiated by the Japanese in 1942 as a way of alleviating unemployment, especially among those who were no longer needed as workers on sugar, tea, and coffee estates (1994: 156–157). But as the Pacific War went badly for the Japanese, the military began to plan a massive defense buildup in the occupied areas. Sato quotes Japanese estimates that, by November 1944, 2.62 million workers had been conscripted to work on a range of projects, including many that were intended to increase agricultural production.

De Jong has put forward a higher figure of 4.1 million for the entire occupation period (2002: 243). Only a small proportion of these would have been sent overseas; most stayed on the island where they had been recruited and often worked only for brief periods. The majority were in Java. Some volunteered in order to earn a wage and receive food. Workers were supposed to get a daily ration of rice of four hundred grams if they were judged to be involved in hard labor, which was probably more than many other Javanese were getting by 1944 and was indeed the same as the household ration given to Japanese males engaged in heavy work (Johnston 1953: 203). But conditions of work were often harsh, and the daily ration actually received may well have been much less than the mandated minimum. Mortality was certainly higher among laborers sent to other parts of Indonesia far from home who received little or no support from local populations.

Mortality was highest for those hapless workers sent out of their own countries to work on projects often thousands of miles from home. Most attention has been concentrated on those who were sent to the notorious "death railway" that was built from Thailand into Burma. Nakahara quotes figures from Allied sources indicating that around 182,500 workers from Southeast Asia worked on this project, in addition to the Allied prisoners of war, mainly from Britain and Australia (1999: 233). Around 73,500 workers from Malaya were transported to the Thai-Burma and Kra railway projects; at least 30 percent died (Kratoska 1998: 184; Bayly and Harper 2004: 405–409). Many of the rest were from Burma, where death rates were also high. In addition, forced labor was used for projects within Malaya. In spite of mounting unemployment and the harsh economic climate, the Japanese in Malaya found few takers for employment even on local public works projects; by early 1945, the majority of the rural labor force was engaged in growing their own food (Kratoska 1998: 186–189).

Conscription and enforced migration were also widespread in Korea, where many rural people were either dragooned into factories as unskilled workers or sent abroad. By 1944, it was estimated that 11.6 percent of the population was residing abroad; the percentage of adults would have been much higher (Cumings 1997: 175). Most of these workers came from rural areas in the south, where high population growth and increasing concentration of landownership was producing a large surplus of labor, which could not be absorbed in agriculture. Large numbers of women from Korea and other occupied territories were forced to become "comfort workers" in military brothels (Hicks 1995). In Taiwan, there was far less movement of labor; there was also less emphasis on heavy industrialization than in Korea, and while indigenous Taiwanese did serve in the Japanese army, numbers were smaller than in Korea.

By 1944, the food situation had become very precarious in many parts of East and Southeast Asia, and hunger was widespread. In Malaya, rice availability fell sharply, but in a relatively land-abundant region it was at least possible to grow other foods; tapioca became an important staple even for the more affluent families (Bayly and Harper 2004: 327–330). Root crops were also widely consumed in Indonesia and the Philippines, but it is probable that their availability did not prevent many premature deaths from hunger and malnutrition. In Java, Japanese procurements amounted to nearly 1.5 million tons in 1943, which was 17 percent of prewar production. This amount fell only slightly in 1944, when a severe drought curtailed production of both rice and other food staples (Sato 1994: 122–123). It was estimated that death rates increased by more than 20 percent in many parts of Java between 1939 and 1944; in some areas in Central and East Java they almost doubled (de Vries 1946; see also Kurosawa-Inomata 1997: 126). Nitisastro cast doubt on the reliability of these estimates, which he considered to be of "only very limited value" but agreed that mortality rates in Java and to a lesser extent other parts of Indonesia increased between 1944 and 1946 (1970: 119). De Jong has cited several eye-witness accounts of starvation in Bandung and Semarang that are similar to those from the contemporaneous Bengal famine (2002: 279–280). Apart from the serious decline in food availability, the drastic decline in medical supplies would also have led to increased death rates.

By 1944, a very severe food situation also prevailed in northern Vietnam. In that year, drought and insects reduced the spring rice crop, and typhoons damaged the main autumn crop (Marr 1995: 96–99). In addition, almost 170,000 hectares of food-crop land had been converted to production of jute, cotton, hemp, and vegetable oils. Dung has quoted estimates that these lands could have yielded 64,000 tons of paddy as well as tens of thousands of tons of maize and sweet potatoes (1995: 592). Both French and Japanese officials were aware of the food supply problem but were slow to act. Northern Vietnam usually depended on food imports from southern Vietnam, and while these were greatly reduced because of Allied air raids on both coastal shipping and overland transport, French and Japanese officials did manage to stockpile rice from the south for their own use. Many landlords and larger farmers also began to stockpile rice in anticipation of further rises in prices. By early 1945, a major famine had taken hold; prices of both rice and other foods including corn and root crops increased far more rapidly than money wages, and many employees in jobs that did not include food rations found themselves starving. Poorer rural families were also in a terrible position. Deaths reached their peak in March–May 1945 and continued up to the Japanese surrender.

The famine in Vietnam is thought to have killed between 600,000 and 2 million people (Pluvier 1974: 280–281). The figure of 2 million was widely used in propaganda by the communist forces after 1945, although Marr has argued that the true figure was lower, probably around the 1 million mark (1995: 104). Dung has suggested that this is too low (1995: 576). A figure of at least 1.5 million is probably more realistic. In Java, de Vries estimated that the years 1943–1945 cost 2.45 million lives, including the deaths of the forced laborers who died outside Java. This figure might also be too high, but it is likely that there were at least two million premature deaths in all Indonesia. American and Philippine authorities estimated that the full death toll during the Japanese occupation was 1.1 million people. Of these, 131,000 had been murdered or tortured to death by the Japanese (Pluvier 1974: 358). If it is assumed that excess deaths in British Malaya, Thailand, and Burma amounted to at least 1 million, then the years of the Japanese occupation led to the premature deaths of more than 5 million people in Southeast Asia. These figures are only rough estimates, and the true figure could have been much higher. What is certain is that the cost of the Japanese occupation, both in lives and in physical destruction, was extremely high.

August 1945 saw the dropping of two devastating nuclear bombs on Japanese cities. The subsequent loss of life and destruction of property finally forced the Japanese government into the humiliation of an unconditional surrender. But in spite of the hardships of the occupation, the Allied troops who returned to Southeast Asia were not greeted as liberators by local populations. Even among those who had not supported the nationalist movements before 1942, the returning armies were seen as simply attempting to restore the colonial status quo of the pre-1942 era. There was little confidence that, if the old colonial governments were reinstated, they would govern Southeast Asia in the interests of the indigenous populations. Many millions, especially the young, wanted a new political and economic order in which Southeast Asians would have much greater power to determine their own destinies. The returning colonial regimes reacted to these demands in very different ways.

The Transition to Independence in Southeast Asia, Korea, and Taiwan

The Allied armies that returned to Burma, Malaya, Indonesia, Indochina, and the Philippines in 1945 found not just mass poverty and starvation, but also considerable economic devastation. The extent of the destruction of infrastructure, factories, and mines varied considerably by region. In Burma, where the retreating British had carried out a scorched earth policy in 1942 and Allied forces had bombed cities and other installations during the reconquest, the economic devastation was long-lasting "and was to impoverish more than one generation" (Bayly and Harper 2004: 180). In the Philippines, the Japanese armed forces put up a savage resistance to the returning American forces led by General MacArthur. Fighting in Manila was especially fierce, and the Japanese, realizing that they were encircled, embarked on a series of atrocities against the civilian population reminiscent of the pillage of Nanking in 1937 (Karnow 1989: 320–321). When the Japanese were finally subdued, much of the city was reduced to rubble.

The Americans had granted the Philippines home rule with the inauguration of the commonwealth in November 1935. It was expected that full independence would follow within ten years. But many observers, after witnessing the devastation brought about by the war and by the American recapture of the islands, doubted that the country could cope with the enormous challenges, both political and economic, that full independence would bring. The American high commissioner, Paul McNutt, was known to be opposed to rapid granting of independence, although some Philippine politicians thought that if the chance was not seized promptly, the Americans might refuse to honor their pledge in the future (Karnow 1989: 334). This argument won the day, and full independence arrived on July 4, 1946. But it was clear that the new republic would have to continue to depend on American economic assistance for reconstruction and also in dealing with internal rebellions, especially in parts of Luzon.

The situation in Indonesia was very different. Key nationalist leaders, such as Sukarno and Hatta, had been released from prison by the Japanese and had cooperated with them in setting up youth groups that, although officially pro-Japan, were in fact fronts for nationalist movements whose aim was full political independence. When Japan surrendered unconditionally in August 1945, there were few Allied troops on Indonesian soil. The older generation of nationalists was uncertain how to act in the political hiatus that followed; their minds were made up for them by youth groups who pressed for an immediate declaration of independence. On August 17, two days after the Japanese surrender, Sukarno stood outside his house in Jakarta and read the Indonesian declaration of independence to a small group of onlookers (Ricklefs 1993: 210).

British forces, most of them Indian, arrived in the latter part of September 1945 and saw their main task as disarming and repatriating the Japanese military before handing back power to the Dutch. By early 1946, it was clear that the Dutch had little interest in negotiating anything but very limited self-government for some parts of the country. Many in the Netherlands, newly liberated after almost five years of German occupation, saw no reason why the Dutch should not continue to govern Indonesia much as they had done before 1942. The nationalist movement was itself split on how to deal with Dutch intransigence. Outside Java some traditional leaders sided openly with the returning Dutch, fearful of their privileges in an Indonesian republic. The scene was set for a bitter and destructive war of attrition between Dutch and republican forces, which was only finally resolved at the end of 1949.

The situation in British Malaya was different again. Even before 1942, it was clear to at least some in Whitehall and in the British business community that the "administrative hotch potch of British territories in Malaya" would at some stage have to be reformed. The Japanese occupation was seen as a chance to work out a new system of governance that would better serve the interests of all the races in the peninsula (Stockwell 1974: 333–335). The new plan that emerged from a Colonial Office planning unit was for a Malayan Union, embracing both the federated and the unfederated states as well as Singapore, Malacca, and Penang. The most radical aspects of the plan involved stripping the Malay sultans of much of their power and granting full citizenship and other constitutional rights to the Chinese and the Indians. The British, on returning to Malaya, tried to implement the plan but ran into fierce opposition, mainly from the Malays and also from elements within the British expatriate business and planter community. It was subsequently argued that, in failing to implement the plan, the British lost an opportunity to create a genuinely multiracial state in Malaya (Stockwell 1984: 69). While a federal constitution was promulgated in 1948, it left the Malays with several important political privileges; the Attlee government made a broad commitment to Malay independence but set no date, even for limited self-government.

There were several reasons why, in contrast to the situation in Indonesia, the Philippines, or Burma, the British both wanted and could afford to stall in Malaya. First, no strong independence movement had emerged during the war that commanded the allegiance of all ethnic groups. The communist-led insurgency, which became known as the "emergency," was led by Chinese but was not supported by the Chinese business community or by the great majority of Malays. Second, at least some British officials, notably the governor-general in Southeast Asia, Malcolm MacDonald, were sympathetic to "moderate" Asian nationalists and anxious to avoid any impression that the British were ganging up with the Dutch and the French to stifle all expressions of Asian nationalism (Stockwell 1984: 74–76). And third, the British realized that, unlike India and Burma, Malaya could play a crucial role in earning dollars for what was then called the sterling area. Export production recovered quickly from wartime problems, and by 1952, export earnings per capita in Malaya were among the highest in the world (Woytinsky and Woytinsky 1955: 63). As Smith has pointed out, the British could afford to let Burma go along with India; in terms of the harsh economic realities of the post-1945 world, it had little value to Britain (1988: 48). But Malaya certainly did. Indeed, Britain's slow decolonization of Malaya has been viewed as "inexplicable without reference to its dollar-earning capacity" (White 2000: 560).

The result was that Burma, devastated by war and plagued by unrest among ethnic minorities, gained independence in October 1947. Aung San, the only leader able to command broad support among the population, had already been assassinated by political rivals, and the new nation was vulnerable to attack both from within and from without. In Malaya, the British adopted a policy of slow progress toward self-government that ultimately paid off; self-government was granted in Malaya in 1957, while two years later, after a sweeping victory in elections, the People's Action Party gained power in Singapore. In 1963, the British granted full independence to the Federation of Malaysia, which included all the British territories in both peninsular Malaya and Borneo, except Brunei. Although Singapore left the federation two years later, federal Malaysia has survived and prospered.

The most prolonged and violent transition to independence was in French Indochina. The French, like the Dutch in Indonesia, were antagonistic to the nationalist leaders who had emerged during the Japanese occupation. The Dutch reluctance to grant independence or even a measure of autonomy to the nationalists was mainly based on the fear that the loss of Indonesia would spell the ruination of the already war-damaged Dutch economy. French reluctance to compromise on sovereignty in Indochina was due more to concerns that any attempt to negotiate with the nationalists there would set a dangerous precedent regarding French territories in North Africa and elsewhere in Africa and the Pacific. Ho Chi Minh pointed out in 1947 that if the French were prepared to do what Britain had done in India or the United States in the Philippines, there was no reason why the relationship with France should not be friendly and cooperative. But many French politicians and military officers were staunch imperialists who could not contemplate any concession to nationalist forces. In addition, by the end of the 1940s, they had gained more support from the United States, now fearful of the spread of communism in Asia.

The American position by the latter part of the 1940s was changing from one of broad anticolonialism and sympathy for Asian independence struggles to a more bellicose anticommunism. National liberation struggles were supported if they were clearly anticommunist but not if they were led by people with communist or left-wing links. It was the effective suppression of the communist uprising in Madiun in East Java by nationalist forces in 1948 that tilted American support toward Sukarno and his government in Indonesia and away from the Dutch (Ricklefs 1993: 230). The French, by contrast, exploited growing American fears about the spread of communism in Asia, especially after the communist triumph in China, by stressing the communist sympathies of the Viet Minh leadership. Thus the United States supported the French creation of a unified state of Vietnam within the French Union with Bao Dai as head of state, in spite of his obvious lack of support among the Vietnamese people. By convincing the United States that their military struggle against the Viet Minh was part of a broader Asian anticommunist struggle, the French gained crucial American military aid (Pluvier 1974: 446–451). Even after their military defeat in 1954, the French were able to prevent the emergence of a unified Vietnam at the Geneva Conference of 1954. It was only in 1975, after another two decades of savage and destructive fighting, that a unified Vietnamese state finally emerged.

Independence in Korea and Taiwan came far more precipitately than in Southeast Asia. The era of Japanese colonialism came to an abrupt end with the surrender of Japan in August 1945. An agreement that Soviet and American troops would both occupy Korea was reached at the Yalta conference; subsequently the Americans and the Russians decided to divide the country into two jurisdictions along the thirty-eighth parallel (Cumings 1997: 186–192). Taiwan, under the terms of the Cairo declaration of December 1943, was handed back to the KMT government on the mainland. Although the Taiwanese were not consulted about this, there is evidence that many on the island at first greeted the decision with euphoria (Lai, Myers, and Wei 1991: 47–48). Even Taiwanese who had benefited from and cooperated with the Japanese regime, to the extent of adopting Japanese names and speaking the Japanese language, felt some relief that they were again joining the mainland, which was the home of their remote ancestors and the source of their culture. But their enthusiasm rapidly turned to bitter disillusion with tragic consequences.

There are several parallels between the situation in both Taiwan and Korea in 1945 and that in the Southeast Asian colonies three years earlier. Just as the Dutch, the British, and the French all lost face as a result of their craven capitulation to or cooperation with the Japanese in 1942, so did the defeated Japanese rapidly lose whatever respect they had hitherto been given by the populations in their erstwhile colonies. The economic consequences of the rupture with Japan for both Taiwan and Korea was even more devastating than the consequences of the break with Europe and the United States had been for the Southeast Asian colonies. Almost all their trade had been conducted with Japan or with its other colonies, and during the 1930s, their economies were developed to serve the needs of the Japanese war machine. Suddenly all these links were severed, Japan itself was an economic ruin, and the two former colonies faced an uncertain economic and political future.

In Taiwan, the KMT government was ill-prepared to tackle the challenge of integrating the island back into the mainland administrative and economic system, which was itself in a chaotic state by 1945. The impact of the Pacific War on the Taiwan economy had begun to be felt by 1943, with farm labor in short supply, irrigation systems neglected, and fertilizer shipments from Japan disrupted (Hsing 1971: 149). Taiwan suffered considerable damage from Allied bombings in early 1945 that destroyed ports, railways, and industrial complexes (Lai, Myers, and Wei 1991: 80–81). Large numbers of people who had worked for the Japanese as officials or members of the police and local militias were unemployed. Taiwan had been dependent on Japan not just for chemical fertilizers, but also for textile materials and machinery; supplies of all these dwindled to nothing by late 1945. One result was a sharp decline in rice output and output of other agricultural staples.

It was estimated that in August 1945, when Taiwan was formally retroceded to China, around three-quarters of the industrial capacity on the island and two-thirds of the power-generating capacity had been destroyed. At least half the railway rolling stock, track, and stations were also out of action (Hsing 1971: 149). In Taiwan as in the Southeast Asian territories under Japanese control, the issue of banknotes expanded rapidly through 1944 and into 1945, with an inevitable acceleration in inflation. Rising prices and shortages of food led to hoarding on the part of many producers. Those on wage incomes in urban areas and many small farmers in rural areas were, like their counterparts to the south, in a desperate situation. The unstable economic situation precipitated unrest, which exploded in antigovernment riots in 1947. These were suppressed with considerable loss of life; the bad relations between Taiwanese and mainlanders persisted after the KMT government was evicted from the mainland in 1949 and moved to Taiwan. Economic instability persisted into 1950; by February of that year, the Taipei wholesale price index had reached 554, compared with 100 in the first half of 1937, and the difference between the official and the market rate of exchange continued to widen (Lin 1973: 34).

The situation on the Korean peninsula over the war years was little better. Ban has estimated that agricultural output in South Korea, which had grown almost 3 percent per annum through the 1930s, fell almost 3.5 percent per annum between 1939 and 1945 (1979: 93). The main reason appears to have been the sharp decline in use of purchased inputs; in 1945, the value of inputs, including fertilizers, other chemical inputs, seeds, and tools, had fallen to less than half their value (in constant 1965 prices) of 1938 (ibid.: table K-4b). Conscription of rural labor, especially from the south, probably also contributed to the output declines. But in spite of output declines, Korean shipments of rice to the Japanese mainland continued until 1945, although in that year they were much reduced, mainly as a result of transport problems. After 1945, both land and labor productivities in South Korean agriculture experienced sustained growth.

CHAPTER 9

The Transition to Independent States

Growth and Structural Change after 1945

Few observers surveying the economic plight of the former colonies of East and Southeast Asia in 1945, or indeed in 1950, could have been very optimistic about their futures. Apart from the devastation of infrastructure brought about by Allied bombing, accelerating inflation, and severe shortages of food and other basic needs, the populations of both the European and Japanese colonies were alienated from their former colonial masters, and, especially among the young, there was a growing desire to acquire more control over their own destinies. But how was this to be done in a world that was rapidly becoming polarized into rigid blocs, controlled by the United States and the Soviet Union? In 1946, only one country appeared to have emerged relatively unscathed from the carnage, and that country, Thailand, had not been directly colonized. Nor had it experienced much economic growth or structural change away from smallholder agriculture in the pre-1940 era. Per capita GDP in 1938 was little changed from that in 1913 and only about 12 percent higher than in 1890 (Manarungsan 1989: 251).

Infrastructure in Thailand was undeveloped compared to most of the colonies in East and Southeast Asia. While there had been some development of railways before 1940, road development was very limited, and the ratio of highway miles to area was very low compared to most other parts of East and Southeast Asia (Andrews 1935: 390). The expansion of rice production was achieved mainly through area expansion; yields remained low by Asian standards. There was little modern industry apart from rice milling. But the pro-Japanese government that was in place during most of the war had managed to avoid at least some of the catastrophes that befell the European and American colonies. Toward the end of the Pacific War, it was replaced by the left-leaning Seri Thai group led by Pridi Bhanomyong, but this government was unable to cope with the shortages, labor unrest, and inflation of the immediate postwar years. It was overthrown by a group of military officers in 1947 (Phongpaichit and Baker 1995: 182–186). Partly because of the subsistence orientation of many farmers and their minimal reliance on purchased inputs and partly because wartime damage to infrastructure was limited, Thailand was the only country in the region where, by 1949, rice production was well above prewar peaks, although the Philippines had just managed to return to prewar output levels in that year (Table 9.1).

Paauw has argued that, by 1950, both the Philippines, with the help of American assistance, and Thailand had returned to prewar output levels in terms of per capita GDP (1963: table 6). The estimates made by Manarungsan confirm that, by 1950, real gross domestic product was around one-third higher than in 1938 (1989: 251); in per capita terms it was roughly the same. In the Philippines, total national product was estimated by Goodstein to have been around 11 percent higher in 1948 than in 1938, although per capita national product was significantly lower (1962: table 1-1). But the Philippines experienced rapid growth of per capita gross national product after 1946; in the decade from 1946 to 1956, it more than doubled, which was almost certainly a faster rate of recovery than in any other part of Asia. Per capita consumption expenditures also doubled, indicating a significant improvement in living standards (National Economic and Development Authority 1978: table 4.1.1). By 1956, total national product was thought to have been around 84 percent higher than in 1938; per capita output was also much higher than in 1938 in spite of rapid population growth after 1945 (Goodstein 1962).

Elsewhere in Southeast Asia, the process of postwar rehabilitation was much slower; indeed, the evidence indicates that by 1959 neither Burma nor Indonesia, nor South Vietnam, nor British Malaya had returned to prewar levels of per capita GDP (van der Eng 2002: 172; Booth 2003a: table 2; Bassino unpublished). In the case of Burma, per capita GDP growth was quite rapid during the 1950s; the slow return to prewar levels was a consequence of the devastation of the 1940s. In Indonesia and South Vietnam, slow growth in per capita GDP in the 1950s, especially the latter part of the decade, also contributed to the slow recovery to prewar output levels (Table 9.2). Maddison's

Table 9.1. Rice Production as a Percentage of the Prewar Peak, 1946–1960

Colony[a]	1946	1949	1955	1960
Cochinchina (1939/1940)	35.4	40.3	60.7	107.9
Burma (1939)	48.4	57.7	75.9	89.2
Taiwan (1938)	63.8	86.7	115.2	136.4
Java (1941)	75.0	86.6	98.0	108.1
British Malaya (1938)	75.9	90.7	102.0	141.3
Philippines (1940/1941)	85.5	106.8	134.1	151.7
Thailand (1941)	86.8	129.3	141.8	152.1

Sources: Taiwan: Executive Yuan 1962: 27; Cochinchina: Wiegersma 1988: 177; Ministry of National Economy 1962: 173; Java: van der Eng 1994: table A1; Central Bureau of Statistics 1968: 93; Burma: Saito and Lee 1999: 81; Thailand: Central Statistical Office 1955: 154; British Malaya: Rose 1985: 208, 216; Philippines: Mears et al. 1974: 355–356.

[a] Figures in parentheses indicate the peak year before 1942.

estimates for Malaysia (i.e., British Malaya excluding Singapore and including Sarawak and North Borneo) indicate that the 1939 level of per capita GDP was not reached again until 1962. Per capita GDP growth in Singapore during the 1950s was also slow (Maddison 2003: 183–185).

Taiwan, having experienced considerable destruction through bombing in the final phase of the Pacific War, also struggled to regain pre-1942 levels of output after the end of the Japanese colonial era. By April 1946, the last Japanese soldier had left Taiwan, and the American Liaison Group also withdrew. The reins of government were handed over to the mainland Chinese KMT regime, who installed General Chen Yi as high commissioner. The result was three years of administrative misrule that severely hindered economic recovery (Kerr 1966: 97–142; Lin 1973: 27–33). Inflation had already taken hold in the final phase of the Japanese era and was fueled after 1946 by large government deficits. According to Kerr, word quickly spread on the mainland that substantial Japanese assets were available for the taking, and thousands of carpetbaggers streamed in, mainly from Shanghai (1966: 97–98). The newcomers had money or could arrange to get it from mainland banks, and working together with the new government, they rapidly acquired many Japanese and joint Japanese-Taiwanese enterprises.

The takeover of Japanese property was done in the name of "Necessary State Socialism," but the corruption and mismanagement was so blatant that it caused immense resentment among many Taiwanese. The presence of thousands of poorly paid and equipped mainland troops also contributed to the looting of property owned by indigenous Taiwanese as well as by the departing Japanese. Food stockpiled by the Japanese army was immediately confiscated, but in addition, many Taiwanese farmers had to give rice and other produce to the government, precipitating food shortages in what had always

Table 9.2. Index of Per Capita GDP, 1950–1970 (1960 = 100)

	1950	1955	1960	1965	1970
Singapore	n.a.	n.a.	100	120.5	196.2
Taiwan	62.3	87.4	100	139.1	183.0
Korea (South)	77.3	96.5	100	119.5	182.5
Thailand	77.2	90.7	100	121.6	159.6
Malaysia	92.7	99.4	100	119.1	133.2
Philippines	72.8	93.1	100	110.7	125.5
Indonesia	85.2	101.1	100	100.0	120.8
Laos	104.7	102.6	100	96.0	115.9
Burma	64.5	83.2	100	111.6	108.9
Vietnam (South)	84.6	96.9	100	112.3	105.2
Cambodia	84.8	86.7	100	104.1	97.6

Source: World Bank 1976.

Note: n.a. = not available.

been a food-surplus island. Mounting inflation also contributed to the woes of urban people who could no longer afford to buy food and other necessities. By 1947, popular resentment had boiled over into armed revolt, which was brutally suppressed. Many educated Taiwanese, who had been the most vocal critics of Chen Yi's misrule, lost their lives.

The final defeat of the KMT on the mainland and the advent of around 1.5 million mainlanders in 1949 did bring some benefits to Taiwan. Many skilled professionals, managers, and administrators arrived who were able to fill at least some of the gaps left by the departing Japanese. Some brought both capital and technical expertise in manufacturing industry. The KMT government was able to impose a monetary reform, which did finally bring down the rate of inflation. Massive American aid permitted the imports of key commodities including soybean, cotton, and fertilizers (Lin 1973: 33–38). Aid and improvements in tax collection reduced the government deficit. Steps were also taken to improve the lot of rural Taiwanese. The Chinese-American Joint Commission on Rural Reconstruction was set up and began to tackle the problems in the rural economy, although the terms of trade facing farmers continued to deteriorate until 1954 (ibid.: 206). Greater availability of fertilizer boosted rice production, although prewar production levels were not regained until the early 1950s (see Table 9.1). Sugar production had not regained prewar levels by 1960; the loss of protected markets in Japan was a blow from which the industry never fully recovered.

By 1953, real per capita income in Taiwan had returned to the prewar peak, in spite of the 60 percent increase in population (Hsing 1971: 152). From 1953 onward, growth in Taiwan was new, rather than simply catching up to prewar levels. Aid inflows played an important role in the rapid recovery and continued growth of the Taiwanese economy between 1946 and 1961; during these years per capita US aid flows were higher than in any other country in the region (Table 9.3). According to Hsing, the Americans, in disbursing project aid, favored infrastructure projects such as electric power and transport

Table 9.3. American Aid Per Capita, 1946–1948, 1949–1952, and 1953–1961 (US dollars, annual averages over the years shown)

	1946–1948	1949–1952	1953–1961
Taiwan	30.92	23.99	35.16
Korea (South)	3.44	6.50	21.19
Vietnam (South)	n.a.	n.a.	18.92
Thailand	0.11	1.29	2.59
Philippines	5.84	8.65	2.21
British Malaya	n.a.	n.a.	0.35
Indonesia	0.31	0.36	0.33

Source: Kang 2002: 43. Population data from World Bank 1976.

Note: n.a. = not available.

(1971: 192–198); in the first part of the 1950s, aid funds covered half of total gross capital formation. But some part of the aid did go to the agricultural sector and especially to the implementation of the land reform program, which is examined more fully below.

In Korea, the post-1945 problems were more serious than in Taiwan and took longer to resolve. The end of Japanese rule and the division of the country "created extreme disorganization in every aspect of Korean society" (Kim and Roemer 1979: 25). The departure of almost all Japanese managers and technicians led to a sharp fall in manufacturing output; many plants had to suspend production completely because of a lack of raw materials and managerial staff. Kim and Roemer have estimated that industrial output in the south in 1948 was only about 15 percent of the 1939 level (ibid.: 27). The southern sector experienced a surge in population, due to refugees from the north and also to the repatriation of migrant workers from Japan and other parts of the former Japanese empire. Food availability per capita declined sharply, and South Korea became dependent on food aid from the United States.

The division of the Korean peninsula together with the communist victories in China created a highly unstable political situation. In 1950, troops from the north crossed the line of partition and tried to set up a unified state. Seoul, the capital of the southern zone, fell to the invading army. The bitter war that followed involved large numbers of foreign troops from the United States and its allies and from China and the Soviet Union. The fighting was brought to an end after three years with an armistice agreement in 1953 that effectively returned the country to the pre-1950 status quo. The war caused massive devastation of private dwellings, industrial plants, and infrastructure. In addition, many people were forced to move from their ancestral homes, and at least 2 million Koreans from both north and south, many of them civilians, perished. It was estimated that real output of agriculture, forestry, mining, and manufacturing in South Korea was only 73 percent of 1940 levels in 1953; in per capita terms, commodity output had fallen by almost half (Kim and Roemer 1979: 35). Such was the fall in productive capacity that "the Korean economy in 1953 could be managed only with a massive inflow of foreign relief and aid" (ibid.: 39).

By the late 1950s, it was clear that, within Southeast Asia, Thailand and the Philippines were undergoing structural change away from agriculture and toward industry (Paauw 1963: 575–577). In Taiwan also, the share of agriculture in GDP was falling and that of industry increasing (Hsing 1971: 274). By 1960, the percentage of GDP accruing from agriculture in the former colonies varied considerably; it was still more than 50 percent in Indonesia and Cambodia but below 30 percent in Burma, Taiwan, the Philippines, and Singapore (Table 9.4). But a fall in the percentage accruing from agriculture did not necessarily mean that there was an increase in the share of manufacturing industry. In a number of countries, the share of the tertiary sector, including government services, had increased rapidly after 1950. In many former colonies, agriculture and manufacturing industry together accounted for only around half of total GDP (Table 9.4).

In 1960, in spite of a sluggish growth performance since 1945, Singapore and the Federation of Malaya had the highest per capita GDP among the former colonial territories, with Taiwan, the Philippines, Thailand, and South Korea behind them (Table 9.5). Indonesia and Burma were well behind South Korea. These two economies remained behind throughout the 1960s. Several observers attributed their poor performance to a failure to relink effectively to the world economy; this argument is examined further below. There was

Table 9.4. Agricultural and Manufacturing Shares of GDP: 1960 and 1970

	Agriculture / GDP		Manufacturing / GDP	
	1960	1970	1960	1970
Indonesia	53.9	47.2	8.4	9.3
Cambodia	51.0	38.3	10.1	11.7
Thailand	39.6	28.3	10.4	12.2
Korea (South)	36.9	28.1	11.2	17.2
Malaysia	33.4	26.5	7.3	11.5
Vietnam (South)	30.4	31.5	9.6	5.6
Philippines	27.8	29.7	16.2	15.6
Burma	27.1	38.0	8.6	10.4
Taiwan	26.4	15.0	13.6	18.7
Singapore	5.7	2.8	8.7	19.1

Source: World Bank 1976.

Note: Although the Federation of Malaysia included Singapore until 1965, the data given here refer to Malaysia excluding Singapore in both 1960 and 1970.

Table 9.5. Per Capita GDP (1985 US dollars), 1955, 1960, 1965, 1970

	1955	1960	1965	1970
Japan	2,108	3,052	4,663	7,676
Singapore	n.a.	1,649	1,866	2,994
Malaysia	1,352	1,497	1,687	2,106
Korea (South)	876	899	1,047	1,694
Thailand	728	969	1,184	1,573
Philippines	1,043	1,165	1,248	1,433
Indonesia	n.a.	589	545	640
Burma	252	315	415	418

Source: Penn World Tables, version 5.6 (from http://datacentre.chass.utoronto.ca)

Note: Although the Federation of Malaysia included Singapore until 1965, the data given here refer to Malaysia excluding Singapore in 1955, 1960, and 1970. Data are adjusted for changes in the terms of trade.

n.a. = not available.

still, in 1960, little evidence pointing to the very different performance of the former colonies in coming decades; few would have predicted the stellar post-1960 performance of South Korea or Taiwan from their growth performance in the 1950s, and few would have forecast the disappointing post-1960 performance of the Philippines. By 1970, this was changing; Taiwan, South Korea, and Singapore all experienced growth in per capita GDP of 80 percent or more during the 1960s, and the share of manufacturing industry in total output had undergone a considerable increase (see Tables 9.2 and 9.4). The Philippines, by contrast, experienced much more modest per capita growth during the 1960s, and the share of manufacturing industry in total output fell slightly.

A further aspect of structural change in Southeast Asia that might help to explain the divergent outcomes after 1960 concerns the role of government. Most of the newly independent countries in Southeast Asia, even the more pro-Western ones, such as the Philippines and Thailand, were inclined toward a more activist view of the state than the colonial powers had been. This involved not just higher levels of public expenditures relative to GDP, but also direct government involvement in production through state-owned enterprises. Planning offices were established throughout the region, and a variety of development plans were produced. To quote a United Nations publication: "The actual extent of planning has varied from country to country. Mainland China and other centrally planned economies of the region have attempted to implement plans affecting their entire economies. In other countries the plans deal only or mainly with the major programmes to be implemented in the public sector and, in several of them, lay down production and investment targets for the private sector" (United Nations ECAFE 1961: 54).

If one of the purposes of the increased emphasis on the role of government in the economy was to bring about an increase in the share of government domestic revenues and expenditures, and especially government investment expenditures, relative to GDP, outcomes by the latter part of the 1950s in different parts of Asia were very mixed. Comparing government revenues and expenditures per capita in the 1950s with those in the 1930s is difficult because exchange rates were overvalued in many parts of Asia after 1950, which makes conversion into dollars problematic. But there is ample evidence that, compared with the colonial regimes, several newly independent countries found domestic revenue mobilization difficult. The rapid increase in world prices for a range of agricultural and mineral products that occurred in the early 1950s as a result of the Korean War led to a windfall increase in government revenues in primary exporting countries, as taxes on foreign trade still accounted for a large proportion of all taxes. But the war boom collapsed rapidly, and in most parts of Southeast Asia, government revenues were less than 15 percent of GDP by 1957 (Table 9.6).

Government expenditures were higher than domestic revenues in most of the former colonies, which reflected the important role of foreign aid, especially in the case of Taiwan and South Korea. It was in these two economies

Table 9.6. Government Expenditures and Revenues as a Percentage of GDP, and Investment and Defense Expenditures as a Percentage of Total Expenditures, 1957

	Percentage of GDP			Percentage of Government Expenditures	
	Government Expenditures	Government Revenues	Government Investment	Investment	Defense
Taiwan	30	20	10	32	34
Burma	25	20	10	39	28
Korea (South)	22	11	9	40	30
Federation of Malaya	19	17	3	25	16
Thailand	16	12	5	29	22
Indonesia	15	12	2	11	15
Cambodia	14	12	n.a.	n.a.	28
Philippines	12	11	3	22	14

Source: United Nations ECAFE 1961: tables 22, 24, 25, 32, 33.

Note: Federation of Malaya excludes Singapore and includes the former federated and unfederated states.

n.a. = not available.

together with Burma that government investment accounted for around 9 percent of GDP in 1957. Elsewhere government investment was below 5 percent of GDP (see Table 9.6). Much of this investment went toward the repair and rebuilding of war-damaged infrastructure; very few of the former colonies in East and Southeast Asia had been able, by the end of the 1950s, to add substantially to the stock of infrastructure that had been in place by the late 1930s. The evidence on installed capacity of electric power illustrates this point. By 1959, there was wide variation in installed capacity per capita, with Singapore and Taiwan at the top of the rankings (Table 9.7). In Taiwan, the figure was about 50 percent higher than the prewar figure, and there was an even more rapid increase in the Philippines, albeit from a lower base. But elsewhere there was little change (see Table 4.7). In South Korea, installed capacity was, in 1959, well below the figure for the whole of Korea in the late 1930s, reflecting both the damage inflicted during the Korean War and the fact that much of the capacity installed in the Japanese era was in the north of the country.

It would be simplistic to argue that the relatively high ratios of government investment to GDP in the latter part of the 1950s were in themselves a crucial determinant of future economic growth. Taiwan, South Korea, and Burma all managed quite high ratios in spite of the fact that around 30 percent of government expenditures in all these economies was devoted to defense. But after 1960, Taiwan and South Korea forged ahead in terms of economic growth, while Burma fell behind. To seek the explanation for this, we have to look in more detail at the way in which these economies responded to the changing opportunities for international trade in the post-1950 world econ-

Table 9.7. Electric Power Generation: Installed Capacity, Total and Per Capita, 1959

Country	Installed Capacity, 1959 (megawatts)	Per Capita (megawatts per million people)
Singapore	152.0 (4.1)	97.3
Taiwan	632.8 (2.1)	61.8
Malayan Federation	307.0 (2.2)	39.0
Philippines	434.7 (2.6)	16.4
South Korea	374.8 (1.4)	15.5
South Vietnam	97.6 (1.5)	7.2
Thailand	160.3 (3.8)	6.2
Burma	105.2 (3.5)	4.8
Cambodia	21.4 (3.2)	4.1
Indonesia	277.0 (1.6)	3.0
Laos	3.6 (1.8)	1.6

Sources: United Nations ECAFE 1962: 28; World Bank 1976.

Note: Figures in parentheses show 1959 installed capacity as a ratio of that in 1951.

omy. We also have to take into account the changes in political leadership that occurred during the 1960s.

Inward- and Outward-Looking Economic Policies

In a well-known paper written in the mid-1960s, the Burmese economist Hla Myint drew a distinction between what he termed the "inward-" and "outward-" looking economies of Southeast Asia. He argued that, by the early 1960s, two discernible patterns of economic development had emerged in Southeast Asia, typified by Burma and Indonesia, on the one hand, and Malaysia, Thailand, and the Philippines, on the other. (He did not explicitly consider the countries of former Indochina, and he did not examine Taiwan and South Korea). Myint pointed out that while all the countries of Southeast Asia shared a common reaction after independence to what might be termed the "colonial economic pattern," the nature of the reaction differed between these two groups. Governments in the Philippines, Thailand, and (British) Malaya

> seemed to have sensed early that it would be easier and quicker to change the economic structure and the pattern of distribution of incomes and economic activities if the total volume of national output were expanding rapidly than in a situation of economic stagnation or slow growth. They also seemed to have realised that, given the basic conditions of their economies, the key to expanding their total national product was to be found in expanding the volume of their exports. Since a large share of these exports was produced by the foreign-owned mines and plantations,

the governments of these countries took care to guarantee the security of foreign property and freedom to remit profits, and generally created a favorable economic environment which encouraged the foreign enterprises not only to continue their existing production but also to undertake new investments, to strike out into new lines of exports and to introduce new methods of production and organization. (Myint 1967: 2–3)

In contrast, Myint continued, the political leaderships of Burma and Indonesia at that time "were obsessed by the fear" that once foreign enterprises were allowed to reestablish themselves or expand their operations, they would resume their old stranglehold over the economy and reimpose the colonial economic pattern whereby most profits were remitted abroad, and the local populations gained little benefit from the exploitation of the economy's abundant natural resources. Myint argued that both countries did little to attract new investment and indeed nationalized many foreign-owned firms. In the latter part of the 1950s, after the failure in the United Nations of a resolution on Indonesian sovereignty over West New Guinea, the Indonesian government proceeded to nationalize all remaining Dutch-owned enterprises in Indonesia and expel almost all their staff (Anspach 1969: 191–192). The Dutch enterprises were, for the most part, converted into state-owned enterprises and have remained in government hands down to the present day. Lacking skilled administrators to run such a wide diversity of companies, including estates, banks, trading houses, and industrial enterprises, many were turned over to the military or to nominees of political parties, often with unfortunate consequences for their management.

Both the Indonesian and Burmese governments also adopted policies hostile to their Chinese and Indian minorities, so that many left either for their ancestral homelands or to settle in third countries. But in spite of much rhetoric supporting "indigenism," policies toward indigenous producers, especially of exports, were also often hostile. In both countries, smallholder producers of export crops were taxed through export taxes and marketing boards, and there was little investment in infrastructure or new cultivation technologies that would directly benefit smallholder producers. The increasingly overvalued exchange rates led to greatly increased smuggling of traded goods in the border regions of Burma, while in Indonesia, many of the export-producing regions outside Java virtually seceded from the national economy and were conducting their own export and import trade with neighboring Malaysia and with the Philippines.

Even among the countries that Myint considered were pursuing "open-type" policies after 1950s, there were considerable differences in both policies and outcomes in the two decades from 1950 to 1970. In their study of the transition in the open dualistic economies of East and Southeast Asia, Paauw and Fei distinguished between those countries characterized by neocolonialism (Malaya and Thailand) and those characterized by economic nationalism (Taiwan and the Philippines) (1973: 77–89). The neocolonial countries continue to rely on free market systems to facilitate the growth of traditional export staples, while the nationalists use controls to facilitate import substitution, leading to the rapid growth of domestic industrial capacity to replace imported goods. Broadly, the neocolonial path was adopted by both Thailand and Malaya because both countries were still, after 1950, characterized by favorable natural resource endowments. In addition, a lack of entrepreneurship and capital among the indigenous population coupled with distrust of the migrant minorities on the part of the political elite militated against the adoption of policies favoring rapid domestic industrialization. In Thailand, state enterprises were the favored vehicle for industrialization until the Sarit regime assumed power in 1957. Thereafter, the government embarked on an import-substitution strategy, with substantial foreign participation, usually through joint ventures with Sino-Thai business groups.

In both the Philippines and Taiwan, alien minorities played a much smaller role in the nonagricultural sectors of the economy, and industrial interests had more political power from the early 1950s onward. But the transition process in these two countries, although broadly within the economic nationalist mold, differed in important respects. In Taiwan, the import-substituting phase was remarkably short; already by the early 1960s agricultural exports accounted for less than 50 percent of all exports (Paauw and Fei 1973: 273). The speed of the transition was in large part due to the supply of entrepreneurs, many of whom had come from the mainland. To begin with, manufactured exports from Taiwan were concentrated in labor-intensive products such as textiles, garments, and footwear. Increasingly after 1960, more technologically sophisticated industrial processes were mastered, and manufactured exports became far more diversified into products that Taiwan had not produced at all, or only in very small quantities, during the import-substitution phase (Nelson and Pack 1999: 418–419).

Apart from the supply of entrepreneurial talent and capital, Paauw and Fei also stressed the crucial role of agricultural modernization in the transition to export-oriented growth (1973: 114–115). They argued that government policies, including land reform, agricultural cooperatives, extension services, and infrastructure investment played an important role in modernizing Taiwanese agriculture, in addition to private initiatives. During the 1950s, Taiwan was able to build on the Japanese legacy in the agricultural sector, and the rapid gains in agricultural productivity facilitated the release of labor into nonagricultural employment. To the extent that this was rural-based, industrialization took place without rapid urbanization, and many rural households were able to diversify their incomes away from total reliance on agriculture without physically relocating to the towns. There is considerable evidence that, since the 1950s, farm households in Taiwan earned their income increasingly from off-farm and nonagricultural sources (Ho 1986: table 4.2).

The transition to export-oriented growth in Taiwan was accompanied by a change in the balance of trade; whereas in the colonial era there had been a large export surplus, throughout the 1950s, imports exceeded exports, often by a large margin (Table 9.8). In the Philippines as well, the balance of trade was negative for most years from 1949 onward (Power and Sicat 1971: 37). Perhaps paradoxically, it was in Burma and Indonesia, the two Southeast Asian economies that had run large current account surpluses in the prewar era, that the balance of trade remained in surplus throughout much of the 1950s (Table 9.8). Although there were large deficits in services in both economies, especially Indonesia, during most of the 1950s, the current account was in surplus (Rosendale 1978: 146). The reasons for these surpluses are not entirely clear; in the early 1950s, they were the result of the rapid surge in export prices as a result of the Korean War boom. Later in the decade, slow overall economic growth together with import controls and a complex multiple exchange rate system appear to have depressed import demand.

In most of the former colonies in East and Southeast Asia, the share of the former metropolitan powers in total exports and imports fell after 1950 (Table 9.9). This reflected a trend toward diversification of trade flows that was common to almost all former colonies in the postindependence period (Kleiman 1976: 478). In those colonies where trade flows before 1940 had been very tightly tethered to the metropolitan power, the decline was quite

Table 9.8. Commodity Export Earnings as a Percentage of Commodity Import Earnings, 1950–1965

	Burma	Indonesia	Taiwan
1950	153	176	n.a.
1951	144	139	n.a.
1952	134	92	58
1953	134	110	68
1954	123	138	48
1955	126	159	70
1956	126	102	57
1957	77	123	67
1958	95	154	71
1959	100	153	66
1960	87	118	69
1961	103	77	67
1962	121	97	75
1963	115	122	108
1964	87	132	114
1965	91	148	89

Sources: Burma: Saito and Lee 1999: 185; Indonesia: Rosendale 1978: 146; Taiwan: Hsing 1971: 279–280.

Note: n.a. = not available.

marked; in Taiwan, for example, Japan's share of total exports fell from more than 90 percent in 1938 to less than 40 percent by 1960. There was a similar fall in the share of imports coming from Japan. By 1960, Taiwan was sourcing more imports from the United States, which was in part at least a reflection of the large American aid flows (Table 9.9). In the Philippines, the share of the United States in total exports fell, while that of Japan rose, although the United States remained the country's most important trading partner. In Indonesia, where the Netherlands only accounted for around 20 percent of export and import trade in 1938, the proportion had fallen to virtually nothing by 1960, reflecting the hostile nature of the bilateral relationship after the expropriation of Dutch assets in 1958–1959.

The transition to rapid export-oriented growth in Taiwan in the 1960s has often been compared with that in South Korea. Certainly the experience of both these economies had become an important model for other developing countries, in Asia and elsewhere, by the 1980s, although there were important differences in the policies they adopted (Wade 1990: 320–325). In the 1950s, South Korea followed a "one-sided policy of import substitution" with export growth playing a minimal role in overall economic growth. In the 1960s, trade and exchange rate policies were reformed, and there was a rapid switch to export-oriented growth, leading some commentators to talk of an "unbalanced export-oriented industrialization strategy" (Kim and Roemer 1979: 136–137). By 1970, manufacturing output was a slightly lower proportion of GDP in South Korea than in Taiwan, although higher than in any Southeast Asian country except Singapore, where per capita GDP was much higher and the agricultural sector tiny (see Table 9.4). Like Taiwan, South Korea after 1960 was extremely successful in increasing exports in sectors that had not developed at all during the colonial and immediate postcolonial years.

Reforming Land Tenure and Promoting Agricultural Growth

In the aftermath of depression, war, and foreign occupations, the problem of land tenure was of paramount importance in the minds of many of the nationalists who came to power in the decade after the Japanese defeat. Even more than in the late 1930s, all the colonial territories in East and Southeast Asia were still basically agricultural economies in 1945, with the majority of their labor forces relying on agriculture for most of their income. Yet there was a widespread conviction that many of those employed in agriculture were somehow being cheated of their just rewards, and in some parts of Asia, this conviction was already spilling over into armed insurrections. The grievances centered on three key issues: tenancy, large estates, and growing landlessness. It was already obvious by the late 1930s that tenancy was widespread in both Taiwan and Korea as well as in Lower Burma and the Philippines (see Table 3.5). But the causes were very different in different colonies. In Burma, tenancy was the result of dispossession of indigenous cultivators by Indian moneylenders, while in Korea it was due to widespread ownership of land by both

Table 9.9. Percentage Breakdown of Exports and Imports by Main Trading Partners, 1938 and 1960

	Percentage of Exports		Percentage of Imports	
	1938	1960	1938	1960
Burma				
United Kingdom	16.9	9.8	20.2	14.3
India[a]	51.0	34.8	49.2	13.0
United States	0.2	0.4	4.4	3.8
Japan	2.3	5.1	8.7	22.5
British Malaya				
United Kingdom	14.1	12.5	18.2	15.0
Other British	17.5	16.2	17.9	17.6
United States	n.a.	11.3	n.a.	4.0
Western Europe	n.a.	20.4	n.a.	9.3
Indonesia				
Netherlands	20.0	0.3	22.2	3.1
United States	14.2	23.0	12.6	15.7
Japan	3.1	4.1	15.0	16.0
Singapore	17.0	23.1	7.6	2.2
French Indochina[b]				
France	47.2	35.8	52.3	21.3
United States	8.6	4.4	5.1	25.5
Japan	3.1	2.8	3.1	21.9
Hong Kong	9.7	8.6	7.2	0.3
Philippines				
United States	83.0	50.9	69.6	44.6
Japan	5.1	23.5	9.6	26.4
Taiwan				
Japan	92.0	37.4	89.4	34.6
United States	0.9	12.5	0.7	40.8
Hong Kong	0.2	11.5	0.0	2.0
Korea[c]				
Japan	73.2	47.4	88.5	21.9
United States	0.4	16.7	1.7	45.4
China[d]	23.7	19.4	6.5	2.0

Sources: Burma: Andrus 1948: 167–176; Central Statistical and Economics Department 1963: tables 110, 115; British Malaya: Department of Statistics 1939: 114; Department of Statistics 1961; Indonesia: Central Bureau of Statistics 1959: 108–109; Central Bureau of Statistics 1968: 206–207; French Indochina: Direction des Services Économiques 1947: 290–292; South Vietnam: Ministry of National Economy 1962: 328–330. Philippines: Bureau of Census and Statistics 1941: table 120; National Economic and Development Authority 1975: table 12.3. Taiwan: Grajdanzev 1942: 144; Hsing 1971: 284–285; Korea: Grajdanzev 1944: 227; Economic Planning Board 1967: 210–211.

Note: n.a. = not available.

[a] 1960 data refer to Pakistan, India, and Sri Lanka.

[b] 1960 data refer to South Vietnam only.

[c] Data refer to 1939 and 1961. The 1961 data refer to South Korea only.

[d] In 1938, China includes Manchuria. In 1960, China refers to Hong Kong and Taiwan only.

indigenous and Japanese landlords. In Taiwan and the Philippines as well as in southern Vietnam, indigenous landlords predominated.

Large estates run along capitalist lines, employing substantial numbers of wage workers and often owned by foreign interests, were important in the development of export crops in British Malaya, Indonesia, South Vietnam, and the Philippines. Increasingly after 1945, they were the focus of intense resentment from various nationalist and radical forces, for whom they exemplified exploitation on the part of either foreign corporations or domestic "comprador capitalists." But should these estates be nationalized and run by domestic corporations, either state-owned or private? Or should they be divided up among smallholder farmers? The case for converting estates into smallholdings was especially strong in regions where population growth was outstripping available supplies of arable land and where landlessness and near landlessness was an increasing problem. They included Java, parts of Sumatra and Sulawesi, and parts of the Philippines and Vietnam. Even in those regions considered land abundant in the pre-1940 era, landlessness was growing, and conflicts over land were increasingly violent after 1945. In North Sumatra, where the postwar migration of Bataks from their traditional homelands added to existing population pressures, demands for the redistribution of estate lands were becoming more pressing, while in the central plains of Thailand, both tenancy and the numbers of landless were increasing (Feith 1962: 293–297; Phongpaichit and Baker 1995: 38–39).

Newly independent or about to become independent governments in East and Southeast Asia reacted to these demands for agrarian reform in different ways. Perhaps the most successful, and certainly the most quoted, example of agrarian reform was that carried out in Taiwan between 1949 and 1953. In 1949, the KMT government enacted a rent reduction program that aimed to reduce rents and increase the security of tenants. This program was followed by the sale of part of the public lands owned by the Japanese state until 1945 to Taiwanese cultivators who had been leasing the land. Then in 1953, the "Land to the Tiller" program was implemented; this consisted of the compulsory purchase of tenanted farm land and its resale to those who were actually cultivating the land (Apthorpe 1979: 521–522). The result of these policies was that, by 1955, more than 80 percent of farmers in Taiwan were either full or part owner-operators, while only 17 percent were pure tenants, compared with 41 percent in 1945 (Mao 1982: table 1).

A number of extravagant claims have been made about the impact of the Taiwanese reform program; a not untypical claim is that it "created the foundation for both economic growth and an equitable distribution of income and wealth" (Orme 1995: 41). In fact, the reform did not have a dramatic impact on the size distribution of operated holdings, which was already quite equal in the Japanese era (Apthorpe 1979: 529). Nor is it clear what the contribution of the reform policies was to subsequent agricultural growth in Taiwan, as a number of other important development programs in the agricultural sector were also being implemented at the same time. Thus it is probably wrong to argue that agrarian reform by itself had a dramatic impact on output per hectare or per worker, both of which increased steadily during the 1950s and 1960s (Lee and Chen 1979: table T-1a). However, the granting of secure title to cultivators undoubtedly did, at the margin, encourage greater use of inputs such as fertilizer and improved seeds and increased the net wealth of many rural families.

In Korea after 1945, the implementation of land reform proceeded rather differently than in either Japan or Taiwan. In the north, a five-hectare limit was placed on holding size, which "did away with perennially high rates of tenancy" (Cumings 1997: 428). It would not have made much difference to operated holding sizes, as by the late 1930s very few operated holdings exceeded five hectares (see Table 3.4). But the cultivators received secure title to land that they could pass on to their children, although the land was "socialized" in the sense that it could not be sold on the market. In the south, the government of President Rhee was not supportive of radical reform, and Rhee vetoed the Land Reform Act of 1949, although this veto was subsequently voted down by the legislative assembly. After the act was passed, implementation was slow, and it was only after the reoccupation of the south by Allied troops that the reform was concluded. Around 970,000 tenant farmers and farm laborers became landowners, and only about 7 percent of farmers were still tenants. The old landlord class was wiped out; although they were compensated with government bonds, for most the value was too low for them to make productive investments in nonagricultural ventures (Boyer and Ahn 1991: 31; Putzel 1992: 81–82).

The Korean reform was a tenancy reform rather than a redistributive land reform (Lee 1979: 494). It had little impact on the size distribution of operated holdings, although as in Taiwan, by conferring much greater security of tenure on cultivators, the reform would have had a positive impact on investment decisions. Efforts by the government in the south to modernize agriculture during the 1950s and 1960s do not appear to have been as successful as in Taiwan, and urban-rural income differentials remained large. These had the effect of encouraging out-migration, and many farm households rented out land that they could not cultivate themselves because the young adults in the household were working outside agriculture. By the end of the 1970s, tenancy was again increasing, although it was still illegal under the terms of the land reform legislation (Boyer and Ahn 1991: 77–79).

There are obvious parallels between the situation in Vietnam and that in Korea after 1950; both countries were divided between communist and noncommunist regimes, and in both the noncommunist governments were dependent on American assistance and advice. In North Vietnam, a land reform program began in 1953 but rapidly led to "major upheavals in rural society," substantial opposition in many areas, and in 1956 the resignation of the first secretary of the Communist Party of Vietnam (Fforde 1989: 11).

Pre-1953 land reform efforts in the north carried out by Vietminh cadres had often been quite successful, as they were based on traditional views of the commune's obligation to redistribute land to those in need. But after 1954 the party's approach to land reform became more doctrinaire and coercive, and less popular with rural people. After 1959, rural cooperatives were formed, and by the early 1960s, more than 90 percent of the rural population in the north had joined cooperatives comprising around 70 percent of the cultivated area (ibid.: 12). How well or badly these functioned is still a matter of some controversy, but with the escalation of the war in the mid-1960s and heavy American bombing, the conditions for implementing sustained rural development policies were hardly propitious.

Matters were rather different in the south. As we have seen, population densities in Cochinchina were much lower than in Tonkin in the late 1930s, although tenancy was widespread (see Table 3.1). After the installation of President Diem in 1956, the Americans pressed him to implement some tenure reforms, and Edward Lansdale, the American who had advised President Magsaysay on land reforms in the Philippines, was brought in to encourage Diem to take a more activist approach (Putzel 1992: 100). An ordinance enacted in 1955 was mainly concerned with confirming the titles of absentee landlords, although it did provide for a maximum rental and for rent reductions in times of crop failure. Many farmers in those parts of the south effectively under Viet Cong control had been paying no rent to absentee landlords at all and were not impressed with the provisions of the ordinance. After further pressure from the Americans, another ordinance was issued that did allow for some redistribution from landlords to tenants, although the ceilings were about thirty times higher than the American advisers wanted (Wiegersma 1988: 181–184). The main problem was that Diem relied on the landlord class and landowning officials for his support. Gradually, those in his government who were genuinely committed to rural reform were marginalized, and by the early 1960s, what little commitment there had been to effective reform had vanished.

In the Philippines, the average holding size was larger than in either Taiwan or Korea in the late 1930s, and around half the land was in holdings under full or partial tenancy (see Table 3.5). Given the continuing influence of the Americans in the country after 1945, it might have been expected that they would push for land reform there as they were doing in both occupied Japan and the former Japanese colonies. But General MacArthur, after his reconquest of the Philippines in 1944, was determined to restore the pre-1942 status quo and did not want to threaten the landlord class that underpinned it (Putzel 1992: 83). The Bell Trade Act, signed in 1945, provided for the resumption of free trade with the United States, thus restoring the power and privileges of the large sugar growers. The first two post-1946 presidents, Roxas and Quirino, were conservatives who thought that the radical peasant movements that had arisen before and during the Japanese occupation could, and should, be destroyed by armed force. They had little time for arguments that land issues were at the heart of the rural unrest and must be addressed directly.

Land reform was placed on the policy agenda in 1950, with the publication of the report of the Bell Mission's survey of the Philippine economy (Putzel 1992: 85). This report recommended substantial land redistribution as a means of ending the agrarian unrest. Experts who had worked on the Japanese land reform were dispatched to Manila; they argued for the abolition of absentee ownership, capping of rentals at 25 percent of the crop value, low ceilings on land retained by former landlords, and government purchase of land for resale to tenants and the landless. As in Japan, Taiwan, and Korea, it was proposed that landlords be compensated with government bonds. Tenants would pay for land they acquired over a period of twenty-five years, at an interest rate of 4 percent. The American advisers argued that implementation of these proposals would give cultivators the incentive to adopt new technologies, while at the same time encouraging former landlords to invest their capital in nonagricultural enterprises.

Putzel has argued that the American advisers "underestimated the degree to which the state was controlled by the landed oligarchy in the Philippines, and the extent of animosity toward reform among policy-makers and US corporate lobbyists in Washington" (1992: 87). When Ramon Magsaysay was elected to the presidency in 1953, it was hoped that he would be more supportive of agrarian reform; he did not come himself from a landowning background, and his political style was more populist than that of his predecessors. But he was both unwilling and unable to overcome the hostility of landowning interests; the agrarian legislation passed in 1954 and 1955 was modest in its aims, being mainly concerned with regulating tenancy agreements. The Land Reform Act of 1955 was more ambitious and created a Land Tenure Administration that would acquire large tenanted rice and corn estates and resell them to tenants. But the provisions of the act were watered down in the congress, with some legislators stating that any redistribution was "communist-inspired" and land reform should be limited to resettlement on virgin lands (ibid.: 92). With the death of Magsaysay in a plane crash in 1957, land reform slipped off the policy agenda until the Marcos era.

In other parts of Southeast Asia, problems of land tenure were also of pressing concern to postcolonial governments. In Burma, not surprisingly given the extent of tenancy in the late 1930s, the government was concerned with eliminating Indian ownership and restoring national ownership of land. This was done not through a Taiwan-style reform but by nationalizing all agricultural land in 1948. However, implementation was slow and the consequences not always beneficial to tenants; some tenants were evicted as a result of land nationalization and became landless laborers (Steinberg 1981: 126). In addition, although nationalization made the state the landlord, it did not always eliminate insecurity of tenure on the part of small cultivators. The Revolutionary Council that came to power in 1962 was committed to improving the conditions of peasant cultivators and in 1965 passed a tenancy law that in effect abolished all tenancy. Although this legislation seemed radical, its main thrust was "to break up the landowner-tenant relationship in order to create a new government-owner-cultivator relationship and, at the same time, to strengthen government control over farmers" (Than and Nishizawa 1990: 90–91).

In Thailand, there was little overt government concern with land tenure issues in the 1950s and 1960s, in spite of the evidence that "the balance of advantage shifted in favor of the landlord" in many rice-growing areas in the delta, and exploitative tenancy agreements were often a step toward complete landlessness (Phongpaichit and Baker 1995: 38). In British Malaya, by contrast, officials became more concerned about land tenure issues in the preparation for self-government. Harper has argued that the debates over political and constitutional reform in the immediate post-1945 years took place "against a backdrop of agrarian crisis and terror" (1999: 94). According to his analysis, the communist rebellion, called an "emergency" by the British, drew its support and sustenance from an array of rural problems. During the Japanese occupation, many of the forest reserves created by the British had been felled for food-crop, especially tapioca, cultivation. Japanese food-crop policies were aggravated by spontaneous migration of people into the interiors of the peninsula; this process had begun during the depression and continued through the war years. Many of these squatters were Chinese. By the late 1940s, the squatter problem was acute in several areas and prevented rubber plantations from expanding the area under higher-yielding varieties (ibid.: 99–100).

To the problems of squatters and illegal deforestation were added problems of widespread tenancy. The survey reported by Wilson found that tenancy was widespread in the rice-growing regions in the northern part of the peninsula and that "less than one half of the padi land of North Malaya is owned by the farmers who cultivate it" (1958: 63). Wilson also found evidence of very uneven distribution of land in the areas where detailed surveys were carried out. Wilson's findings were confirmed by the 1960 Agricultural Census, which found that only about one-third of all wet paddy land in peninsular Malaya was owner-cultivated (Hill 1967: 101). A much higher proportion of land under rubber and coconut cultivation was owner-operated, although Hill has queried the accuracy of these findings. He argued that the high degree of tenancy, especially in the paddy areas, was the result of historical forces dating from the nineteenth century, when Malay entrepreneurs had secured land grants from the sultans and brought in many families from Java, Sumatra, and southern Borneo to cultivate them. Their descendants continued as tenant cultivators, while the descendants of the original landlords, often minor members of the royal households or hajis, continued as landlords and often extended their landholdings. Hill stressed that the colonial land legislation, and especially the Malay Reservation Acts, would not have affected

Malay landlords, as the legislation was only intended to prevent non-Malays from acquiring agricultural land (ibid.: 106).

Probably nowhere in Asia in the years after the Japanese occupation were land problems more complex and politically fraught than in Indonesia. At least in British Malaya, arable land was still in abundant supply relative to the numbers wishing to cultivate it, even if access to land was inequitable, and land legislation often favored expatriate corporations over locals, whether Malay or Chinese. The situation was very different in many parts of Indonesia. The Dutch had bequeathed to independent Indonesia two distinct legal systems, one based on Dutch law and one on traditional or *adat* law, as it had been interpreted by colonial legal scholars. Although Dutch colonial officials tried to preserve traditional legal systems, especially as they related to land matters, they also realized that, with growing commercialization of the indigenous economy, land was increasingly becoming a marketable commodity. By the 1920s, the official records showed that there were over 400,000 land transactions per year in Java and Bali (Booth 1998: 300). Perhaps surprisingly, writers such as Boeke did not accept this as evidence of the existence of a land market (1953: 131), although quite a high proportion of these transactions were sales rather than legacies or gifts. The Dutch agrarian legislation of 1870 permitted the leasing of land to Dutch and other foreign corporations, although foreigners were not able to purchase agricultural land outright.

By 1940, large estates in Indonesia controlled about 2.9 million hectares of land in Indonesia, of which only about 1.2 million hectares were actually under cultivation. Outside Java, only about 40 percent of land controlled by estates was planted (see Table 3.9). By contrast, many families in Java, Bali, and other parts of the country either possessed no land at all or cultivated only very small parcels, from which they could not make an adequate living. Some colonial agricultural experts, aware of the growing landlessness in Java and the widespread indigenous resentment about land issues, advocated the conversion of land under both annual and perennial crops to food-crop agriculture. This happened to some extent during the Japanese occupation and the ensuing struggle against the Dutch, with squatters occupying land that had been under both annual crops (tobacco and sugar) and tree crops (tea, coffee, and rubber).

In 1950, the government faced a very difficult problem regarding estate land. Under the terms of the Round Table Conference Agreements of 1949, the Indonesian negotiators had pledged to honor existing legal titles to land; in addition, the pressing need to earn foreign exchange and attract more foreign investment encouraged the new government to accommodate the demands of Dutch and other foreign-owned estate and mining companies (Feith 1962: 293). But that meant expelling many thousands of squatters, most of whom had few other means of making a living. The scene was set for bitter and protracted struggles, which lasted throughout the period of parliamentary democracy. Perhaps surprisingly, given the populist inclinations of most of the post-1950 cabinets, government policy tended to protect the large estates. When in the late 1950s the government took over most Dutch-owned companies, including estates, they continued to be operated as estates, often managed by the military. The option of dividing up the land, amounting to well over 1 million hectares, among smallholder cultivators does not seem to have been seriously considered.

This failure is all the more surprising when we consider the position of the smallholder cultivator of cash crops in postindependence Indonesia. By the 1950s, smallholders were producing 88 percent of output of tobacco, 77 percent of coffee, and 65 percent of rubber (Booth 1988: table 6.5). Of the main export crops, only sugar and tea were still largely produced by estates, although output of both crops remained well below pre-1940 levels throughout the 1950s. While the failure to break up large estates in the Philippines or South Vietnam can be explained by the dominant position of large landowners in the government and the legislature, this was far less the case in Indonesia. The failure to redistribute estate land was in large part due to the urban bias of the principal decision makers; they simply did not appreciate that smallholder producers were potentially far more efficient than the large estates. In addition, both military and civilian officials saw the estates as important sources of patronage in an increasingly difficult economic environment. As they were largely ignorant of the problems, both technical and socioeconomic, facing the estate sector, it is hardly surprising that most of the new managers had at best patchy success in reviving its fortunes.

In January 1960, the Supreme Advisory Council of President Sukarno held a special session devoted to land reform; after this the government moved quickly to introduce new agrarian legislation. Its intention was to unify the dualistic legacy from the Dutch colonial era and convert all land rights into a single system based on *adat* law but modified by principles introduced in the new law (Gautama and Harsono 1973: 24). The new legislation introduced both land ceilings (depending on the density of population) and minimum holding sizes (of two hectares). As Mortimer has pointed out, it was an arithmetical impossibility to provide two hectares to every rural family in Java, even if vacant estate land was redistributed, lower land ceilings than five hectares imposed, and land grants to village officials abolished (1974: 287). The Indonesian Communist Party (PKI) did in fact advocate these more radical reforms, although it did not advocate the formation of agricultural collectives. "If the PKI leaders shared the Leninist view that land reform was no more than a necessary concession to the proprietary instincts of the peasantry along the way to collectivization, they did not show it" (ibid.: 288). Instead they supported a "land to the tiller" policy and supported the demands of squatters on former estate and forest land, small landowners who had lost their land through pawning, and landless laborers. Partly as a result of PKI agitation, some 1 million hectares of agricultural land had been redistributed to around

1 million people by 1968, although some of this might have been reoccupied subsequently by former owners (Utrecht 1969: 84).

The modest achievements of land reform policies in most parts of Southeast Asia in the critical two decades following 1945 were thus the result of powerful vested interests in governments and legislatures who opposed radical redistribution, on the one hand, and an inability on the part of many urban-based nationalists, including those from left-wing parties, to appreciate the nature and extent of the problems in rural areas, on the other. A surprising number maintained the colonial belief that estates were a more efficient form of agricultural production, in spite of the evidence to the contrary. In addition, in Indonesia, Malaya, and the Philippines, there was a tendency on the part of well-intentioned reformers to believe that problems of landlessness in densely settled regions could be solved by moving people to those parts of the country deemed to have abundant supplies of empty land. These attitudes can be contrasted with the situation in Taiwan, where land reform was implemented quickly and efficiently by the KMT government, whose members had few vested interests to protect or few illusions that land settlement was a viable option.

The failure to implement land reform in the Philippines did not have an adverse impact on agricultural growth, which was in fact quite rapid in the 1950s and 1960s. Total output growth was 4 percent per annum during these two decades, which was slower than in South Korea and Taiwan but faster than in many other parts of Asia (David and Barker 1979: table 5.2). But growth in both output per hectare and output per worker in the agricultural sector was much slower in the Philippines than in the two former Japanese colonies (Table 9.10). Much of the agricultural growth in the Philippines during these two decades was due to increases in land and labor rather than to growth in factor productivity. The slow growth in agricultural productivity combined with the skewed access to land and the large number of landless rural families, estimated by Bautista to be 20 percent of all rural households in 1965 (1994: 99), meant that by the early 1960s poverty levels were still

Table 9.10. Post-1946 Growth of Agricultural Output, Arable Land per Worker, Yields per Hectare, and Output per Worker: Taiwan, South Korea, and the Philippines

		Annual Average Growth of		
	Total Output	Arable Land per Worker	Yields per Hectare	Output per Worker
Taiwan (1946–1970)	5.6	−0.6	5.2	4.6
South Korea (1953–1969)	4.4	−0.7	3.3	2.5
Philippines (1950–1969)	4.0	0.2	1.3	1.5

Sources: Lee and Chen 1979: tables 3.1, 3.5, 3.7, 3.8a); Ban 1979: tables 4.1, 4.6, 4.7; David and Barker 1979: tables 5.4, 5.5a, 5.6.

high in rural areas of the Philippines. The proportion of the population under the poverty line was estimated to be 64 percent in 1961; this had fallen only slightly to 57 percent by 1971 (Balisacan 1993: 297).

By the early 1970s, there were clear differences between the size distribution of landholdings in Taiwan and in most parts of Southeast Asia. In 1975, only 4 percent of land was in holdings over five hectares in Taiwan compared with 34 percent in the Philippines, 23 percent in Indonesia, and 24 percent in Thailand (Booth 2002: table 2). Agricultural growth in Taiwan was accompanied by considerable diversification of farm household income away from dependence on agricultural incomes. While this was also happening in other parts of Asia, the "linkage ratio" between growth in agricultural incomes and growth in other sources of income for agricultural households appeared to be considerably lower than in Taiwan (ibid.: table 4). The land reform program appeared to have brought about an egalitarian distribution of ownership of agricultural land, while the rapid growth of employment opportunities in nonagricultural activities meant that most rural households experienced growth in nonagricultural incomes at the same time that agricultural incomes were increasing. This benign outcome did not occur to anything like the same extent in other parts of Asia.

Eradicating the Legacy of the Plural Economy

It was stressed in the previous chapter that the Japanese occupation facilitated the rise of an aggressive form of indigenism in several parts of Southeast Asia. This was due in part to the expropriation of almost all enterprises owned by European and American interests and in part to the harsh treatment of many ethnic Chinese businesspeople. In addition, the Japanese approach to economic policy making in the occupied territories was dirigiste in the extreme and relied on a range of economic controls embracing most aspects of production and distribution. Even if this controlled economy proved incapable of supplying basic needs to the great majority of the population across Southeast Asia, it still presented nationalists across the region with an alternative model to the apparently more laissez-faire approach of the colonial powers (Golay, Anspach, Pfanner, and Ayal 1969: 455–456). In spite of the increasing economic dislocation in the last phase of the Japanese period, some shrewd and determined indigenous businesspeople in various parts of Southeast Asia were able to turn a chaotic situation to their own advantage and establish viable enterprises.

On the political front, the fierce devotion to emperor, armed forces, and nation, which inspired the Japanese military, made a deep impression on many young people in Southeast Asia, and this intense nationalism inevitably affected the way they viewed economic problems. After 1945, the relationship between indigenous business groups, the Chinese, and foreign businesses, especially those originating from the colonial power, could never be the same as it was before 1942. The forces of indigenism were probably strongest in Indonesia, where grievances against both the Dutch and the Chinese were intense, and in Burma, where not just Indians and Chinese, but also some minority ethnic groups such as the Karens, were considered to have been accorded favorable treatment in the colonial era. But they were not entirely absent elsewhere in the former colonies or in Thailand, the only Southeast Asian country to have escaped direct colonial control.

In most of the former colonies in Southeast Asia, the independent governments wanted to eradicate what they saw as the pernicious legacy of the plural economy, with its apparent tight relationship between ethnicity and economic role. It has been suggested that the drive toward rapid indigenism was essentially an elite phenomenon, "originating with and promoted by politicians seeking power for other ends and by members of a narrow indigenous entrepreneurial element who are motivated by avarice to expropriate alien wealth" (Golay, Anspach, Pfanner, and Ayal 1969: 447). While this was probably true, especially in Indonesia and Burma, it could hardly be denied that in both countries there was considerable grassroots antagonism against the role of the Chinese and the Indians respectively. In Burma, this antagonism was in large part due to the Indian expropriation of indigenous cultivators. In Indonesia, it resulted from the role of the Chinese in rural areas as traders and moneylenders together with the widespread perception among many nationalists that Chinese businesses had received preferential treatment under the Dutch. In 1956, the former minister of the interior in the Natsir cabinet, Assaat, made a direct attack on the role of the Chinese in Indonesia, which triggered a number of violent demonstrations against Chinese businesses; these attacks continued well into the 1960s (Feith 1962: 481–487; Mackie 1976).

In both Burma and Indonesia, the decade after independence witnessed much political rhetoric about socialism and popular control over the means of production. In Burma, there was a strong government push during the 1950s, even before the military regime assumed power, to take over both British and Indian firms, and to establish new state enterprises in manufacturing. By 1960, it was estimated that more than 90 percent of industry was Burmese-owned. But it was clear that many private businesses and state enterprises were poorly managed and that government industrial policy suffered from a lack of coordination. The Revolutionary Government that assumed control in the early 1960s, after a brief period of apparent openness to both domestic and foreign private enterprise, abruptly reversed its policy and after 1963 prevented the establishment of any new private enterprise in manufacturing industry (Pfanner 1969: 231–232).

The main problem facing governments in Burma and elsewhere who wished to promote both indigenous private enterprises and state enterprises was the acute shortage of managerial expertise. Few indigenous Indonesians, Thais, Burmese, Malays, Vietnamese, or even Filipinos had had much experience running large-scale productive enterprises, and many of the state corporations created throughout Southeast Asia between 1945 and 1960 were financial failures. In Thailand, Burma, and Indonesia, many managers were former army officers and treated the enterprises they were supposed to be running as sources of personal enrichment and patronage. Ayal has pointed out that, even before 1940, the Thai experience confirmed the basic correlation between premature indigenism and corruption, a correlation that was to become more obvious in other parts of the region after 1950 (1969: 338–339).

In Indonesia, the 1945 constitution had enshrined the "family principle" of economic organization, and some nationalist leaders regarded cooperatives as an "excellent expression of Indonesian social ideals" even though the peasant economy in Indonesia had, during the latter part of the colonial era, been increasingly based on private ownership of land and production for the market, whether domestic or foreign (Mackie 1964: 44–45). Perhaps because the spirit of private enterprise was so strong in rural areas, little was achieved with agricultural cooperatives during the 1950s, and, as we have seen, there was little pressure for the establishment of collective farms, even on the part of the Indonesian Communist Party. Instead in the early 1950s, government policy was directed more to the fostering of indigenous entrepreneurs in the nonagricultural economy. The so-called Benteng program, established immediately after independence, was at first directed mainly toward getting more indigenous Indonesians involved in the lucrative import and export trade, which had been dominated in colonial times by the big Dutch trading houses and to a lesser extent by the Chinese.

Anspach has discussed the failings of the program in detail. As he pointed out, there was concern, even among some nationalist politicians, at the blatant racial bias of the Benteng measures and the unwillingness to encourage Chinese businesses even when their owners had adopted Indonesian nationality (1969: 168–179). In addition, the lingering support for cooperatives, especially strong with Vice President Hatta, meant that some key politicians tended to oppose any plan to encourage private enterprise, whatever the ownership. The distaste of the Hatta camp for hothouse development of indigenous entrepreneurs was no doubt strengthened by the growing evidence that many of the so-called indigenous businesses that got access to import licenses were simply fronts for more experienced Chinese companies. In fact, close cooperation between Chinese businessmen and Indonesian powerholders began during the latter part of the 1940s, when nationalists leaders established links with *totok* traders in order to secure food and other essential materials for the struggle against the Dutch (Twang 1998: 324–327). It was the less culturally integrated *totok*, rather than the older, established, Dutch-speaking *peranakan* business groups, who adjusted more quickly to the often hostile political climate of the 1950s.

President Sukarno exploited the growing public frustration at the perceived failure of indigenist policies after he brought the period of constitutional democracy to an end in 1958 and ushered in the Guided Economy. From then on, indigenist goals became intertwined with the aim of implementing Indonesian socialism, although as Anspach has pointed out, for most of the Indonesian political elite, socialism meant little more than "an emotional predilection, a vestigial sentiment from the revolutionary struggle against the capitalistic Dutch" (1969: 126). In fact, the decades of the 1950s and the 1960s almost certainly witnessed an attenuation of the role of government in the Indonesian economy. Government expenditures relative to GDP were already low in Indonesia in comparison with several other former colonies in the late 1950s (see Table 9.6). After 1960, in spite of the increased rhetoric about Indonesian socialism, revenues and expenditures fell further relative to GDP. In 1960, output from government enterprises, including those expropriated from the Dutch, amounted to only about 20 percent of total output (Booth 1998: figure 4.1, table 4.9).

In several respects, British Malaya in the late 1950s offered a stark contrast to the situation in both Burma and Indonesia as well as that in Thailand. The Chinese and to a lesser extent the Indian presence was much larger than elsewhere in Southeast Asia, and indigenous Malays comprised a much lower proportion of the nonagricultural labor force than in other colonies in the 1930s (see Tables 6.2 and 6.4). It might have been expected that indigenist policies would have been stronger there than in other parts of Southeast Asia. But according to Golay, Anspach, Pfanner, and Ayal, the forces of indigenism were comparatively weak, and there was little or no socialist content to such indigenist policies as were implemented (1969: 454). Pressures on foreign and especially British enterprises were hardly draconian. Indeed White argued that, by 1957, the British had achieved something approximating neocolonialism or "informal empire" (1996: 269).

The Alliance government maintained open economic policies, a competitive exchange rate, and a friendly attitude to foreign investment. In 1962, Malaya was the sixth largest recipient of direct foreign investment from Britain. Estate companies that had been established in the colonial era, far from being threatened with takeovers by the government, were encouraged to undertake replanting and expansion of their activities. Although Malaya's share of world rubber production, both natural and synthetic, was only 18.2 percent in 1960 compared with 44.5 percent during the 1930s, the Alliance government recognized that both rubber and tin would continue to be important earners of foreign exchange in the 1960s and that investment in both industries should be encouraged, whatever its provenance. These attitudes were unacceptable to more radical nationalists in the wider Malay world, especially President Sukarno, whose policy of confronting the new Malaysian Federation when it was formed in 1963 was based on a fear that it was simply a front for the neocolonial ambitions of Britain and the other former colonial powers in the region.

In the 1950s, the government of what was still British Malaya had to be urged by international development agencies to assume more responsibility for encouraging manufacturing industry. The report by the International Bank for Reconstruction and Development (as the World Bank was then known), published in 1955, recommended a two-pronged approach. On the one hand, the government should provide infrastructure including water, electric power, roads, and so on, while, on the other hand, it should "foster individual enterprise" through measures such as provision of technical and market research for secondary industry, investment in appropriate education and training programs, support for foreign investors in sectors where their technical know-how could be crucial, and also the judicious use of tariff protection. On this last point, the report stressed that the tariff should be used as a means of encouraging development and not as a way of supporting "hopelessly high-cost industries" (International Bank for Reconstruction and Development 1955: 123). Here the bank seemed to be echoing the belief, strongly held by many British colonial officials, that most infant industries never grew up and that most colonies should remain primary producers (Meredith 1975: 497).

Tariff protection was an especially difficult issue because those parts of British Malaya that had developed as free ports, especially Singapore and Penang, were fearful that with independence their free port status would be removed and their consumers forced to pay high tariffs on imported goods or buy high-cost manufactures from other parts of Malaya. These fears were part of the reason for Singapore's departure from the Federation of Malaysia in 1965. But the Malay political elites who dominated policy making just before independence were themselves ambivalent about encouraging rapid industrialization because they knew that it would be the Chinese who would seize the opportunities provided by tariff protection. Some were also concerned about the impact of industrial protection on the urban-rural terms of trade and about the welfare effects on small rural producers, the great majority of whom were Malay. As Golay has argued, the insecurity felt by the Malay leadership also caused them to accept and even encourage the continuing large Western stake in the economy (1969a: 346).

The situation in the Philippines was different again. By the late 1930s, almost 45 percent of the assets of nonagricultural enterprises in the Philippines were owned by Filipino citizens (Golay 1969b: table 1). This was a far higher proportion than in any other colonial territory in East or Southeast Asia. Certainly many of the large owners of both agricultural estates and nonagricultural enterprises were of mixed Filipino and Chinese or Spanish descent, but the ethnicity issue was less politically fraught in the Philippines after 1945 than in many other parts of the region. This was mainly because ethnic Chinese were fewer in number than in many other parts of Southeast Asia and not really perceived as a major threat by postindependence governments. The most overtly anti-Chinese legislation was the Retail Trade Nationalization Law, enacted in 1954, which restricted retail trade to Filipino businesses after 1964. But many noncitizen Chinese who owned medium- and large-scale firms got around the legislation, usually by seeking naturalization

(Yoshihara 1994: 28–32). By the late 1960s, younger members of Chinese families were integrating reasonably well into the broader Philippine society.

A shared religion and a similar educational background helped in assimilating the Chinese in the Philippines; in addition, many in the governing elite had some Chinese and Spanish ancestry and harbored little resentment toward those of mixed or foreign blood if they were prepared to take citizenship and embrace Philippine cultural values. This lack of xenophobia was also reflected in the attitudes of the government and business elites toward foreign and especially American companies. Most of the politicians who attained power after 1946 in the Philippines harbored little overt hostility to these enterprises. In addition, they had virtually no sympathy for socialist policies or even for government taking an activist role in the economy. As we have seen, land reform policies made little progress in the period from the late 1940s to the late 1960s. In the late 1950s, government expenditure relative to GDP was the lowest in the region (see Table 9.6). By and large the political forces that had come to power in the last phase of the American period remained in control after 1946 and became over time an entrenched barrier to further structural transformation of the economy. In this sense, American colonialism was, as Kang has argued, "pervasive and yet, ultimately, nontransformative" (2002: 27).

In the two decades after 1946, it could be argued, the lack of aggressive economic nationalism in the Philippines served the country well. There was substantial economic growth during this period. After the implementation of high levels of protection through extensive import and foreign exchange controls after 1949, the manufacturing sector grew rapidly, and by 1960 manufacturing accounted for a higher proportion of GDP than in any other former colonial territory in Asia (Golay 1969b: 33; see also Table 9.4). Export growth slowed as a result of the overvaluation of the peso, and gradually the export sector was taken over by Philippine interests. It was these interests that ultimately pushed through the removal of exchange and import controls in 1962 and the substantial devaluation of the peso. It was much easier for the government of the day to undertake such measures once the export sector was seen to be in Philippine hands. At this point it might have appeared that pressures of indigenism, such as they were, were driving the Philippines in the direction of a more open and competitive economy. But in spite of these policy changes, it proved impossible for the Philippines to move into the kind of high-speed industrial growth achieved by Taiwan and South Korea after 1960. The benefits of the devaluation of 1962 were rapidly eroded by high inflation (Power and Sicat 1971: 52), thus providing only a transitory boost to both existing and new export industries.

In both Taiwan and South Korea, forces of indigenism were weaker than in much of Southeast Asia, mainly because the dominant Japanese presence had left virtually no room for any other foreign participation in either economy. There was no equivalent of the large migrant Indian or Chinese presence, and there was no foreign investment apart from that of the Japanese. Thus the abrupt departure of the colonial power in 1945 left large holes in both economies, which were filled in different ways in the two former colonies. In Taiwan, the Chen Yi administration that took over from the departing Japanese was imbued by the "statist economic ideas" used in KMT circles to interpret Sun Yat-sen's doctrine of fostering the people's livelihood (Lai, Myers, and Wei 1991: 84). Officials were concerned with building up a patronage network for migrants from the mainland but were also imbued with an ideological bias in favor of a planned economy. Publicly owned firms soon controlled more than 70 percent of all industrial and agricultural enterprises. In addition, a new Monopoly Bureau controlled the supply and marketing of salt, camphor, opium, matches, liquor, and tobacco. The government also imposed strict regulations on private trade.

By the end of 1946, the Chen Yi administration probably controlled "even more economic activity than had the Japanese" (Lai, Myers, and Wei 1991: 87). Even before the wave of refugees from the mainland in 1949, many mainlanders were employed in the bureaucracy, including the state enterprises. Steinhoff has estimated that the numbers of mainlanders employed by state enterprises more than doubled between 1946 and 1949; in 1949 they accounted for more than one-third of the total (1980: 61). Many lacked experience in the jobs they were allocated, and a process of rationalization of employment began in the early 1950s. Numbers of both mainlanders and Taiwanese working in the state enterprises fell. It is probable that some moved into private sector activities, although these were largely the province of indigenous Taiwanese. After the land reform was implemented, Taiwanese landlords received compensation for the land they had surrendered in the form of government bonds and stock in former Japanese companies; some of them at least used these assets to build up new enterprises (ibid.: 59).

Taiwanese and mainlanders did not meld easily into a unified nation. They were in many cases divided by language; many indigenous Taiwanese had little command of Mandarin and were more fluent in Japanese (Wade 1990: 232). Few mainlanders who arrived in 1949 understood either Japanese or the local dialects. After the ruthless suppression of the 1947 uprising, there was little appetite on the part of the native Taiwanese for further political dissent. Rather they acquiesced in a division of labor that saw the mainland arrivals disproportionately represented in the civil service, the military, and key professions such as teaching. In this sense, the arrivals from the mainland replaced the Japanese, who had accounted for around half the government and professional jobs in the colonial era (see Table 6.4). Indigenous Taiwanese found it easier to move into industry and commerce, where they had, in spite of considerable discrimination, been able to make some headway under the Japanese. For example, Taiwan Plastic, which grew into a vast conglomerate after 1960, was founded by a businessman who began as a rice trader in the

Japanese era (Kobayashi 1996: 331). By the mid-1970s, more than 70 percent of the three hundred largest companies in Taiwan were controlled by native Taiwanese (Wade 1990: 262).

In a divided Korea, the situation was different again. In North Korea, the adoption of a strict socialist model led to the elimination of most forms of private enterprise by the end of the 1950s. In South Korea, most scholars have viewed the postarmistice years as characterized by rampant cronyism, where Japanese properties and aid dollars, largely from the United States, were distributed to business groups friendly to the Rhee regime at very low prices. It was thus possible for firms with the right connections to make "massive profits with no further effort than a bit of paper work in ordering imports" (Jones and Sakong 1980: 277). In addition, businesses with good political and bureaucratic connections received low interest loans, tax benefits, and other privileges. This was a situation not unlike that which the Benteng program created in Indonesia, although in the Korean case large inflows of foreign aid greatly added to the opportunities for rent seeking. Jones and Sakong have drawn a parallel between the charismatic political talents of Rhee and those of Sukarno, and argued that both were better suited to the creation and integration of a new nation than the development of an existing one (ibid.: 41).

Jones and Sakong point out that this situation changed with the advent of the Park government (1980: 276). Under Park, firms were expected to make a convincing argument that the privileges conferred on them would be used productively. Good connections with the bureaucracy were still important, but as the supply of potential entrepreneurs increased, an element of competition was introduced into the process of securing the necessary government-controlled inputs. At least some Koreans who had moved into business in the latter part of the colonial era or in the immediate aftermath of the Pacific War found that the business climate under Park allowed them to develop their business ventures without the impediments that hampered them under previous regimes. The introduction of a more open and competitive market for foreign exchange and a decline in aid flows eliminated an important cause of rent-seeking behavior. The Park government remained distrustful of foreign, and particularly Japanese, domination and did not encourage foreign firms to establish businesses in Korea. The absence of multinational companies in manufacturing, trade, and commerce created more space for indigenous firms. In this respect, Korea differed from Taiwan and even more from Southeast Asia after 1960.

It is striking how many of the policy debates in the former colonial territories in the decade after 1945 revolved around issues of ownership of productive assets (foreign or local, state or private, indigenous or migrant Asian). But it was clear, at least to the more thoughtful nationalists, that whatever their ultimate ownership, if assets were to be properly managed, it would be necessary to develop a domestic class of professional managers and technically trained workers. Throughout the region, whether in the former Japanese colonies or in Southeast Asia, colonial educational legacies especially at the tertiary level were at best modest and at worst nonexistent. It might have been true, as Jones and Sakong have argued in the Korean case, that potential managers and technicians might have learned by watching rather than by doing in the Japanese factories established in the late colonial era (1980: 18). But such knowledge as the indigenous workers picked up was rapidly dissipated, not just in Korea but in other former colonies as well, through the disturbed years of the 1940s and 1950s. What was required was a dramatically increased supply of workers with the kinds of technical skills that modern industry and commerce demanded in the second part of the twentieth century.

The main exception to the shortage of skilled workers was the Philippines, where, in the mid-1950s, numbers of graduates in science and technology per 100,000 people were roughly the same as in Japan and substantially higher than elsewhere in Asia (Table 9.11). This was the result of the high secondary and tertiary enrollments there in the late colonial era. But in Taiwan and South Korea, gross enrollment ratios at the primary level (numbers of children enrolled as a percentage of total numbers in the seven to twelve age groups) had already caught up with the Philippines by the mid-1950s, and in South Korea gross enrollment ratios at the secondary level were higher (Table 9.11). The growth in educational enrollments in South Korea from the 1950s onward meant that, by the 1970s, almost half the male labor force had at least secondary education (Booth 2003b: 153).

Even in economies such as South Korea and Taiwan where, by the late 1960s and early 1970s, the nonagricultural sectors of the economy were growing rapidly, it was not always easy to match the output of the educational

Table 9.11. Educational Enrollments and Science and Technology Graduates in Asia, c. 1955

| | Gross Enrollment Ratios | | Science and Technology |
	Primary	Secondary	Graduates per 100,000 People
Japan	64	94	34.9
Philippines	54	25	34.2
India	27	18	18.1
Korea (South)	54	36	17.2
Taiwan	54	24	14.3
China	36	8	4.8
Thailand	51	14	3.3
Vietnam (South)	21	4	0.6
British Malaya	49	18	n.a.
Indonesia	39	8	n.a.
Burma	24	9	n.a.

Sources: United Nations UNESCO 1964: 103–105; United Nations ECAFE 1962: 34.

Note: n.a. = not available.

system with the requirements of the labor market. A labor force survey carried out in South Korea in 1974 found that, although open unemployment was only around 6.5 percent, a further 13 percent of workers were "underutilized" in the sense that there was a mismatch between their qualifications and the work they were doing. In the Philippines, where growth was slower during the 1960s, a 1968 survey found that around 10 percent of employed workers were underutilized using the mismatch criterion. Many were also working quite short hours (Hauser 1977: table 5). While rapid expansion of access to education for the indigenous population was viewed by many postindependence politicians as one means of eradicating the legacy of the plural economy, finding productive jobs for the output of the education system proved more difficult than many had realized.

CHAPTER 10

Conclusions

M uch of the literature on economic development in East and Southeast Asia written during the 1970s and 1980s tended to emphasize the economic policies adopted by the different governments that came to power in the postindependence era. Most economists wanting to explain the rapid growth of Taiwan, South Korea, Hong Kong, and Singapore from 1960 onward focused particularly on macroeconomic and exchange rate policies and on reforms of the trade regime. It was argued that prudent fiscal and monetary policies reduced inflation and permitted governments to improve infrastructure and expand access to education, while the exchange rate regime and "open-type" trade policies provided an incentive climate conducive to the rapid growth of exports. These policy lessons were then disseminated by international development organizations and by leading academics to other parts of the developing world. They became influential in other parts of Southeast Asia during the 1970s and 1980s, and by the early 1990s, economies such as Malaysia, Indonesia, and Thailand had also achieved considerable success in accelerating the growth of manufactured exports. The World Bank (1993) attributed this success to getting the basics of economic policy right; their influential report on the "East Asian Miracle" argued that this policy package offered lessons to other, less successful, parts of the developing world.

The success of the "East Asian" model was used not just by the World Bank but by many orthodox economists in Asia and elsewhere to challenge the influence of dependency theory, which argued that the antidevelopmental policies adopted by many colonial and postcolonial regimes in Latin America and elsewhere had left a legacy that made it unlikely that any underdeveloped economy in the second part of the twentieth century would benefit from trade and investment links with the developed world. But as Kohli argued, in their criticisms of dependency theory, many economists "threw out the proverbial baby with the bathwater; they threw out the colonial pasts of the developing world. Instead of asking, could the roots of varying performances be located in a variety of colonial pasts, most developmentalists now focus on the nature of post-WWII states, social structures, and policy choices as the primary explanations of divergent performances" (1994: 1288).

Kohli's remarks were aimed not just at mainstream economists, but also at some of their critics, such as Amsden (1989), whom he considered to have underestimated the importance of the Japanese legacy to the fashioning of the South Korean developmental state under Park. But other scholars have been inclined to see more discontinuities than continuities in the Korean story. Haggard, Kang, and Moon have argued that the few entrepreneurs who did manage to build up successful enterprises during the Japanese era would probably have emerged anyway, even if Japan had not been in charge (1997: 868). They are unimpressed with Kohli's argument that the lineages of the developmental state in South Korea can be traced back to the Japanese and see the policies that emerged in the 1960s as being very much the product of their time and place.

It has not been the purpose of this study to examine the specific debate over the Japanese colonial legacy in Korea or indeed in Taiwan, where there is greater consensus on the achievements of the Japanese, especially in agriculture and infrastructure development. My aim has been rather to place the debate concerning Japanese colonialism in a wider perspective through an examination of the record of other colonial regimes in Southeast Asia. By reviewing what was achieved and not achieved in British, Dutch, French, and American colonial possessions as well as in nominally independent Thailand, I argue that we are in a better position to assess the colonial legacies bequeathed to independent states throughout East and Southeast Asia. That the legacies were extremely mixed is hardly surprising, as most colonial regimes were pursuing a range of policies that changed over time as both internal and external circumstances changed.

In all cases, colonial economic policies reflected the pressures at work on the metropolitan powers, whether from business groups, political parties, or various lobby groups, some of which were, by the early twentieth century, suspicious of the economic benefits of colonial ventures to the metropolitan economies. Thus many of the differences noted in this study reflect the very different aims and interests that the various colonial powers had in their Asian colonies in the early decades of the twentieth century. These interests also changed over time, as a result of both political changes in the metropolitan economies and changes in the international economy. The severe depression in the advanced capitalist economies in the early 1930s had an especially important impact on the Southeast Asian colonies because exports made a significant contribution to total GDP, and falling demand for and prices of commodities such as sugar, rubber, and tin affected both government revenues and the incomes of many millions of small producers as well as employees of large estates and mining companies. Colonial governments were forced not just to intervene in commodity markets, but also to use various devices to encourage the emergence of new industries, especially in manufacturing.

These variations in policies both over time and across colonial jurisdictions mean that many of the generalizations in the literature about the economic impact of colonialism have to be modified in the light of actual experience. In Chapter 3, the process of accommodating growing populations in agriculture was discussed, in both Taiwan and Korea and in various parts of Southeast Asia. It was argued that, in spite of much rhetoric about the desirability of creating a prosperous farming sector with cultivators owning secure title to their land, this goal remained elusive in many parts of the region until the 1940s. Tenancy was widespread, and in the most densely settled areas, many cultivators owned either no land at all or such tiny parcels of land that it was impossible for them to scrape even a bare subsistence. They were forced to seek wage work where it was available or engage in various kinds of self-employment in cottage industry or trade.

The classical concept of vent for surplus was used by Myint to analyze the process by which unused land was brought under cultivation of export crops in the late nineteenth and early twentieth centuries. It involved the replication of existing technologies over more land and was not entirely applicable to either Taiwan or Korea, where much of the growth in production of rice for export came from cultivation of new varieties on existing land. In addition, even in the more land-abundant parts of Southeast Asia, the rapid growth in demand for export crops had made land a valuable and highly contested factor of production by the early twentieth century. Powerful business groups, often owned or backed by citizens of the colonial power, secured land from native cultivators, sometimes by using legal titling procedures that the indigenous populations did not understand or recognize. The result was that indigenous smallholders were sometimes not only prevented from expanding their own holdings but dispossessed of the land they were already cultivating.

Governments reacted to these problems in various ways. Probably the strongest reaction was in British Malaya, where the Malay Reservation Enactments placed strict controls on land alienation within the designated Malay reserves. But this policy was designed not so much to facilitate the cultivation of export crops by indigenous Malays as to encourage them to grow more rice, which was usually less profitable. Elsewhere colonial governments were inclined to a more laissez-faire approach to land matters, although in Indonesia the Dutch colonial government prevented land sales of indigenous land to foreigners including Chinese. Broadly speaking, as was argued in Chapter 4, governments in all the East and Southeast Asian colonies in the early part of the twentieth century were taking a much more activist role in the economy. Revenue sources were diversified, and expenditures were devoted to a range of infrastructure projects as well as to education and health services. It was shown in Chapter 7 that the outcomes in terms of increased enrollments and improved health indicators, such as infant mortality rates, were often substantial, although by the 1930s they varied considerably by colony.

It was argued in Chapter 5 that there was wide variation in balance of payments outcomes between colonies, which suggests that care should be exercised in making generalizations about "colonial drains." Even between the two Japanese colonies, there was a considerable difference. Taiwan ran large balance of payments surpluses for most years from 1915 through 1938, which were used in part to fund private capital outflows. In Korea, the current account was usually in deficit, and after 1930 these deficits became larger, reflecting the huge capital inflows from Japan into heavy industry and infrastructure development, especially in the north. Within the Southeast Asian colonies, there was also considerable variation in balance of payments outcomes. Although we do not have complete balance of payments for Burma, there can be little doubt that a substantial surplus was generated during the first four decades of the twentieth century, and part of this surplus was used to fund government remittances to New Delhi. In Indonesia, as in Taiwan, the balance of payments surpluses were used mainly to fund private capital outflow.

As was pointed out in Chapter 7, a well-informed observer, looking at the achievements, both economic and social, of the various colonial regimes in East and Southeast Asia in the late 1930s, would almost certainly have put Taiwan and the Philippines at the top of the list. Taiwan was impressive, not just for its social achievements, but also for the progress made in agricultural productivity. This in turn was the result of considerable investment in rural infrastructure as well as in the dissemination of high-yielding varieties of rice. No other Asian colony had similar success in achieving higher rice yields, although there was some progress in Korea and Java in increasing cropping ratios and disseminating improved seeds. Java, from the late nineteenth century to the 1930s, also achieved remarkable results in developing new, higher-yielding sugar varieties, But on the negative side, the Japanese in Taiwan also made little effort to develop the entrepreneurial capacities of the indigenous population. There was, for example, no equivalent of the popular credit system that the Dutch had developed in Java. In the Philippines, where American involvement in industry and commerce was far less pervasive than Japanese involvement in Taiwan, indigenous Filipinos (admittedly including many of mixed Chinese and Spanish descent) owned a considerable share of nonagricultural assets in the economy by the late 1930s.

Fitting Thailand into the Southeast Asian picture is complicated by the fact that it was never formally a colony, although some writers have argued that the "Thai government acted as if it were a colonial government to preserve its own continuity and to maintain domestic stability" (Resnick 1970: 66). When one evaluates economic development in Thailand during the first four decades of the twentieth century in a comparative perspective, there is some evidence that the Thai government was even more Catholic than the pope in implementing strictly conservative fiscal and monetary policy. In part this might have reflected the presence of British financial advisers, but in addition it appears that the government was reluctant to embark on any policy that might possibly have affected its sovereignty, including foreign borrowing for infrastructure projects, such as irrigation or road development, which would have yielded rates of return higher than the cost of borrowing. Nor were they keen to encourage foreign investment, either in estate agriculture or in industry. Thus the sorts of policy initiatives that the Dutch pursued in Indonesia after 1901 were not, by and large, viewed favorably by the Thai governing elite until well after the end of the Pacific War.

During the early part of the 1940s, the world turned upside down for many in Southeast Asia. While the ignominious defeat at the hands of the Japanese of the Dutch, British, and American colonial regimes may have been welcomed by many, Japanese rule turned out to be an unmitigated disaster for the great majority of people in the region. The indiscriminate use of military scrip together with increased shortages of food and other basic needs led to mounting inflation. The Japanese broke up the regional rice trade networks within Southeast Asia that had evolved over the previous decades and forced many regions to become largely self-sufficient in food. While some land that had been used to grow tree crops was converted to food production, such land was usually not suitable for rice. Millions had to rely on root crops or whatever else they could grow locally. By 1945, many civilians in both urban and rural areas were dying of hunger and disease. In addition, many men were conscripted to work as laborers on public works projects; hunger and maltreatment led to many deaths in their ranks as well.

It was hardly surprising that, by the time of the Japanese surrender in August 1945, many people in the Southeast Asian colonies had decided that no foreign power, either European or Asian, could be trusted to govern them in their own interests. But the path to independence throughout the region was far from smooth. In the Philippines, the Americans honored previous pledges and granted complete independence in 1946, and the British gave Burma independence along with the rest of what had been British India. But both the Dutch and the French wanted to retain control over their Southeast Asian colonies. Bloody conflicts followed that were only resolved by the intervention of outside powers. The Dutch government, under considerable international pressure, conceded independence to Indonesia in late 1949; in French Indochina, the settlement reached at Geneva in 1954 provided only a temporary lull in a struggle that lasted three decades, until 1975. In the two Japanese colonies, the end of Japanese colonial rule was followed by a brutal takeover by KMT forces in Taiwan and partition and a destructive war in Korea.

In the early 1950s, it was far from obvious that any former colony in East and Southeast Asia or Thailand had favorable economic prospects. The Philippines presented the most optimistic picture; the economy had recovered rapidly from the damage of war, with substantial American aid, and by the mid-1950s had the highest per capita GDP in the region, after British Malaya, which was still a colony. The other former colonies took longer to catch up to prewar output, and some, including Indonesia and Burma, had not done so by 1960. Virtually everywhere in Southeast Asia, disputes over land became more frequent and often more violent in the decade after 1945. Only in South Korea and Taiwan were the governments that emerged after the Pacific War both willing and able to push through effective land reforms. In both countries, cultivated holdings were mainly small and tenancy widespread. The land reforms were thus mainly reforms in tenancy, with the large landlords being dispossessed and compensated with government bonds. In Southeast Asia, governments struggled with the problem of agrarian reform through the 1950s and 1960s, but vested interests were very powerful, and little was achieved. Only in communist-controlled North Vietnam was there substantial land redistribution, although the government's attempts to set up collective farms met with considerable resistance and had to be modified.

In all the newly independent states in East and Southeast Asia, economic nationalism was pervasive, but it took very different forms. In South Korea and several parts of Southeast Asia, there was considerable hostility to foreign multinational firms, and foreign investment was not encouraged. In Indonesia, hostility to the continuing presence of Dutch companies in the estates sector, in manufacturing, and in banking and trade boiled over in the late 1950s into wholesale nationalization of Dutch assets. In other parts of Southeast Asia, attitudes were less hostile but were hardly supportive of large-scale inflows of foreign capital. Policies changed in Thailand in the late 1950s when General Sarit took over and set up the Board of Investment. By far the most friendly policies toward foreign investment were in British Malaya, where the government encouraged investment not just by British firms, but also by other European and American multinationals. When Singapore seceded from the Malaysian Federation in 1965, the government there made even more determined efforts to sell Singapore as a base for the Southeast Asian operations of foreign multinationals.

Given all the changes, both economic and political, that swept through the former colonies of East and Southeast Asia in the two decades after the end of the Pacific War, it might appear that the evidence strongly supports those who argue that the legacies of colonialism, whether positive or negative, were rapidly eroded after 1945. While debates continued until the 1990s about what policies were crucial in accelerating growth in the two Japanese colonies after 1960, many participants appeared to argue that the Japanese legacy was only of minor importance. A large conference volume, produced in 1981 by a leading research institute in Taiwan, that examined the "experiences and lessons" of economic development in Taiwan had very little to say about the Japanese era at all (Academia Sinica 1981). Most of the participants at the conference stressed macroeconomic and trade policies, while some also touched on the "grim battle for survival in Taiwan which put anti-colonialism largely out of people's minds" (Arndt 1981: 137). This situation was contrasted with the situation in Indonesia in the 1950s, where a "backward-looking anti-colonialism" was used by politicians to gain support for indigenist policies, many of which were damaging to economic growth.

Such views can be contested; it is arguable that the battle for survival in Taiwan after 1949 was as much a battle on the part of native Taiwanese against the KMT government as one by the island as a whole against the mainland. But the fact remains that the KMT government, although dominated by mainlanders, did adopt policies that supported the Taiwanese business class in their efforts to diversify exports and move into a sustained process of export-led growth. Credit for moving toward more open economic policies has often been given to key policy makers such as K. Y. Yin, the minister of economics who was able to persuade his political colleagues of the need for a policy shift in the late 1950s (Galenson 1981: 77). But to the extent that these technocrats were advocating "open-type" trade policies and a stronger role for both indigenous Taiwanese and foreign private enterprise in the economy, they were in fact supporting an economic policy package that was the antithesis of what had been practiced under the Japanese until 1945.

In several parts of Southeast Asia, the strong economic nationalism that emerged after 1945 was a reaction against colonial policies that had created the plural economy and the economic subordination of indigenous populations. Economic nationalism took different forms in different countries; in many parts of the region, state enterprises were encouraged as a means of diluting the influence of Chinese and other foreign businesses. But these were frequently badly managed and in some cases used as vehicles for the enrichment of their managers, political parties, and the military. The disappointing economic performance of many state enterprises led to another round of reaction in the 1960s. In Thailand and Indonesia, new economic strategies were adopted that were more supportive of foreign investment, and joint ventures were formed between foreign and domestic partners, who were often of Chinese descent. But in Burma the reaction took the form of even more inward-looking policies that strengthened the hold of the military over the economy and further isolated the country from the regional and global economy (Booth 2003a: 149–153).

In Korea, the regime of Park Chung Hee had at best dubious democratic credentials and treated its political opponents harshly. But it did give high priority to rapid economic growth as a policy goal, and it awarded various types of subsidies to companies willing and able to meet reasonably strict performance criteria. As Kang has argued, political considerations were often just as important as merit in the decisions as to which conglomerate received government assistance and how much (2002: 97). The lavish assistance provided to the favored few resulted in a number of inefficiencies, including chronic overcapacity. In addition, the agricultural sector was neglected, and considerable poverty remained in rural areas until the 1980s. But compared with several economies that in 1960 had a higher per capita GDP than South Korea, including both the Philippines and Malaysia, by 1995 the South Korean economy had performed consistently better and had not just achieved higher per capita GDP, but also managed to penetrate world markets with a range of products, from consumer electronics to ships and motor vehicles, manufactured and marketed under Korean brand names. In this sense, South Korea had forged ahead of most of the other former colonies of East and Southeast Asia. While some of the entrepreneuers behind the successes of the large Korean conglomerates may have had their start in the colonial era, most were "new men" in the sense that they had embarked on new initiatives in new industries after 1945.

Kang attributes at least part of the Korean success to a "mindset that was hell-bent on catching up to the Japanese" (2002: 186). Thus one important aspect of the Japanese legacy was that it provided its former colonies with a powerful example of rapid recovery from the appalling destruction of war and of sustained economic growth through the successful penetration of world markets for manufactures, together with a strong desire to compete with and outperform that example. In the Philippines, by contrast, it has been argued that the American colonial regime "blocked Americans from plundering the archipelago, but did nothing to prohibit its exploitation by Filipinos" (Karnow 1989: 223). Critics of the American legacy have argued that the political model that the Americans bequeathed to the Philippines was one of representative democracy, but the elected representatives were largely, if not entirely, drawn from landowners and business families (Hawes 1987: 25). Thus they could, and did, manage the economy largely in their own interests. Catching up with the American economy or that of Japan was not viewed as a priority.

While there is some truth in these arguments, they do not seem entirely satisfactory in explaining postindependence outcomes across East and Southeast Asia. After all, however dysfunctional the American-style political system in the Philippines proved to be for economic development, the Philippine economy was hardly a complete economic failure until the early 1980s. The Philippines recovered faster from the devastation of the war than any other part of Asia, and economic growth was not much below the Asian average in the three decades from 1950 to 1980 (Balisacan and Hill 2003: 7). The poor performance in the 1980s has been attributed to Marcos, but it was Marcos who set aside the American political legacy when he closed down the congress and declared martial law in 1972. Indeed, disillusion with the American political model as a means of achieving rapid economic success seems to have been widespread among the Philippine political elite by the 1970s. Karnow has argued that Marcos' main political opponent, Benigno Aquino, was also doubtful that the Philippines could develop rapidly with an American-style constitution and openly admired more authoritarian rulers in prewar Europe and postwar Asia (1989: 360).

In any comparative study of economic development, it is unwise to be too seduced by the attractions of historical determinism. If economies are to grow at a sustained rate over decades and if the expanded output is to be used to improve living standards for the great majority of the population, then it is essential that a political leadership emerge that gives economic growth high priority in policy making. Such leaders did emerge in Japan in the 1950s and in most parts of East and Southeast Asia over the last four decades of the twentieth century. They gave high priority to rapid economic growth as a means of catching up with the more advanced economies and produced the growth miracle that received so much attention in the literature on Asian economic development until 1997. The main exceptions to the "East Asian model" were Burma and the Philippines, but in neither case does it seem plausible to blame the failure to sustain rapid economic growth under Ne Win and Marcos on the British or American colonial legacies in these two countries. Had these two leaders had different policy priorities, they could have produced sustained growth, as Suharto was able to do in Indonesia and Park in South Korea. That they did not follow growth-promoting policies was a reflection of their own personalities and predilections; other leaders could well have chosen different policies, with different results, not just for economic growth but also for the welfare of their citizens.

Bibliography

Academica Sinica. 1981. *Conference on Experience and Lessons of Economic Development in Taiwan*. Taipei: Academica Sinica.

Acemoglu, Daron, Simon Johnson, and James A. Robinson. 2001. "The Colonial Origins of Comparative Development: An Empirical Investigation." *American Economic Review* 91: 1369–1401.

Adas, Michael. 1974. *The Burma Delta: Economic Development and Social Change on an Asian Rice Frontier, 1852–1941*. Madison: University of Wisconsin Press.

———. 1998. "Improving on the Civilising Mission? Assumptions of United States Exceptionalism in the Colonisation of the Philippines." *Itinerario* 22 (4): 44–66.

Alatas, Syed Hussein. 1977. *The Myth of the Lazy Native*. London: Frank Cass.

Alexander, Jennifer, and Paul Alexander. 1991. "Protecting Peasants from Capitalism: The Subordination of Javanese Traders by the Colonial State." *Comparative Studies in Society and History* 33: 370–394.

Amsden, Alice. 1985. "The State and Taiwan's Economic Development." In Peter B. Evans, D. Rueschemeyer, and T. Skopcol, eds., *Bringing the State Back In*. New York: Cambridge University Press.

———. 1989. *Asia's Next Giant: South Korea and Late Industrialization*. New York: Oxford University Press.

Anderson, Kym, and Rod Tyers. 1992. "Japanese Rice Policy in the Interwar Period: Some Consequences of Imperial Self Sufficiency." *Japan and the World Economy* 4: 103–127.

Andrews, James M. 1935. *Siam: Second Rural Survey 1934–1935*. Bangkok: Bangkok Times Press Ltd.

Andrus, J. R. 1948. *Burmese Economic Life*. Stanford: Stanford University Press.

Angoulvant, Gabriel 1926. *Les Indes néerlandaises: Leur rôle dans l'économie internationale*. Paris: Le Monde Nouveau.

Anh, Nguyen The. 1998. "Japanese Food Policies and the 1945 Great Famine in Indochina." In Paul Kratoska, ed., *Food Supplies and the Japanese Occupation in South-East Asia*. Basingstoke: Macmillan Press.

Anspach, Ralph. 1969. "Indonesia." In Frank H. Golay, Ralph Anspach, M. Ruth Pfanner, and Eliezer B. Ayal, *Underdevelopment and Economic Nationalism in Southeast Asia*. Ithaca: Cornell University Press.

Apthorpe, Raymond. 1979. "The Burden of Land Reform in Taiwan: An Asian Model Land Reform Re-analysed." *World Development* 7: 519–530.

Arndt, H. W. 1981. "Discussants." In *Conference on Experience and Lessons of Economic Development in Taiwan.* Taipei: Academica Sinica.

Ayal, Eliezer B. 1969. "Thailand." In Frank H. Golay, Ralph Anspach, M. Ruth Pfanner, and Eliezer B. Ayal, *Underdevelopment and Economic Nationalism in Southeast Asia.* Ithaca: Cornell University Press.

Aye Hlaing. 1964. "Trends of Economic Growth and Income Distribution in Burma, 1870–1940." *Journal of the Burma Research Society* 47 (June): 89–148.

———. 1965. "An Economic and Statistical Analysis of Economic Development of Burma under British Rule." Ph.D. dissertation, University of London.

Aziz, Ungku A. 1964. "Poverty and Rural Development in Malaysia." *Kajian Ekonomi Malaysia* 1 (1): 70–105.

Balisacan, Arsenio M. 1993. "Agricultural Growth and Rural Performance: A Philippine Perspective." *Journal of Philippine Development* 20 (2): 289–317.

Balisacan, Arsenio, and Hal Hill. 2003. "An Introduction to Key Issues." In Arsenio Balisacan and Hal Hill, eds., *The Philippine Economy: Development, Policies and Challenges.* New York: Oxford University Press.

Ban, Sung Hwan. 1979. "Agricultural Growth in Korea, 1918–1971." In Yujiro Hayami, V. W. Ruttan, and Herman Southworth, eds., *Agricultural Growth in Japan, Taiwan, Korea and the Philippines.* Honolulu: University of Hawai'i Press.

Banens, Maks. 2000. "Vietnam: A Reconstruction of Its Twentieth Century Population History." In Jean-Pascal Bassino, Jean-Dominique Giacometti, and K. Odaka, eds., *Quantitative Economic History of Vietnam, 1900–1990.* Tokyo: Hitotsubashi University, Institute of Economic Research.

Bank of Chosen. 1920. *Economic History of Chosen.* Seoul: Bank of Chosen.

Barclay, George. 1954. *Colonial Development and Population in Taiwan.* Princeton: Princeton University Press.

Barker, Randolph, Robert Herdt, and Beth Rose. 1985. *The Rice Economy of Asia.* Washington, D.C.: Resources for the Future, Inc.

Barlow, Colin, and John Drabble. 1990. "Government and the Emerging Rubber Industries in Indonesia and Malaysia." In Anne Booth, W. O'Malley, and Anna Weidemann, *Indonesian Economic History in the Dutch Colonial Era.* Monograph Series 35. New Haven: Yale University Southeast Asian Studies.

Barnett, H. L. 1947. *Malayan Agricultural Statistics.* Kuala Lumpur: Department of Agriculture.

Bassino, Jean-Pascal. 1998. *Exchange Rates and Exchange Rate Policies in Vietnam under French Rule (1895–1954).* Discussion Paper D98-8. Tokyo: Hitotsubashi University Institute of Economic Research.

———. 2000a. "Estimates of Indochina's and Vietnam's Balance of Payments, 1890–1945: Investigating the Extent of the French Drain in Vietnam." In Jean-Pascal Bassino, Jean-Dominique Giacometti, and K. Odaka, eds., *Quan-*

titative Economic History of Vietnam 1900–1990. Tokyo: Hitotsubashi University, Institute of Economic Research.

———. 2000b. "Public Finance in Vietnam under French Rule, 1895–1954." In Jean-Pascal Bassino, Jean-Dominique Giacometti, and K. Odaka, eds., *Quantitative Economic History of Vietnam 1900–1990*. Tokyo: Hitotsubashi University, Institute of Economic Research.

———. Unpublished. "National Income Estimates of Vietnam, 1890–1970." C. 1999.

Bassino, Jean-Pascal, and Bui Thi Lan Huong. 2000. "Estimates of Indochina's and Vietnam's International Trade (1890–1946)." In Jean-Pascal Bassino, Jean-Dominique Giacometti, and K. Odaka, eds., *Quantitative Economic History of Vietnam 1900–1990*. Tokyo: Hitotsubashi University, Institute of Economic Research.

Batson, Benjamin A. 1984. *The End of the Absolute Monarchy in Siam*. Singapore: Oxford University Press.

Bauer, Peter B. 1948. *The Rubber Industry: A Study in Competition and Monopoly*. London: Longmans, Green.

Bautista, Romeo M. 1994. "Dynamics of Rural Development: Analytical and Policy Issues." *Journal of Philippine Development* 21 (1 and 2): 93–134.

Baxter, James. 1941. *Report on Indian Migration*. Rangoon: Government Printing and Stationery.

Bayly, Christopher, and Tim Harper. 2004. *Forgotten Armies: The Fall of British Asia, 1941–1945*. London: Allen Lane.

Beasley, W. G. 1987. *Japanese Imperialism 1894–1945*. Oxford: Clarendon Press.

Benda, Harry. 1966. "The Pattern of Administrative Reform in the Closing Years of Dutch Rule in Indonesia." *Journal of Asian Studies* 25: 589–605.

———. 1967. "The Japanese Interregnum in Southeast Asia." In Grant K. Goodman, comp., *Imperial Japan and Asia: A Reassessment*. New York: East Asia Institute, Columbia University.

Benham, Frederic. 1951. *The National Income of Malaya, 1947–49 (with a Note on 1950)*. Singapore: Government Printing Office.

Birnberg, Thomas B., and Stephen A. Resnick. 1975. *Colonial Development: An Econometric Study*. New Haven: Yale University Press.

Boeke, J. H. 1927. "Objective and Personal Elements in Colonial Welfare Policy." Translated and reprinted in *Indonesian Economics: The Concept of Dualism in Theory and Practice*. The Hague: W. van Hoeve, 1966.

———. 1953. *Economics and Economic Policy of Dual Societies: As Exemplified by Indonesia*. Haarlem: H. D. Tjeenk Willink and Sons.

Boomgaard, Peter. 1988. "Treacherous Cane: The Java Sugar Industry between 1914 and 1940." In Bill Albert and Adrian Graves, eds., *The World Sugar Economy in War and Depression 1914–40*. London: Routledge.

———. 1991. "The Non-agricultural Side of an Agricultural Economy: Java, 1500–1900." In Paul Alexander, Peter Boomgaard, and Ben White, eds., *In the*

Shadow of Agriculture: Non-farm Activities in the Javanese Economy, Past and Present. Amsterdam: Royal Tropical Institute.

———. 1993. "Upliftment down the Drain? Effects of Welfare Measures in Late Colonial Indonesia." In Jan-Paul Dirkse, Frans Husken, and Mario Rutten, eds., *Development and Social Welfare: Indonesia's Experiences under the New Order.* Leiden: KITLV Press.

Boomgaard, P[eter], and A. J. Gooszen. 1991. *Changing Economy in Indonesia,* vol. 11: *Population Trends, 1795–1942.* Amsterdam: Royal Tropical Institute.

Boomgaard, Peter, and J. L. van Zanden. 1990. *Changing Economy in Indonesia,* vol. 10: *Food Crops and Arable Lands, Java, 1815–1942.* Amsterdam: Royal Tropical Institute.

Booth, Anne. 1988. *Agricultural Development in Indonesia.* Sydney: Allen and Unwin in association with the Asian Studies Association of Australia.

———. 1990. "The Evolution of Fiscal Policy and the Role of Government in the Colonial Economy." In Anne Booth, W. J. O'Malley, and Anna Weidemann, eds., *Indonesian Economic History in the Dutch Colonial Era.* Monograph Series 35. New Haven: Yale University Southeast Asian Studies.

———. 1994. "Japanese Import Penetration and Dutch Response: Some Aspects of Economic Policymaking in Colonial Indonesia." In S. Sugiyama and M. Guerrero, eds., *International Commercial Rivalry in Southeast Asia in the Interwar Period.* Monograph Series 39. New Haven: Yale Southeast Asia Studies.

———. 1998. *The Indonesian Economy in the Nineteenth and Twentieth Centuries: A History of Missed Opportunities.* London: Macmillan.

———. 2000. "Crisis and Response: A Study of Foreign Trade and Exchange Rate Policies in Three Southeast Asian Colonies in the 1930s." In Peter Boomgaard and Ian Brown, eds., *Weathering the Storm: The Economies of Southeast Asia in the 1930s Depression.* Leiden: KITLV Press.

———. 2002. "Rethinking the Role of Agriculture in the 'East Asian Model': Why is Southeast Asia Different from Northeast Asia?" *ASEAN Economic Bulletin* 19:1 (April): 40–51.

———. 2003a. "The Burma Development Disaster in Comparative Historical Perspective." *Southeast Asia Research* 11 (2): 141–171.

———. 2003b. "Education, Equality and Economic Development in the Asia-Pacific Economies." In Martin Andersson and Christer Gunnarsson, eds., *Development and Structural Change in the Asia-Pacific.* London: RoutledgeCurzon.

———. 2003c. "Four Colonies and a Kingdom: A Comparison of Fiscal, Trade and Exchange Rate Policies in South East Asia in the 1930s." *Modern Asian Studies* 37 (2): 429–460.

———. 2005. *Did It Really Help to Be a Japanese Colony? East Asian Economic Performance in Historical Perspective.* Working Paper Series, no. 43. Singapore: Asia Research Institute, National University of Singapore (http://www.ari.nus.edu .sg/docs/wps/).

———. 2007. "Night Watchman, Extractive or Developmental State? Some Evidence from Late Colonial South East Asia." *Economic History Review* 60 (2): 241–266.

Boyer, William W., and Byong Man Anh. 1991. *Rural Development in South Korea: A Sociopolitcal Analysis.* Newark: University of Delaware Press.

Brocheux, Pierre. 1975. "Le prolétariat des plantations d'hévéas au Vietnam méridional: Aspects sociaux et politiques." *Le mouvement social,* no. 90 (January–March).

———. 1995. *The Mekong Delta: Ecology, Economy and Revolution, 1860–1960.* Madison: University of Wisconsin.

Brown, Ian. 1988. *The Elite and the Economy in Siam c. 1890–1920.* Singapore: Oxford University Press.

———. 1993. "The End of the Opium Farm in Siam, 1905–7." In John Butcher and Howard Dick, eds., *The Rise and Fall of Revenue Farming.* Basingstoke: Macmillan Press.

———. 1994. "The British Merchant Community in Singapore and Japanese Commercial Expansion in the 1930s." In S. Sugiyama and M. Guerrero, eds., *International Commercial Rivalry in Southeast Asia in the Interwar Period.* Monograph Series 39. New Haven: Yale Southeast Asia Studies.

———. 2000. "Material Conditions in Lower Burma during the Economic Crisis of the Early 1930s: What the Cotton Textile Import Figures Reveal." In Peter Boomgaard and Ian Brown, eds., *Weathering the Storm: The Economies of Southeast Asia in the 1930s Depression.* Leiden: KITLV Press.

Brudnoy, David. 1970. "Japan's Experiment in Korea." *Monumenta Nipponica* 25: 155–195.

Bureau of Census and Statistics. 1941. *Yearbook of Philippine Statistics 1940.* Manila: Commonwealth of the Philippines, Bureau of Census and Statistics.

———. 1947. *Yearbook of Philippine Statistics 1946.* Manila: Republic of the Philippines, Bureau of Census and Statistics.

———. 1960. *Handbook of Philippine Statistics, 1903–1959.* Manila: Bureau of Census and Statistics.

Burger, D. H. 1939. "The Government's Native Economic Policy." Translated and reprinted in *Indonesian Economics: The Concept of Dualism in Theory and Practice.* The Hague: W. van Hoeve, 1966.

Butcher, John. 1993. "Revenue Farming and the Changing state in Southeast Asia." In John Butcher and Howard Dick, eds., *The Rise and Fall of Revenue Farming.* Basingstoke: Macmillan Press.

Butcher, John, and Howard Dick, eds., 1993. *The Rise and Fall of Revenue Farming.* Basingstoke: Macmillan Press.

Carr, Carolle, and Ramon H. Myers. 1973. "The Agricultural Transformation in Taiwan: The Case of Ponlai Rice, 1922–42." In R. T. Shand, ed., *Technical Change in Asian Agriculture.* Canberra: Australian National University Press.

Central Bureau of Statistics. 1939. *The Living Conditions of Municipally Employed Coolies in Batavia in 1937.* Bulletin 177. Batavia: Central Bureau of Statistics, as translated in *The Indonesian Town: Studies in Urban Sociology*. The Hague: van Hoeve, 1958.

———. 1947. *Statistical Pocketbook of Indonesia, 1941*. Batavia: G. Kolff and Co.

———. 1959. *Statistical Pocketbook of Indonesia, 1959*. Jakarta: Central Bureau of Statistics.

———. 1968. *Statistical Pocketbook of Indonesia, 1964–1967*. Jakarta: Central Bureau of Statistics.

Central Service of Statistics. 1940. *Statistical Yearbook of Thailand, No. 20*. Bangkok: Central Service of Statistics.

———. C. 1946. *Statistical Yearbook of Thailand*, no. 21: *1939–40 to 1944*. Bangkok: Central Service of Statistics.

Central Statistical and Economics Department. 1963. *Statistical Yearbook 1961*. Rangoon: New Secretariat.

Central Statistical Office. 1955. *Statistical Yearbook of Thailand*, no. 22: *1945–55*. Bangkok: Central Statistical Office.

Cha, Myung Soon. 1998. "Imperial Policy or World Price Shocks? Explaining Interwar Korean Consumption Trend." *Journal of Economic History* 58:3 (September): 731–754.

Chandra, Bipan. 1968. "A Reinterpretation of Nineteenth-Century Indian Economic History." *Indian Economic and Social History Review* 5 (1): 35–75.

Chang, Han-Yu. 1969. "A Study of the Living Conditions of Farmers in Taiwan, 1931–1950." *The Developing Economies* 7 (1): 35–62.

Chang, Han-Yu, and Ramon Myers. 1963. "Japanese Colonial Development Policy in Taiwan, 1895–1906: A Case of Bureaucratic Entrepreneurship." *Journal of Asian Studies* 22 (4): 433–449.

Chang, Yunshik. 1966. "Population in Early Modernization: Korea." Ph.D. dissertation, Princeton University.

———. 1971. "Colonization as Planned Changed: The Korean Case." *Modern Asian Studies* 5 (2): 161–186.

———. 1977. "Planned Economic Transformation and Population Change." In C. I. Eugene Kim and Doretha Mortimore, eds., *Korea's Response to Japan: The Colonial Period 1910–1945*. Michigan: Center for Korean Studies, Western Michigan University.

Chaudhuri, K. N. 1983. "Foreign Trade and the Balance of Payments (1757–1947)." In Dharma Kumar, ed., *The Cambridge Economic History of India*, vol. 2: *C.1757–c. 1970*. Cambridge: Cambridge University Press.

Chung, Young-Iob. 2006. *Korea under Siege, 1876–1945: Capital Formation and Economic Transformation*. New York: Oxford University Press.

Clark, Grover C. 1936. *The Balance Sheets of Imperialism: Facts and Figures on Colonies*. New York: Columbia University Press.

Colonial Reports. 1929. *Colonial Reports: Annual No. 1415: Unfederated Malay States Reports for 1927*. London: HM Stationery Office.

Commonwealth of the Philippines, Commission of the Census. 1941. *Summary for the Philippines and General Report for the Census of Population and Agriculture, 1939.* Manila: Bureau of Printing, May.

Corpuz, O. D. 1997. *An Economic History of the Philippines.* Quezon City: University of the Philippines Press.

Creutzberg, P. 1975. *Changing Economy of Indonesia,* vol. 1: *Indonesia's Export Crops, 1816–1940.* The Hague: Martinus Nijhoff.

———. 1976. *Changing Economy of Indonesia,* vol. 2: *Public Finance: 1816–1939.* The Hague: Martinus Nijhoff.

———. 1978. *Changing Economy of Indonesia,* vol. 3: *Rice Prices.* The Hague: Martinus Nijhoff.

Cribb, Robert. 1993. "Development Policy in the Early Twentieth Century." In Jan-Paul Dirkse, Frans Husken, and Mario Rutten, eds., *Development and Social Welfare: Indonesia's Experiences under the New Order.* Leiden: KITLV Press.

Cumings, Bruce. 1984a. "The Legacy of Japanese Colonialism in Korea." In Ramon H. Myers and Mark R. Peattie, eds., *The Japanese Colonial Empire, 1895–1945.* Princeton: Princeton University Press.

———. 1984b. "The Origins and Development of the Northeast Asian Political Economy: Industrial Sectors, Product Cycles, and Political Consequences." *International Organization* 38 (1): 1–40.

———. 1997. *Korea's Place in the Sun: A Modern History.* New York: W. W. Norton and Company.

———. 1999. "Colonial Formations and Deformations: Korea, Taiwan, and Vietnam." In *Parallax Visions: Making Sense of American–East Asian Relations.* Durham: Duke University Press.

David, Cristina C., and Randolph Barker. 1979. "Agricultural Growth in the Philippines, 1948–1971." In Yujiro Hayami, V. W. Ruttan, and Herman Southworth, eds., *Agricultural Growth in Japan, Taiwan, Korea and the Philippines.* Honolulu: University of Hawai'i Press.

Davis, Dwight. 1932. "Reports on Good Will Trip." *Annual Report of the Governor General of the Philippine Islands 1931,* appendix 1. Washington, D.C.: United States Government Printing Office.

Department of Economic Affairs. 1936. *Census of 1930 in the Netherlands Indies.* Vol. 8. Batavia: Department of Economic Affairs.

———. 1938. *Prices, Price Indexes and Exchange Rates in Java, 1913–1937.* Bulletin of the Central Bureau of Statistics, no. 146. Batavia: Department of Economic Affairs.

———. 1941. *Statistical Abstract of the Netherlands Indies.* Batavia: Department of Economic Affairs.

———. 1947. *Statistical Pocketbook of Indonesia 1941.* Batavia: G. Kolff and Co. for the Central Bureau of Statistics.

Department of Statistics. 1936. *Malayan Year Book 1936.* Singapore: Government Printing Office for the Department of Statistics, Straits Settlements and Federated Malay States.

———. 1939. *Malayan Year Book 1939.* Singapore: Government Printing Office for the Department of Statistics, Straits Settlements and Federated Malay States.

———. 1961. *Malayan Statistics April 1961.* Singapore: Government Printer for the Department of Statistics.

Descours-Gatin, Chantal. 1992. *Quand l'opium finançait la colonisation en Indochine.* Paris: Éditions l'Harmattan.

Dick, Howard. 2002. *Surabaya, City of Work: A Socioeconomic History, 1900–2000.* Athens: Ohio University Press.

Dick, Howard, Vincent J. H. Houben, J. Thomas Lindblad, and Thee Kian Wie. 2002. *The Emergence of a National Economy: An Economic History of Indonesia, 1800–2000.* Sydney: Allen and Unwin; and Honolulu: University of Hawai'i Press.

Direction des Services Économiques. 1947. *Annuaire statistique de l'Indochine, 1943–1946.* Hanoi.

Doeppers, Daniel F. 1984. *Manila 1900–1941: Social Change in a Late Colonial Metropolis.* Manila: Ateneo de Manila University Press.

Dormois, Jean-Pierre, and Francois Crouzet. 1998. "The Significance of the French Colonial Empire for French Economic Development (1815–1960)." *Revista de historia economica* 16: pp. 323–349.

Doumer, Paul A. 1902. *Rapport: Situation de l'Indochine, 1897–1901.* Hanoi: F-H. Schneider.

Drabble, John H. 1973. *Rubber in Malaya, 1876–1922.* Kuala Lumpur: Oxford University Press.

———. 1991. *Malayan Rubber: The Interwar Years.* Basingstoke: Macmillan Press.

———. 2000. *An Economic History of Malaysia, c. 1800–1990: The Transition to Modern Economic Growth.* Basingstoke: Macmillan Press.

Drake, P. J. 1972. "Natural Resources versus Foreign Borrowing in Economic Development." *Economic Journal* 82: 951–962.

Dros, Nico. 1992. *Changing Economy in Indonesia,* vol. 13: Wages 1820–1940. Amsterdam: Royal Tropical Institute.

Dung, Bui Minh. 1995. "Japan's Role in the Vietnamese Starvation of 1944–45." *Modern Asian Studies* 29 (3): 573–618.

Eckert, Carter J. 1991. *Offspring of Empire: The Koch'ang Kims and the Colonial Origins of Korean Capitalism, 1876–1945.* Seattle: University of Washington Press.

———. 1996. "Total War, Industrialisation, and Social Change in Late Colonial Korea." In Peter Duus, Ramon H. Myers, and Mark R. Peattie, *The Japanese Wartime Empire, 1931–1945.* Princeton: Princeton University Press.

Economic Planning Board. 1967. *Korea Statistical Yearbook 1967.* Seoul: Bureau of Statistics, Economic Planning Board.

Elson, Robert E. 1992. "International Commerce, the State and Society: Economic and Social Change." In Nicholas Tarling, ed., *The Cambridge History of Southeast Asia,* vol. 3: *From c. 1800 to the 1930s.* Cambridge: Cambridge University Press.

Emerson, Rupert. 1937. *Malaysia: A Study in Direct and Indirect Rule*. New York: Macmillan.

Eng, Pierre van der. 1991. "An Observer of Sixty-Five Years of Socio-Economic Change in Indonesia: Egbert de Vries." *Bulletin of Indonesian Economic Studies* 27 (1): 39–56.

———. 1993. *Food Consumption and the Standard of Living in Indonesia, 1880–1990*. Economics Division Working Paper, 93/1. Canberra: Research School of Pacific Studies, Australian National University.

———. 1994. *Food Supply in Java during the War and Decolonisation, 1940–1950*. Hull: Centre for Southeast Asian Studies.

———. 1996. *Agricultural Growth in Indonesia*. Basingstoke: Macmillan Press.

———. 2002. "Indonesia's Growth Performance in the Twentieth Century." In A. Maddison, D. Rao, and W. Shepherd, eds., *The Asian Economies in the Twentieth Century*. Cheltenham: Edward Elgar.

Espino, Jose M. 1933. *The American Tariff Policy in the Philippines*. Manila: Institute of Pacific Relations.

Evans, L. W. 1939. *Federated Malay States, Report of the Registrar General of Births and Deaths for the Year 1938*. Kuala Lumpur: FMS Government Press.

Evenson, Robert E., and Y. Kislev. 1975. *Agricultural Research and Productivity*. New Haven: Yale University Press.

Executive Yuan. 1962. *Taiwan Statistical Data Book, 1962*. Taipei, Republic of China.

Feith, Herbert. 1962. *The Decline of Constitutional Democracy in Indonesia*. Ithaca: Cornell University Press.

Feeny, David. 1982. *The Political Economy of Productivity: Thai Agricultural Development, 1880–1975*. Vancouver: University of British Columbia Press.

Fernando, M. R., and David Bulbeck. 1992. *Chinese Economic Activity in Netherlands India: Selected Translations from the Dutch*. Data Paper Series No. 2, Sources for the Economic History of Southeast Asia. Singapore: Institute of Sutheast Asian Studies.

Fforde, Adam. 1989. *The Agrarian Question in North Vietnam, 1974–79*. Armonk: M. E. Sharpe Inc.

Findlay, Ronald, and M. Lundhal. 1994. "Natural Resources, "Vent-for-Surplus" and the Staples Theory." In G. M. Meier, ed., *From Classical Economics to Development Economics*. New York: St. Martin's Press.

Flux, A. W. 1899. "The Flag and Trade: A Summary Review of the Trade of the Chief Colonial Empires." *Journal of the Royal Statistical Society* 62: 489–522.

Foreign Affairs Association. 1944. "Chosen (Korea)." In *The Japanese Yearbook 1943–44*. Tokyo: The Foreign Affairs Association of Japan.

Foster, Anne L. 2003. "Models for Governing: Opium and Colonial Policies in Southeast Asia, 1898–1910." In Julian Go and Anne L. Foster, eds., *The American Colonial State in the Philippines: Global Perspectives*. Durham: Duke University Press.

Fowler, John A. 1923. *Netherlands East Indies and British Malaya: A Commercial and Industrial Handbook.* Washington, D.C.: Government Printing Office for the Department of Commerce.

Fraser, H. 1939. *Annual Report on the Social and Economic Progress of the People of the Federated Malay States for 1938.* Kuala Lumpur: FMS Government Press.

Friend, Theodore. 1963. "The Philippine Sugar Industry and the Politics of Independence, 1929–35." *Journal of Asian Studies* 22: 179–192.

———. 1965. *Between Two Empires: The Ordeal of the Philippines, 1929–1946.* New Haven: Yale University Press.

Fukao, Kyoji, Debin Ma, and Tangjun Yuan. 2005. *International Comparison in Historical Perspective: Reconstructing the 1934–36 Benchmark Purchasing Power Parity for Japan, Korea and Taiwan.* Discussion Paper Series 66. Tokyo: Hitotsubsashi University Research Unit for Statistical Analysis in Social Sciences.

Furnivall, J. S. 1934a. *Studies in the Social and Economic Development of the Netherlands East Indies, 3d: The Land Revenue System.* Rangoon: Burma Book Club Ltd.

———. 1934b. *Studies in the Social and Economic Development of the Netherlands East Indies, 3b: State and Private Money Lending in Netherlands India.* Rangoon: Burma Book Club Ltd.

———. 1934c. *Studies in the Social and Economic Development of the Netherlands East Indies, 3c: State Pawnshops in Netherlands India.* Rangoon: Burma Book Club Ltd.

———. 1943. *Educational Progress in Southeast Asia.* New York: Institute of Pacific Relations.

———. 1948. *Colonial Policy and Practice: A Comparative Study of Burma and Netherlands India.* Cambridge: Cambridge University Press.

———. 1957. *An Introduction to the Political Economy of Burma.* Rangoon: Peoples' Literature Committee and House.

Galenson, Walter, ed. 1979. *Economic Growth and Structural Change in Taiwan.* Ithaca: Cornell University Press.

———. 1981. "How to Develop Successfully: The Taiwan Model." In *Conference on Experience and Lessons of Economic Development in Taiwan.* Taipei: Academica Sinica.

Gann, Lewis H. 1984. "Western and Japanese Colonialism: Some Preliminary Comparisons." In Ramon H. Myers and Mark R. Peattie, eds., *The Japanese Colonial Empire, 1895–1945.* Princeton: Princeton University Press.

Gautama, Sudargo, and Budi Harsono. 1971. *Survey of Indonesian Law: Agrarian Law.* Bandung: Padjajaran University Law School.

Geertz, Clifford. 1963. *Agricultural Involution: The Processes of Ecological Change in Indonesia.* Berkeley: University of California Press.

Gelderen, J. van. 1927. "The Economics of the Tropical Colony." Translated and reprinted in *Indonesian Economics: The Concept of Dualism in Theory and Practice.* The Hague: W. van Hoeve, 1966.

———. 1939. *The Recent Development of Foreign Economic Policy in the Netherlands East Indies.* London: Longmans, Green and Co.

German, R. L. 1936. *Handbook to British Malaya, 1935.* London: Malayan Information Agency.

Giacometti, Jean Dominique. 2000a. "Sources and Estimations for Economic Rural History of Vietnam in the First Half of the Twentieth Century." In Jean-Pascal Bassino, Jean-Dominique Giacometti, and K. Odaka, eds., *Quantitative Economic History of Vietnam, 1900–1990.* Tokyo: Hitotsubashi University, Institute of Economic Research.

———. 2000b. "Wages and Consumer Prices for Urban and Industrial Workers in Vietnam under French Rule (1895–1954)." In Jean-Pascal Bassino, Jean-Dominique Giacometti, and K. Odaka, eds., *Quantitative Economic History of Vietnam 1900–1990.* Tokyo: Hitotsubashi University, Institute of Economic Research.

Gill, Insong. 1998. "Stature, Consumption, and the Standard of Living in Colonial Korea." In John Komlos and Joerg Baten, eds., *The Biological Standard of Living in Comparative Perspective.* Stuttgart: Franz Steiner Verlag.

Golay, Frank. 1976. "Southeast Asia: The 'Colonial Drain' Revisited." In C. D. Cowan and O. W. Wolters, eds., *Southeast Asian History and Historiography.* Ithaca: Cornell University Press.

———. 1969a. "Malaya." In Frank H. Golay, Ralph Anspach, M. Ruth Pfanner, and Eliezer B. Ayal, *Underdevelopment and Economic Nationalism in Southeast Asia.* Ithaca: Cornell University Press.

———. 1969b. "The Philippines." In Frank H. Golay, Ralph Anspach, M. Ruth Pfanner, and Eliezer B. Ayal, *Underdevelopment and Economic Nationalism in Southeast Asia.* Ithaca: Cornell University Press.

Golay, Frank, Ralph Aspach, M. Ruth Pfanner, and Eliezer B. Ayal. 1969. "Summing Up." In Frank Golay, Ralph Anspach, M. Ruth Pfanner, and Eliezer B. Ayal, *Underdevelopment and Economic Nationalism in Southeast Asia.* Ithaca: Cornell University Press.

Gonggrijp, G. 1931. "Répartition des activités économiques entre les colonies et la métropole." *Proceedings of the Institut Colonial International, XXI Session.* Paris, May.

Goodman, Grant K. 1983. "America's Permissive Colonialism: Japanese Business in the Philippines, 1899–1941." In Norman Owen, ed., *The Philippine Economy and the United States: Studies in Past and Present Interactions.* Michigan Papers on South and Southeast Asia, no. 22. Ann Arbor: University of Michigan: Center for South and Southeast Asian Studies.

———. 1988. "The Japanese Occupation of the Philippines: Commonwealth Sustained." *Philippine Studies* 36: 98–104.

Goodstein, Marvin E. 1962. *The Pace and Pattern of Philippine Economic Growth: 1938, 1948 and 1956.* Data Paper Number 48 (July). Ithaca: Cornell University Southeast Asia Program.

Gooszen, Hans. 1999. *A Demographic History of the Indonesian Archipelago, 1880– 1942*. Singapore: Institute of Southeast Asian Studies.

Gordon, Alec. 1979. "The Collapse of Java's Colonial Sugar System and the Breakdown of Independent Indonesia's Economy." In Francien Anrooij et al., eds., *Between People and Statistics: Essays on Modern Indonesian History*. The Hague: Martinus Nijhoff.

Goudal, Jean. 1938. *Labour Conditions in Indo-china*. Studies and Reports Series B (Economic Conditions), no. 26. Geneva: International Labour Office.

Gourou, Pierre. 1945a. *Land Utilization in French Indochina*. New York: Institute of Pacific Relations.

———. 1945b. "The Standard of Living in the Delta of the Tonkin (French Indo-China)." Paper presented to the ninth conference of the Institute of Pacific Relations, French Paper No. 4, Institute of Pacific Relations, New York.

Gragert, Edwin H. 1994. *Landownership under Colonial Rule: Korea's Japanese Experience, 1900–1935*. Honolulu: University of Hawai'i Press.

Grajdanzev, Andrew J. 1942. *Formosa Today: An Analysis of the Economic Development and Strategic Importance of Japan's Tropical Colony*. New York: Institute of Pacific Relations.

———. 1944. *Modern Korea*. New York: Institute of Pacific Relations.

Gran, Guy. 1975. "Vietnam and the Capitalist Route to Modernity: Village Cochinchina, 1880–1940." Ph.D. dissertation, University of Wisconsin, Madison.

Grist, D. H. 1941. *Malayan Agricultural Statistics, 1940*. Kuala Lumpur: Department of Agriculture, Straits Settlements and Federated Malay States.

Guerrero, Milagros. 1994. "Japanese-American Trade Rivalry in the Philippines, 1919–1941." In S. Sugiyama and M. Guerrero, eds., *International Commercial Rivalry in Southeast Asia in the Interwar Period*. Monograph Series 39. New Haven: Yale Southeast Asia Studies.

Haggard, Stephan, David Kang, and Chung-In Moon. 1997. "Japanese Colonialism and Korean Development: A Critique." *World Development* 25 (6): 867–881.

Hanson, John R. 1980. *Trade in Transition: Exports from the Third World*. New York: Academic Press.

Harper, T. N. 1999. *The End of Empire and the Making of Malaya*. Cambridge: Cambridge University Press.

Hauser, Philip M. 1977. "The Measurement of Labour Utilization—More Empirical Results." *Malayan Economic Review* 22 (1): 10–25.

Hawes, Gary. 1987. *The Philippine State and the Marcos Regime: The Politics of Export*. Ithaca: Cornell University Press.

Hayami, Yujiro. 1973. "Development and Diffusion of High Yielding Rice Varieties in Japan, Korea and Taiwan, 1890–1940." In R. T. Shand, ed., *Technical Change in Asian Agriculture*. Canberra: Australian National University Press.

Hayami, Yujiro, and Vernon W. Ruttan. 1979. "Agricultural Growth in Four Countries." In Yujiro Hayami, V. W. Ruttan, and Herman Southworth, eds., *Agricultural Growth in Japan, Taiwan, Korea and the Philippines*. Honolulu: University of Hawai'i Press.

Henry, Yves. 1926. "Le crédit populaire agricole et commercial aux Indes néerlandaises." *Bulletin économique de l'Indochine* 29: 69–124.

———. 1932. *Économie agricole de l'Indochine.* Hanoi: Gouvernement Général de l'Indochine.

Hicks, George. 1995. *The Comfort Women: Sex Slaves of the Japanese Imperial Forces.* Singapore: Heinemann Asia.

Hicks, George L., and Geoffrey McNicoll. 1971. *Trade and Growth in the Philipines: An Open Dual Economy.* Ithaca: Cornell University Press.

Higgins, Benjamin. 1956. "The Dualistic Theory of Underdeveloped Areas." *Economic Development and Cultural Change,* January, 99–112.

Hill, R. D. 1967. "Agricultural Land Tenure in West Malaysia." *Malayan Economic Review* 12:1 (April): 99–116.

Hirschman, Albert O. 1977. "A Generalized Linkage Approach to Development, with Special Reference to Staples." *Economic Development and Cultural Change* (supplement), 25: 67–98.

Ho, Samuel Pao-san. 1971. "The Development Policy of the Japanese Colonial Government in Taiwan, 1895–1945." In Gustav Ranis, ed., *Government and Economic Development.* New Haven: Yale University Press.

———. 1978. *The Economic Development of Taiwan, 1860–1970.* New Haven: Yale University Press.

———. 1984. "Colonialism and Development: Korea, Taiwan, and Kwantung." In Ramon H. Myers and Mark R. Peattie, eds., *The Japanese Colonial Empire, 1895–1945.* Princeton: Princeton University Press.

———. 1986. "Off-Farm Employment and Farm Households in Taiwan." In Richard T. Shand, ed., *Off-Farm Employment in the Development of Rural Asia.* Canberra: National Centre for Development Studies, Australian National University.

Hooley, Richard. 1968. "Long-Term Growth of the Philippine Economy, 1902–1961." *The Philippine Economic Journal* 7 (1): 1–24.

———. 1996. "A Century of Philippine Foreign Trade: A Quantitative Analysis." In E. de Dios and R. Fabella, eds., *Choice, Growth and Development: Essays in Honour of Jose Encarnacion.* Quezon City: University of the Philippines Press.

Hopkins, A. G. 1973. *An Economic History of West Africa.* Harlow: Longman.

Houben, Vincent J. H. 1999. "The Quality of Coolie Life: An Assessment of Labour Conditions, 1910–1938." In Vincent J. H. Houben, J. Thomas Lindblad, et al., eds., *Coolie Labour in Colonial Indonesia: A Study of Labour Relations in the Outer Islands, c. 1900–1940.* Wiesbaden: Harrassowitz Verlag.

Howe, Christopher. 1996. *The Origins of Japanese Trade Supremacy: Development and Technology in Asia from 1540 to the Pacific War.* London: Hurst and Company.

———. 2001. "Taiwan in the Twentieth Century: Model or Victim? Development Problems in a Small Asian Economy." *China Quarterly* 165: 37–60.

Hsing, Mo-Huan. 1971. "Taiwan: Industrialization and Trade Policies." In John H. Power, G. P. Sicat, and Mo-Huan Hsing, *The Philippines, Taiwan: Industrialization and Trade Policies.* London: Oxford University Press.

Huff, W. G. 1994. *Economic Growth of Singapore.* Cambridge: Cambridge University Press.

———. 2002. "Boom-or-Bust Commodities in Pre–World War II Malaya." *Journal of Economic History* 62: 1074–1115.

———. 2003. "Monetization and Financial Development before the Second World War." *Economic History Review* 56: 300–345.

Hunt, Chester L. 1988. "Education and Economic Development in the Early American Period in the Philippines." *Philippine Studies* 36: 352–364.

Hunter, Alex. 1966. "The Indonesian Oil Industry." *Australian Economic Papers* 5 (1): 59–106.

Husken, Frans. 1994. "Declining Welfare in Java: Government and Private Enquiries, 1903–1914." In Robert Cribb, ed., *The Late Colonial State in Indonesia.* Leiden: KITLV Press.

Hutchcroft, Paul D. 2000. "Colonial Masters, National Politicos, and Provincial Lords: Central Authority and Local Autonomy in the American Philippines, 1900–1913." *Journal of Asian Studies,* 59 (2): 277–306.

Hymer, Stephen H., and Stephen A. Resnick. 1971. "International Trade and Uneven Development." In J. Bhagwati et al., eds., *Trade, Balance of Payments and Growth.* Amsterdam: North Holland.

Ingleson, John. 1988. "Urban Java during the Depression." *Journal of Southeast Asian Studies* 19 (2): 292–309.

Ingram, J. 1964. "Thailand's Rice Trade and the Allocation of Resources." In C. D. Cowan, ed., *The Economic Development of South-East Asia.* London: George Allen and Unwin.

———. 1971. *Economic Change in Thailand, 1850–1970.* Kuala Lumpur: Oxford University Press.

International Bank for Reconstruction and Development. 1955. *The Economic Development of Malaya.* Baltimore: Johns Hopkins University Press.

Jackson, James C. 1968. *Planters and Speculators: Chinese and European Agricultural Enterprise in Malaya 1786–1921.* Kuala Lumpur: University of Malaysia Press.

Japan Statistical Association. 1987. *Historical Statistics of Japan.* Vol. 3. Tokyo: Nihon Tokei Kyokai.

Johnston, B. F. 1953. *Japanese Food Management in World War II.* Stanford: Stanford University Press.

Joint Preparatory Committee. 1938. *Joint Preparatory Committee on Philippine Affairs, Report of May 20, 1938.* Washington, D.C.: United States Government Printing Office.

Jones, Leroy P., and Il Sakong. 1980. *Government, Business, and Entrepreneurship in Economic Development: The Korean Case.* Cambridge: Harvard University Press for the Council on East Asian Studies, Harvard University.

Jong, L. de. 2002. *The Collapse of a Colonial Society: The Dutch in Indonesia during the Second World War.* Leiden: KITLV Press.

Jose, Ricardo Trota. 1998. "Food Production and Food Distribution Programmes in the Philippines during the Japanese Occupation." In Paul Kratoska, ed., *Food Supplies and the Japanese Occupation in South-East Asia*. Basingstoke: Macmillan Press.

Juhn, Daniel Sungil. 1973. "The Development of Korean Entrepreneurship." In Andrew C. Nahm, ed., *Korea under Japanese Colonial Rule*. Michigan: Center for Korean Studies, Western Michigan University.

———. 1977. "Nationalism and Korean Businessmen." In C. I. Eugene Kim and Doretha Mortimore, eds., *Korea's Response to Japan: The Colonial Period 1910–1945*. Michigan: Center for Korean Studies, Western Michigan University.

Ka, Chih-Ming. 1995. *Japanese Colonialism in Taiwan: Land Tenure, Development, and Dependency, 1895–1945*. Boulder: Westview Press.

Kahin, George McTurnan. 1952. *Nationalism and Revolution in Indonesia*. Ithaca: Cornell University Press.

Kang, David C. 2002. *Crony Capitalism: Corruption and Development in South Korea and the Philippines*. Cambridge: Cambridge University Press.

Karnow, Stanley. 1989. *In Our Image: America's Empire in the Philippines*. New York: Random House Inc.

Kemperman, Jeroen. 2002. "Introduction." In L. de Jong, *The Collapse of a Colonial Society: The Dutch in Indonesia during the Second World War*. Leiden: KITLV Press.

Kerr, George H. 1942. "Formosa: Colonial Laboratory." *Far Eastern Survey*, February 23, pp. 50–55

———. 1966. *Formosa Betrayed*. London: Eyre and Spottiswoode.

Khor, Kok-Peng. 1983. *The Malaysian Economy: Structures and Dependence*. Kuala Lumpur: Marican and Sons.

Kim, Jongchol. 1985. *Education and Development: Some Essays and Thoughts on Korean Education*. Seoul: Seoul National University Press.

Kim, Kwang Suk. 1973. "An Analysis of Economic Change in Korea." In Andrew C. Nahm, ed., *Korea under Japanese Colonial Rule*. Michigan: Center for Korean Studies, Western Michigan University.

Kim, Kwang Suk, and Michael Roemer. 1979. *Growth and Structural Transformation*. Cambridge: Harvard University Press for the Council on East Asian Studies, Harvard University.

Kimura, Mitsuhiko. 1989. "Public Finance in Korea under Japanese Rule: Deficit in the Colonial Account and Colonial Taxation." *Explorations in Economic History* 26: 285–310.

———. 1993. "Standards of Living in Colonial Korea: Did the Masses Become Worse Off or Better Off under Japanese Rule?" *Journal of Economic History* 53 (3): 629–652.

Kindleberger, Charles P. 1987. *The World in Depression 1929–1939*. Harmondsworth: Penguin Books.

Kleiman, Ephraim. 1976. "Trade and the Decline of Colonialism." *Economic Journal* 86 (September): 459–480.

Kobayashi, Hideo. 1996. "The Postwar Economic Legacy of Japan's Wartime Empire." In Peter Duus, Ramon H. Myers, and Mark R. Peattie, eds., *The Japanese Wartime Empire, 1931–1945*. Princeton: Princeton University Press.

Kohli, Atul. 1994. "Where Do High Growth Political Economies Come From? The Japanese Lineage of Korea's "Developmental State." *World Development* 22 (9): 1269–1293.

———. 2004. *State-Directed Development: Political Power and Industrialization in the Global Periphery*. Cambridge: Cambridge University Press.

Kolff, G. H. van der. 1941. "Brown and White Economy: Unity in Diversity." Translated and reprinted in *Indonesian Economics: The Concept of Dualism in Theory and Practice*. The Hague: W. van Hoeve, 1966.

Korthals Altes, W. L. 1987. *Changing Economy of Indonesia*, vol. 7: *Balance of Payments 1822–1939*. Amsterdam: Royal Tropical Institute.

———. 1991. *Changing Economy of Indonesia*, vol. 12a: *General Trade Statistics 1822–1940*. Amsterdam: Royal Tropical Institute.

Kratoska, Paul H. 1998. *The Japanese Occupation of Malaya*. London: Hurst and Company.

———. 2000. "Imperial Unity versus Local Autonomy: British Malaya and the Depression of the 1930s." In Peter Boomgaard and Ian Brown, eds., *Weathering the Storm: The Economies of Southeast Asia in the 1930s Depression*. Leiden: KITLV Press.

Kuitenbrouwer, Maarten. 1991. *The Netherlands and the Rise of Modern Imperialism: Colonies and Foreign Policy, 1870–1902*. New York and Oxford: Berg.

Kurasawa-Inomata, Aiko. 1997. "Rice Shortage and Transportation." In Peter Post and Elly Touwen-Bouwsma, eds., *Japan, Indonesia and the War: Myths and Realities*. Leiden: KITLV Press.

Kurihara, Kenneth. 1945. *Labor in the Philippine Economy*. Stanford: Stanford University Press.

Laanen, J. T. M. van. 1980. *Changing Economy in Indonesia*, vol. 6: *Money and Banking, 1816–1940*. The Hague: Martinus Nijhoff.

———. 1990. "Between the Java Bank and the Chinese Moneylender: Banking and Credit in Colonial Indonesia." In Anne Booth, W. O'Malley, and Anna Weidemann, *Indonesian Economic History in the Dutch Colonial Era*. Monograph Series 35. New Haven: Yale University Southeast Asian Studies.

Lai, Tse-Hai, Ramon H. Myers, and Wei Wou. 1991. *A Tragic Beginning: The Taiwan Uprising of February 28, 1947*. Stanford: Stanford University Press.

Lal, Deepak. 1988. *The Hindu Equilibrium*, vol. 1: *Cultural Stability and Economic Stagnation*. Oxford: Oxford University Press.

Larkin, John A. 1993. *Sugar and the Origins of Modern Philippine Society*. Berkeley: University of California Press.

Lava, Horacio. 1938. *Levels of Living in the Ilocos Region*. Study No. 1, Philippine Council of the Institute of Pacific Relations. Manila: College of Business Administration, University of the Philippines.

Lebra, Joyce C. 1975. *Japan's Greater East Asia Co-Prosperity Sphere in World War II: Selected Readings and Documents*. Kuala Lumpur: Oxford University Press.

Lee, Eddy. 1979. "Egalitarian Peasant Farming and Rural Development: The Case of Korea." *World Development* 7: 493–517.

Lee, Hoon K. 1936. *Land Utilization and Rural Economy in Korea*. Chicago: University of Chicago Press.

Lee, Kuan Yew. 1998. *The Singapore Story: Memoirs of Lee Kuan Yew*. Singapore: Times Editions.

Lee, Teng-hui, and Yueh-eh Chen. 1979. "Agricultural Growth in Taiwan, 1911–1972." In Yujiro Hayami, V. W. Ruttan, and Herman Southworth, eds., *Agricultural Growth in Japan, Taiwan, Korea and the Philippines*. Honolulu: University of Hawai'i Press.

Leff, Nathanial H. 1982. *Underdevelopment and Development in Brazil,* vol. 2: *Reassessing the Obstacles to Economic Development*. London: George Allen and Unwin.

Legarda, Benito J. 1999. *After the Galleons: Foreign Trade, Economic Change and Entrepreneurship in the Nineteenth Century Philippines*. Manila: Ateneo de Manila University Press.

Levin, Jonathan V. 1960. *The Export Economies: Their Pattern of Development in Historical Perspective*. Cambridge: Harvard University Press.

Lewis, W. A. 1976. "Development and Distribution." In Alec Cairncross and Mohinder Puri, eds., *Employment, Income Distribution and Development Strategy: Problems of the Developing Countries*. London: Macmillan Press.

Li, Dun-Jen. 1982. *British Malaya: An Economic Analysis*. Kuala Lumpur: Institut Analisa Sosial.

Lim, Chong-Yah. 1967. *Economic Development of Modern Malaya*. Kuala Lumpur: Oxford University Press.

Lim, Teck-Ghee. 1977. *Peasants and Their Agricultural Economy in Colonial Malaya, 1874–1941*. Kuala Lumpur: Oxford University Press.

Lin, Ching-yuan. 1973. *Industrialization in Taiwan, 1946–72: Trade and Import-Substitution Policies for Developing Countries.,* New York: Praeger Publishers.

Lindblad, J. Thomas. 1998. *Foreign Investment in Southeast Asia in the Twentieth Century*. Basingstoke: Macmillan Press.

———. 1999a. "Coolies in Deli: Labour Conditions in Western Enterprises in East Sumatra, 1910–1938." In Vincent J. H. Houben, J. Thomas Lindblad, et al., eds., *Coolie Labour in Colonial Indonesia: A Study of Labour Relations in the Outer Islands, c. 1900–1940*. Wiesbaden: Harrassowitz Verlag.

———. 1999b. "New Destinations: Conditions of Coolie Labour outside East Sumatra, 1910–38." In Vincent J. H. Houben, J. Thomas Lindblad, et al., eds., *Coolie Labour in Colonial Indonesia: A Study of Labour Relations in the Outer Islands, c. 1900–1940*. Wiesbaden: Harrassowitz Verlag.

Lindert, Peter. 2004. *Growing Public*. Cambridge: Cambridge University Press.

Luton, Harry. 1971. "American Internal Revenue Policy in the Philippines to

1916." In Norman G. Owen, ed., *Compadre Colonialism: Studies on the Philippines under American Rule*. Michigan Papers on South and Southeast Asia, no. 3. Ann Arbor.

Mackie, J. A. C. 1964. "The Indonesian Economy: 1950–1963." Reprinted in Bruce Glassburner, ed., *The Economy of Indonesia: Selected Readings*. Ithaca: Cornell University Press.

———. 1976. "Anti-Chinese Outbreaks in Indonesia, 1959–68." In J. A. C. Mackie, ed., *The Chinese in Indonesia: Five Essays*. Hong Kong: Heinemann Educational Books (Asia) Ltd.

———. 1991. "Towkays and Tycoons: The Chinese in Indonesian Economic Life in the 1920s and the 1980s." In *Indonesia,* special issue: *The Role of the Chinese in Shaping Modern Indonesian Life*. Ithaca: Cornell University Modern Indonesia Project.

Maddison, Angus. 1990. "The Colonial Burden: A Comparative Perspective." In Maurice Scott and Deepak Lal, eds., *Public Policy and Economic Development: Essays in Honour of Ian Little*. Oxford: Oxford University Press.

———. 2003. *The World Economy: Historical Statistics*. Paris: OECD Development Centre.

Manarungsan, Sompop. 1989. "Economic Development of Thailand, 1850–1950." Ph.D. dissertation, State University of Groningen.

———. 2000. "The Rice Economy of Thailand in the 1930s Depression." In Peter Boomgaard and Ian Brown, eds., *Weathering the Storm: The Economies of Southeast Asia in the 1930s Depression*. Leiden: KITLV Press.

Manderson, Lenore. 1996. *Sickness and the State: Health and Illness in Colonial Malaya, 1870–1940*. Cambridge: Cambridge University Press.

Mao, Yu-kang. 1982. "Land Reform and Agricultural Development in Taiwan." In Chi-Ming Hou and Tzong-Shian Yu, eds., *Agricultural Development in China, Japan and Korea*. Tapei: Academica Sinica.

Marr, David. 1995. *Vietnam 1945: The Quest for Power*. Berkeley: University of California Press.

Marseille, Jacques. 1984. *Empire colonial et capitalisme français: Histoire d'un divorce*. Paris: Albin Michel.

May, Glenn Anthony. 1980. *Social Engineering in the Philippines: The Aims, Execution, and Impact of American Colonial Policy, 1900–1913*. Westport: Greenwood Press.

Maxwell, W. George. 1922. *Annual Report for the Federated Malay States for 1921*. Kuala Lumpur: Government Printer.

McCoy, Alfred W. 1992. "Sugar Barons: Formation of a Native Planter Class in the Colonial Philippines." In E. Valentine Daniel, Henry Bernstein, and Tom Brass, eds., *Plantations, Proletarians and Peasants in Colonial Asia*. London: Frank Cass.

McLennan, Marshall S. 1969. "Land and Tenancy in the Central Luzon Plain." *Philippine Studies* 17 (4): 651–682.

———. 1980. *The Central Luzon Plain: Land and Society on the Inland Frontier.* Manila: Alemar-Phoenix Publishing House.

McNamara, Dennis L. 1988. "Entrepreneurship in Colonial Korea: Kim Yon-su." *Modern Asian Studies* 22 (1): 165–177.

———. 1990. *The Colonial Origins of Korean Enterprise, 1910–1945.* Cambridge: Cambridge University Press.

Mears, Leon A. 1961. *Rice Marketing in the Republic of Indonesia.* Jakarta: Institute for Economic and Social Research, University of Indonesia.

Mears, Leon, M. Agabin, T. L. Anden, and R. C. Marquez. 1974. *The Rice Economy of the Philippines.* Manila: University of the Philippines Press.

Meredith, David. 1975. "The British Government and Colonial Economic Policy, 1919–39." *Economic History Review,* new series, 28:3 (August): 484–499.

———. 1996. "British Trade Diversion Policy and the 'Colonial Issue' in the 1930s." *Journal of European Economic History* 25:1 (Spring): 33–66.

Mertens, Walter. 1978. "Population Census Data on Agricultural Activities in Indonesia." *Majalah Demografi Indonesia,* no. 9 (June).

Metzer, Jacob. 1998. *The Divided Economy of Mandatory Palestine.* Cambridge: Cambridge University Press.

Ministry of National Economy. 1962. *Annual Statistics of Vietnam,* vol. 9: 1960/61. Saigon: Ministry of National Economy, Republic of Vietnam.

Miranda, Evelyn A. 1991. "American Economic Imperialism and the Development of the Philippine Oligarchy: The Filipino Legislative Elite, 1900–1935." *Kabar Seberang,* no. 21, 55–68.

Mitchell, B. R. 1998. *International Historical Statistics: Europe, 1750–1993.* Fourth edition. Basingstoke: Macmillan.

———. 2003. *International Historical Statistics: The Americas, 1750–2000.* Fifth edition. Basingstoke: Macmillan.

Mitchell, Kate L. 1942. *An Economic Survey of the Pacific Area,* part 3: *Industrialization of the Western Pacific Area.* New York: Institute of Pacific Relations.

Mizoguchi, Toshiyuki. 1972. "Consumer Prices and Real Wages in Taiwan and Korea under Japanese Rule." *Hitotsubashi Journal of Economics* 13 (June): 40–65.

———. 1974. "Foreign Trade in Taiwan and Korea under Japanese Rule." *Hitotsubashi Journal of Economics* 15 (February): 37–53.

Mizoguchi, Toshiyuki, and Mataji Umemura, eds. 1988. *Basic Economic Statistics of Former Japanese Colonies, 1895–1938: Estimates and Findings.* Tokyo: Toyo Keizai Shinposhain.

Mizoguchi, Toshiyuki, and Yuzo Yamamoto. 1984. "Capital Formation in Taiwan and Korea." In Ramon H. Myers and Mark R. Peattie, eds., *The Japanese Colonial Empire, 1895–1945.* Princeton: Princeton University Press.

Morgan, Stephen, and Shiyung Liu. 2005. "Was Japanese Colonialism Good for the Taiwanese? Stature and the Standard of Living in Taiwan, 1895–1945." Working paper, University of Melbourne (forthcoming, *China Quarterly*).

Morris, Morris D. 1963. "Towards a Re-interpretation of Nineteenth Century Indian Economic History." *Journal of Economic History* 23 (4): 606–618.

Mortimer, Rex. 1974. *Indonesian Communism under Soekarno: Ideology and Politics.* Ithaca: Cornell University Press.

Moulton, Harold G. 1931. *Japan: An Economic and Financial Appraisal.* Washington, D.C.: Brookings Institution.

Murray, Martin J. 1980. *The Development of Capitalism in Colonial Indochina (1870–1940).* Berkeley: University of California Press.

Myers, R[amon] H. 1969. "Taiwan." In R. T. Shand, *Agricultural Development in Asia.* Canberra: Australian National University Press.

———. 1970. "Agrarian Policy and Agricultural Transformation: Mainland China and Taiwan 1895–1945." *Journal of the Institute of Chinese Studies of the Chinese University of Hong Kong* 3 (2): 521–542.

Myers, Ramon H., and Adrienne Ching. 1964. "Agricultural Development in Taiwan under Japanese Colonial Rule." *Journal of Asian Studies* 23 (August): 555–570.

Myers, Ramon H., and Mark R. Peattie, eds., 1984. *The Japanese Colonial Empire, 1895–1945.* Princeton: Princeton University Press.

Myers, Ramon, and Saburo Yamada. 1984. "Agricultural Development in the Empire." In Ramon H. Myers and Mark R. Peattie, eds., *The Japanese Colonial Empire, 1895–1945.* Princeton: Princeton University Press.

Myint, Hla. 1958. "The "Classical Theory" of International Trade and the Underdeveloped Countries." *Economic Journal* 68 (June): 317–337.

———. 1967. "The Inward and Outward-Looking Countries of Southeast Asia." *Malayan Economic Review* 12 (April): 1–13.

———. 1987. "Neo-classical Development Analysis: Its Strengths and Limitations." In Gerald M. Meier, ed., *Pioneers in Development.* Second series. New York: Oxford University Press.

Nakahara, Michiko. 1999. "Labour Recruitment in Malaya under the Japanese Occupation: The Case of the Burma-Siam Railway." In K. S. Jomo, ed., *Rethinking Malaysia.* Kuala Lumpur: Malaysian Social Science Association.

National Economic and Development Authority. 1975. *NEDA Statistical Yearbook of the Philippines 1974.* Manila: National Economic and Development Authority.

———. 1978. *The National Income Accounts, CY 1946–1975.* Philippine National Income Series, no. 5. Manila: National Economic and Development Authority.

National Planning Commission. 1959. *A Study of the Social and Economic History of Burma (British Burma),* part 6b: 1913–23. Rangoon: National Planning Commission, Ministry of National Planning.

———. 1960a. *A Study of the Social and Economic History of Burma (British Burma),* part 7: 1923–31. Rangoon: National Planning Commission, Ministry of National Planning.

———. 1960b. *A Study of the Social and Economic History of Burma (British Burma),* part 8: *British Burma from the Rebellion of 1931 to the Japanese Invasion of 1941.* Rangoon: National Planning Commission, Ministry of National Planning.

Nelson, R., and Howard Pack. 1999. "The Asian Miracle and Modern Growth Theory." *Economic Journal* 109 (July): 416–436.

Ngo Vinh Long. 1991. *Before the Revolution: The Vietnamese Peasants under the French.* New York: Columbia University Press.

Niel, Robert van. 1956. *Living Conditions of Plantation Workers in 1939–40: Final Report of the Coolie Budget Commission.* Translation Series, Modern Indonesia Project. Ithaca: Cornell.

Nitisastro, Widjojo. 1970. *Population Trends in Indonesia.* Ithaca: Cornell University Press.

Norlund, Irene. 1991. "The French Empire, the Colonial State in Vietnam and Economic Policy: 1885–1940." *Australian Economic History Review* 31 (1): 72–89.

———. 2000. "Rice and the Colonial Lobby: The Economic Crisis in French Indochina in the 1920s and 1930s." In Peter Boomgaard and Ian Brown, eds., *Weathering the Storm: The Economies of Southeast Asia in the 1930s Depression.* Leiden: KITLV Press.

Normandin, A. 1916. "Étude comparative du problème de l'hydraulique agricole à Java, aux Indes britanniques en l'Indochine." *Bulletin économique de l'Indochine,* vol. 16.

Office of the Prime Minister. 1958. *A Study of the Social and Economic History of Burma (British Burma),* part 6a: 1897–1913. Rangoon: Office of the Prime Minister.

Ohkawa, K., M. Shinohara, with L. Meissner, eds. 1979. *Patterns of Japanese Economic Development: A Quantitative Appraisal.* New Haven: Yale University Press.

Orme, John. 1995. "Growth with Equity Megapolicies in Taiwan: Land Reform and Export-Led Growth." In John D. Montgomery and Dennis A. Rondinelli, eds., *Great Policies: Strategic Innovations in Asia and the Pacific Basin.* Westport: Praeger.

Owen, Norman G. 1971. "The Rice Industry in Mainland Southeast Asia 1850–1914." *Journal of the Siam Society* 59 (2): 75–143.

———. 1972. "Philippine Economic Development and American Policy: A Reappraisal." *Solidarity* 7 (9): 49–64.

Paauw, Douglas. 1963. "Economic Progress in Southeast Asia." *Journal of Asian Studies* 23 (November): 69–92.

Paauw, Douglas, and John C. H. Fei. 1973. *The Transition in Open Dualistic Economies: Theory and Southeast Asian Experience.* New Haven: Yale University Press.

Palmore, James A., Ramesh Chander, and Dorothy Fernandez. 1975. *The Demographic Situation in Malaysia.* East-West Population Institute, Reprint Series 70. Honolulu: University of Hawai'i.

Panglaykim, J., and I. Palmer. 1989. "Study of Entrepreneurship in Developing Countries: The Development of One Chinese Concern in Indonesia." In Yoshihara Kunio, ed., *Oei Tiong Ham Concern: The First Business Empire of Southeast Asia.* Kyoto: Center for Southeast Asian Studies, Kyoto University.

Park, Soon-Won. 1999. "Colonial Industrial Growth and the Emergence of the

Korean Working Class." In Gi-Wool Shin and Michael Robinson, eds., *Colonial Modernity in Korea*. Cambridge: Harvard University Asia Center.

Paulus, J. 1909. "Finance." In Arnold Wright, ed., *Twentieth Century Impressions of Netherlands India*. London: Lloyd's Greater Britain Publishing Company.

Peattie, Mark R. 1984. "Introduction." In Ramon H. Myers and Mark R. Peattie, eds., *The Japanese Colonial Empire, 1895–1945*. Princeton: Princeton University Press.

Pelzer, Karl. 1945. *Pioneer Settlement in the Asiatic Tropics*. New York: American Geographical Society.

———. 1978. *Planter and Peasant: Colonial Policy and the Agrarian Struggle in East Sumatra 1863–1947*. The Hague: M. Nijhoff.

Pfanner, M. Ruth. 1969. "Burma." In Frank H. Golay, Ralph Anspach, M. Ruth Pfanner, and Eliezer B. Ayal, *Underdevelopment and Economic Nationalism in Southeast Asia*. Ithaca: Cornell University Press.

Phongpaichit, Pasuk, and Chris Baker. 1995. *Thailand: Economy and Politics*. Kuala Lumpur: Oxford University Press.

Pluvier, Jan. 1974. *Southeast Asia from Colonialism to Independence*. Kuala Lumpur: Oxford University Press.

Polak, J. J. 1943. "The National Income of the Netherlands Indies, 1921–39." Reprinted in P. Creutzberg, ed., *Changing Economy of Indonesia*, vol. 5: *National Income*. The Hague: M. Nijhoff.

Popkin, Samuel L. 1979. *The Rational Peasant: The Political Economy of Rural Society in Vietnam*. Berkeley: University of California Press.

Post, Peter. 1997. "The Formation of the Pribumi Business Elite in Indonesia, 1930s–1940s." In Peter Post and Elly Touwen-Bouwsma, eds., *Japan, Indonesia and the War: Myths and Realities*. Leiden: KITLV Press.

Pouyane, A. A. 1926. "Les travaux publics de l'Indochine." *Bulletin économique de l'Indochine*, 169–320.

Power, John H., and Gerardo P. Sicat. 1971. "The Philippines: Industrialization and Trade Policies." In John H. Power, G. P. Sicat, and Mo-Huan Hsing, *The Philippines and Taiwan: Industrialization and Trade Policies*. London: Oxford University Press.

Purcell, Victor. 1965. *The Chinese in Southeast Asia*. Second edition. Kuala Lumpur: Oxford University Press.

Putzel, James. 1992. *A Captive Land: The Politics of Agrarian Reform in the Philippines*. New York: Monthly Review Press.

Rahm, Henry A. 1952. "L'action de la France en Indochine." *Bulletin économique de l'Indochine* 55 (1): 10–109.

Ranis, Gustav. 2002. "The Trade-Growth Nexus in Taiwan's Development." In Erik Thorbecke and Henry Wan, eds., *Taiwan's Development Experience: Lessons on Roles of Government and Market*. Boston: Kluwer Academic Publishers.

Reddy, K. N. 1972. *The Growth of Public Expenditure in India, 1872–1968*. New Delhi: Sterling Publishers.

Reid, Anthony. 1993. *Southeast Asia in the Age of Commerce, 1450–1680,* vol. 2: *Expansion and Crisis.* New Haven: Yale University Press.

———. 2001. "South-East Asian Population History and the Colonial Impact." In T. J. Liu, James Lee, David Sven Reher, Osamu Saito, and Wang Feng, eds., *Asian Population History.* Oxford: Oxford University Press.

Resnick, Stephen A. 1970. "The Decline of Rural Industry under Export Expansion: A Comparison among Burma, Philippines and Thailand, 1870–1938." *Journal of Economic History* 30 (1): 51–73.

Reynolds, Lloyd G. 1983. "The Spread of Economic Growth to the Third World: 1850–1980." *Journal of Economic Literature* 21 (September): 941–980.

Richter, Hazel. 1976. *Burma's Rice Surplus: Accounting for the Decline.* Working Paper No. 3. Canberra: Development Studies Centre, Australian National University.

Ricklefs, M. C. 1993. *A History of Modern Indonesia since c. 1300.* Second edition. Basingstoke: Macmillan Press.

Robequain, Charles. 1944. *The Economic Development of French Indo-China.* London: Oxford University Press.

Roff, W. R. 1974. *The Origins of Malay Nationalism.* Kuala Lumpur: Penerbit Universiti Malaya.

Rose, Beth. 1985. *Appendix to the Rice Economy of Asia.* Washington, D.C.: Resources for the Future.

Rosendale, Phyllis. 1978. "The Indonesian Balance of Payments, 1950–1976: Some New Estimates." Ph.D. dissertation, Australian National University.

Rudner, Martin. 1994. *Malaysian Development: A Retrospective.* Ottawa: Carleton University Press.

Runes, I. T. 1939. *General Standards of Living and Wages of Workers in the Philippine Sugar Industry.* Manila: Philippine Council, Institute of Pacific Relations.

Rush, James. 1991. "Placing the Chinese in Java on the Eve of the Twentieth Century." In *Indonesia,* special issue: *The Role of the Chinese in Shaping Modern Indonesian Life.* Ithaca: Cornell University Modern Indonesia Project.

Sadli, M. 1971. "Reflections on Boeke's Theory of Dualistic Economies." In Bruce Glassburner, ed., *The Economy of Indonesia: Selected Readings.* Ithaca: Cornell University Press.

Saito, T., and Lee Kin Kiong. 1999. *Statistics on the Burmese Economy: The Nineteenth and Twentieth Centuries.* Singapore: Institute of Southeast Asian Studies.

Sansom, Robert L. 1970. *The Economics of Insurgency in the Mekong Delta of Vietnam.* Cambridge: MIT Press.

Sato, Shigeru. 1994. *War, Nationalism and Peasants: Java under the Japanese Occupation.* Sydney: Allen and Unwin for the Asian Studies Association of Australia.

Schneider, Adam. 1998. "The Taiwan Government-General and Prewar Japanese Economic Expansion in South China and Southeast Asia, 1900–1936." In Harald Fuess, ed., *The Japanese Empire in East Asia and Its Postwar Legacy.* Munich: Iudicium Verlag.

Schweitzer, Thomas A. 1971. "French Colonialist Lobby in the 1930s: The Economic Foundation of Imperialism." Ph.D. dissertation, University of Wisconsin, Madison.

Schwulst, E. B. 1932. "Report on the Budget and Financial Policies of French Indo-China, Siam, Federated Malay States and the Netherlands East Indies." In *Report of the Governor General of the Philippine Islands 1931*. Washington, D.C.: United States Government Printing Office.

Service de la Statistique Générale. 1947. *Annuaire statistique de l'Indochine, 1943–46*. Hanoi: Imprimerie d'Extrême-Orient.

Shein Maung, Myint Myint Thant, and Tin Tin Sein. 1969. "'Provincial Contract System' of British Indian Empire, in Relation to Burma: A Case of Fiscal Exploitation." *Journal of the Burma Research Society* 53 (December): 1–27.

Shepherd, Jack. 1941. *Industry in South East Asia*. New York: Institute of Pacific Relations.

Siahaan, Bisuk. 1996. *Industrialisasi di Indonesia: Sejak Hutang Kehormatan Sampai Banting Stir* (Industrialisation in Indonesia: From the debt of honor to the reversal of direction). Jakarta: Pustaka Data.

Siamwalla, Ammar. 1972. *Land, Labour and Capital in Three Rice-Growing Deltas of Southeast Asia 1800–1940*. Centre Discussion Paper No. 150. New Haven: Yale University Economic Growth Center.

Simoni, H. 1929. *Le role du capital dans la mise en valeur de l'Indochine*. Paris: Helms.

Smith, R. B. 1988. "Some Contrasts between Burma and Malaya in British Policy Towards South-East Asia, 1942–1946." In R. B. Smith and A. J. Stockwell, eds., *British Policy and the Transfer of Power in Asia: Documentary Perspectives*. London: School of Oriental and African Studies.

Smith, Sheila. 1976. "An Extension of the Vent-for-Surplus Model in Relation to Long-Run Structural Change in Nigeria." *Oxford Economic Papers* 28 (3): 426–446.

Snodgrass, Donald R. 1980. *Inequality and Economic Development in Malaysia*. Kuala Lumpur: Oxford University Press.

Statistics Department. 1936. *Malayan Yearbook 1936*. Singapore: Straits Settlements and FMS Department of Statistics.

———. 1939. *Malayan Yearbook 1939*. Singapore: Straits Settlements and FMS Department of Statistics.

Steinberg, David I. 1981. *Burma's Road Toward Development: Growth and Ideology under Military Rule*. Boulder: Westview Press.

Steinhoff, Manfred. 1980. *Prestige and Profit: The Development of Entrepreneurial Abilities in Taiwan, 1880–1972*. Canberra: Development Studies Centre, Australian National University.

Stockwell, A. J. 1974. "Colonial Planning during World War II: The Case of Malaysia." *Journal of Imperial and Commonwealth History* 2 (3): 333–351.

———. 1984. "British Imperial Policy and Decolonization in Malaya, 1942–52." *Journal of Imperial and Commonwealth History* 13 (1): 68–87.

Stoler, Ann. 1985. *Capitalism and Confrontation in Sumatra's Plantation Belt*. New Haven: Yale University Press.

Sugiyama, Shinya. 1994. "The Expansion of Japan's Cotton Textile Exports into Southeast Asia." In S. Sugiyama and M. C. Guerrero, eds., *International Commercial Rivalry in Southeast Asia in the Interwar Period*. Monograph Series 39. New Haven: Yale Southeast Asian Studies.

Sugiyama, Shinya, and M. C. Guerrero, eds., 1994. *International Commercial Rivalry in Southeast Asia in the Interwar Period*. Monograph Series 39. New Haven: Yale Southeast Asian Studies.

Suh, Sang-Chul. 1978. *Growth and Structural Changes in the Korean Economy, 1910–1940*. Cambridge: Harvard University Press.

Sundaram, Jomo Kwame. 1988. *A Question of Class: Capital, the State and Uneven Development in Malaya*. New York: Monthly Review Press.

Sundrum, R. M. 1957. *Population Statistics of Burma*. Economics Research Project, Statistical Paper No 3. Rangoon: Economics, Statistics, and Commerce Departments, University of Rangoon.

Suryadinata, Leo. 1972. "Indonesian Chinese Education: Past and Present." *Indonesia*, October, 49–71.

Svedberg, Peter. 1981. "Colonial Enforcement of Foreign Direct Investment." *The Manchester School* 49 (1): 21–33.

———. 1982. "The Profitability of U.K. Foreign Direct Investment under Colonialism." *Journal of Development Economics* 11: 273–286.

Swan, William L. 1988. "Aspects of Japan's Pre-war Economic Relations with Thailand." In Chaiwat Kamchoo and E. Bruce Reynolds, eds., *Thai-Japanese Relations in Historical Perspective*. Monograph Number 41. Bangkok: Chulalongkorn University Institute of Asian Studies.

———. 1989. "Thai-Japan Monetary Relations at the Start of the Pacific War." *Modern Asian Studies* 23 (2): 313–347.

———. 1996. "Japan's Intentions for Its Greater East Asia Co-Prosperity Sphere as Indicated in Its Policy Plans for Thailand." *Journal of Southeast Asian Studies* 27 (1): 139–149.

Takada, Yoko. 2000. "Historical Agrarian Economy of Cochinchina." In Jean-Pascal Bassino, Jean-Dominique Giacometti, and K. Odaka, eds., *Quantitative Economic History of Vietnam 1900–1990*. Tokyo: Hitotsubashi University, Institute of Economic Research.

Tarling, Nicholas. 2001. *A Sudden Rampage: The Japanese Occupation of Southeast Asia 1941–1945*. London: C. Hurst and Co.

Than, Mya, and Nobuyoshi Nishizawa. 1990. "Agricultural Policy Reforms and Agricultural Development in Myanmar." In Mya Than and Joseph L. H. Tan, eds., *Myanmar: Dilemmas and Options*. Singapore: Institute of Southeast Asian Studies.

Thoburn, John T. 1977. *Primary Commodity Exports and Economic Development: Theory, Evidence and a Study of Malaysia*. London: John Wiley and Sons.

Thompson, Virginia. 1937. *French Indo-China*. London: George Allen and Unwin.

Touzet, Andre. 1934. *L'économie indochinoise et la grande crise universelle*. Paris: Marcel Giard.

Tsunoda, Jun. 1980. "The Navy's Role in the Southern Strategy." In James William

Morley, ed., *The Fateful Choice: Japan's Advance into Southeast Asia, 1939–1941*. New York: Columbia University Press.

Tsurumi, E. Patricia. 1984. "Colonial Education in Korea and Taiwan." In Ramon H. Myers and Mark R. Peattie, eds., *The Japanese Colonial Empire, 1895–1945*. Princeton: Princeton University Press.

Twang, Peck-Yang. 1998. *The Chinese Business Elite in Indonesia and the Transition to Independence, 1940–1950*. Kuala Lumpur: Oxford University Press.

UNDP. 2003. *Human Development Report, 2003*. New York: Oxford University Press for the United Nations Development Program.

United Nations ECAFE. 1961. *Economic Survey of Asian and the Far East, 1960*. Bangkok: United Nations Economic Commission for Asia and the Far East.

———. 1962. *Economic Survey of Asian and the Far East, 1961*. Bangkok: United Nations Economic Commission for Asia and the Far East.

United Nations UNESCO. 1964. *UNESCO Statistical Yearbook 1963*. Paris: United Nations Education, Scientific, and Cultural Organization.

United States Tariff Commission. 1937. *United States–Philippines Trade with Special Reference to the Philippine Independence Act and Other Recent Legislation*. Report 118, United States Tariff Commission. Washington, D.C.: United States Government Printing Office.

Utrecht, Ernst. 1969. "Land Reform in Indonesia." *Bulletin of Indonesian Economic Studies* 5 (3): 71–88.

Vichitvong na Pombhejara. 1978. "Thailand's Monetary Development in the 1930s." In Vichitvong na Pombhejara, ed., *Readings in Thailand's Political Economy*. Bangkok: Bangkok Printing Enterprises.

Vinacke, Harold M. 1928. *A History of the Far East in Modern Times*. New York: Alfred A. Knopf.

Vlieland, C. A. 1932. *British Malaya: A Report on the 1931 Census and on Certain Problems of Vital Statistics*. London: Crown Agents.

Vries, E. de. 1946. "Geboorte en Sterfte onder de Japansche Bezitting." *Economisch Weekblad*, May 4, pp. 60–61.

Wade, Robert. 1990. *Governing the Market: Economic Theory and the Role of Government in East Asian Industrialization*. Princeton: Princeton University Press.

Warr, Peter G. 1989. "Export Processing Zones: The Economics of Enclave Manufacturing." *World Bank Research Observer* 4: 65–88.

Wertheim, W. F. 1964. "Betting on the Strong." In Wertheim, *East-West Parallels: Sociological Approaches to Modern Asia*. The Hague: W. van Hoeve.

Wesseling, H. L. 1988. "The Giant That Was a Dwarf, or the Strange History of Dutch Imperialism." In Andrew Porter and Robert Holland, eds., *Theory and Practice in the History of European Expansion Overseas: Essays in Honour of Ronald Robinson*. London: Frank Cass.

White, Nicholas J. 1996. *Business, Government and the End of Empire: Malaya, 1942–1957*. Kuala Lumpur: Oxford University Press.

———. 1999. "Gentlemanly Capitalism and Empire in the Twentieth Century: The Forgotten Case of Malaya, 1914–1965." In Raymond E. Dummett, ed.,

Gentlemanly Capitalism and British Imperialism: The New Debate on Empire. Harlow: Addison Wesley Longman Ltd.

———. 2000. "The Business and the Politics of Decolonisation: The British Experience in the Twentieth Century." *Economic History Review,* new series, 53:3 (August): 544–564.

Wiegersma, Nancy. 1988. *Vietnam: Peasant Land, Peasant Revolution.* New York: St. Martin's Press.

Williams, Lea. 1952. "Chinese Entrepreneurs in Indonesia." *Explorations in Entrepreneurial History* 5 (1): 34–60.

Williamson, Jeffrey G. 1998. "Real Wages and Relative Factor Prices in the Third World 1820–1940: Asia." Discussion Paper Number 1844, Harvard Institute of Economic Research, Harvard University. August.

———. 2000. "Globalization, Factor Prices and Living Standards in Asia before 1940." In A. J. H. Latham and Heita Kawakatsu, eds., *Asia Pacific Dynamism, 1550–2000.* London: Routledge.

Wilson, Constance M. 1983. *Thailand: A Handbook of Historical Statistics.* Boston: G. K. Hall.

Wilson, T. B. 1958. *The Economics of Padi Production in North Malaya,* part 1: *Land Tenure, Rents, Land Use and Fragmentation.* Kuala Lumpur: Ministry of Agriculture and Cooperatives.

Woo, Jung-en. 1991. *Race to the Swift: State Finance in Korean Industrialization.* New York: Columbia University Press.

Wood, Leonard. 1926. *Report of Governor General of Philippine Islands, 1924.* Washington, D.C.: Government Printing Office.

World Bank. 1976. *World Tables 1976.* Washington, D.C.: World Bank.

———. 1993. *The East Asian Miracle: Economic Growth and Public Policy.* New York: Oxford University Press.

Woytinsky, W. S., and E. S. Woytinsky. 1955. *World Commerce and Governments: Trends and Outlooks.* New York: Twentieth Century Fund.

Wyndham, H. A. 1933. *Native Education: Ceylon, Java, Formosa, the Philippines, French Indo-China, and British Malaya.* London: Oxford University Press.

Yoshihara, Kunio. 1989. "Introduction." In Yoshihara Kunio, ed., *Oei Tiong Ham Concern: The First Business Empire of Southeast Asia.* Kyoto: Center for Southeast Asian Studies, Kyoto University.

———. 1994. *The Nation and Economic Growth: The Philippines and Thailand.* Kuala Lumpur: Oxford University Press.

Zablan, Z. C. 1978. "Trends and Differential in Mortality." In *Population of the Philippines.* Country Monograph Series No. 5. Bangkok: United Nations Economic Commission for Asia and the Pacific.

Zimmerman, Carle C. 1999. *Siam Rural Economic Survey 1930–31.* Bangkok: White Lotus (reprint of original edition).

Index

About the Author

For many years Anne Booth's research and teaching have revolved around the comparative economic development of Southeast Asia in the twentieth century, with a special focus on Indonesia. She has taught at the University of Singapore and Australian National University, and since 1991 she has been professor of economics at the School of Oriental and African Studies, University of London. She has published several books and numerous articles.